From Eton to Ypres

The Letters and Diaries of Lt Col Wilfrid Abel Smith, Grenadier Guards, 1914–15

Charles Abel Smith

To my children, Marina, Nicholas and Edmund, so that
they and their generation may continue to remember

Cover illustrations: 2nd Battalion leaving Le Havre (Grenadier Guards);
Wilfrid Abel Smith photographed in 1914, and Goldings in 1885
(Author's collection).

First published 2016
This paperback edition published 2017

The History Press
The Mill, Brimscombe Port
Stroud, Gloucestershire, GL5 2QG
www.thehistorypress.co.uk

British Library Cataloguing in Publication Data.
A catalogue record for this book is available from the British Library.

ISBN 978 0 7509 8179 8

Typesetting and origination by The History Press
Printed and bound by CPI Group (UK) Ltd

Contents

Foreword

I was invited to write this foreword because Lieutenant Colonel Abel Smith was a cousin of mine and I spent six years of the Second World War in the 2nd Battalion Grenadier Guards.

The letters and diaries of Lieutenant Colonel Abel Smith are a vivid reminder, more than 100 years since the start of the First World War, of the particular horrors of that conflict. Trench warfare must have been one of the most appalling manifestations of war and this comes over very clearly in Lieutenant Colonel Abel Smith's diary entries. What also comes through clearly is the courage, stamina and determination needed through those long periods in the trenches and the resolution and discipline to keep going.

An example, on Christmas Eve 1914, he records: 'We are in a beastly place. We took over the Indian trenches last night. It is all slush and water, in some places up to your waist. Tonight it's freezing hard, to make it worse and plenty of bullets flying about.'

He must have been an outstanding commanding officer and a very brave man, as clearly demonstrated by the moving tributes to him from his colleagues and battalion.

Lord Carrington
29 September 2015

Acknowledgements

I am very grateful to Lord Carrington for agreeing to write a foreword.

I must also record my thanks to Henry Hanning for all his support in helping me to produce this book. He is the last serving Grenadier descendant of Wilfrid and was for many years a regimental historian, publishing the much-acclaimed 350-year history of the regiment, *The British Grenadiers*, in 2006. Many thanks also to Robert and Anne Abel Smith for their support and encouragement.

Philip Wright, the Grenadiers' Regimental Archivist, has been tireless in his assistance and I would like to thank him for his permission to print various extracts of his research together with photographs from the Grenadier Guards collection.

I am very grateful to Dorothy Abel Smith, John Abel Smith, Sue Kendall, Gordon Lee-Steere, Edward Gordon Lennox, Jane Jago, Celia Lassen, Jerry Murland, Michael Maslinski, Sir Timothy Ruggles-Brise, Mark Wagner and Lord Astor for providing me with information about their forebears and allowing me to print letters and photographs from their collections.

In addition, I would like to thank Roddy Fisher, Keeper of the Eton Photograph Archive, for his help in providing me with photographs from the Eton collection.

I owe a debt of gratitude to Michael Leventhal for his faith in this book and the production team at The History Press, including Chrissy McMorris, Lauren Newby and Andrew Latimer, for turning it into the finished article.

Finally, a big thank you to my wife, Julia, for all her support in helping me to write this book.

Wilfrid's Family Tree
Showing Main Characters

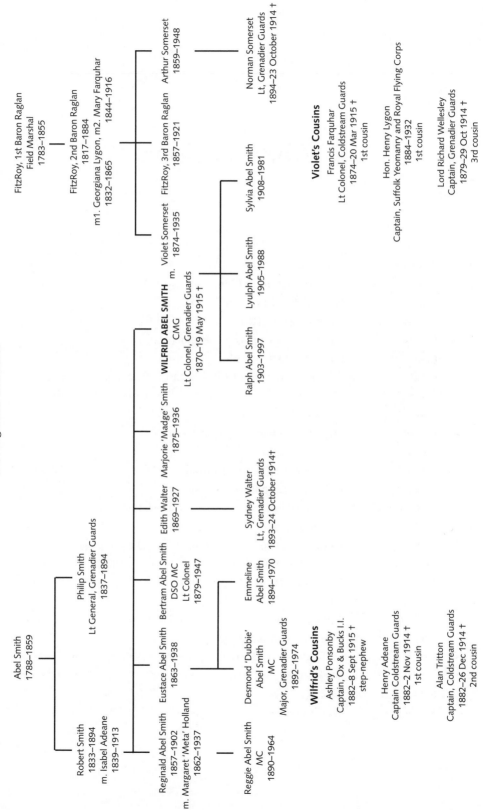

Abel Smith
1788–1859

Robert Smith
1833–1894
m. Isabel Adeane
1839–1913

Philip Smith
Lt General, Grenadier Guards
1837–1894

Reginald Abel Smith
1857–1902
m. Margaret 'Meta' Holland
1862–1937

Eustace Abel Smith
1863–1938

Bertram Abel Smith
DSO MC
Lt Colonel
1879–1947

Edith Walter
1869–1927

Marjorie 'Madge' Smith
1875–1936

WILFRID ABEL SMITH
CMG
Lt Colonel, Grenadier Guards
1870–19 May 1915 †

Reggie Abel Smith
MC
1890–1964

Desmond 'Dubbie'
Abel Smith
MC
Major, Grenadier Guards
1892–1974

Emmeline
Abel Smith
1894–1970

Sydney Walter
Lt, Grenadier Guards
1893–24 October 1914†

Ralph Abel Smith
1903–1997

Lyulph Abel Smith
1905–1988

Sylvia Abel Smith
1908–1981

FitzRoy, 1st Baron Raglan
Field Marshal
1783–1855

FitzRoy, 2nd Baron Raglan
1817–1884
m1. Georgiana Lygon, m2. Mary Farquhar
1832–1865   1844–1916

FitzRoy, 3rd Baron Raglan
1857–1921

Arthur Somerset
1859–1948

Violet Somerset
1874–1935   m.

Norman Somerset
Lt, Grenadier Guards
1894–23 October 1914 †

Wilfrid's Cousins

Ashley Ponsonby
Captain, Ox & Bucks I.I.
1882–8 Sept 1915 †
step-nephew

Henry Adeane
Captain Coldstream Guards
1882–2 Nov 1914 †
1st cousin

Alan Tritton
Captain, Coldstream Guards
1882–26 Dec 1914 †
2nd cousin

Violet's Cousins

Francis Farquhar
Lt Colonel, Coldstream Guards
1874–20 Mar 1915 †
1st cousin

Hon. Henry Lygon
Captain, Suffolk Yeomanry and Royal Flying Corps
1884–1932
1st cousin

Lord Richard Wellesley
Captain, Grenadier Guards
1879–29 Oct 1914 †
3rd cousin

Abbreviations

AA	Assistant Adjutant
AAG	Assistant Adjutant General
BEF	British Expeditionary Force
C. Gds	Coldstream Guards
CIGS	Chief of the Imperial General Staff
C-in-C	Commander-in-Chief
CMG	Companion of the Order of St Michael and St George
C-of-S	Chief of Staff
Coy	Company
DAAG	Deputy Assistant Adjutant General
d.o.w.	died of wounds
DSO	Distinguished Service Order
EEF	Egyptian Expeditionary Force
G. Gds	Grenadier Guards
GOC	General Officer Commanding
GOC-in-C	General Officer Commanding-in-Chief
GSO 1, 2 or 3	General Staff Officer 1st, 2nd or 3rd Grade
I. Gds	Irish Guards
k.i.a.	killed in action
MC	Military Cross
OC	Officer Commanding
Ox. L.I.	Oxfordshire and Buckinghamshire Light Infantry
QMG	Quartermaster General
S. Gds	Scots Guards
W. Gds	Welsh Guards

Introduction

Wilfrid Abel Smith was regarded as one of the finest commanding officers on the Western Front. He took over 2nd Battalion Grenadier Guards in September 1914 whilst they were fighting on the slopes of the River Aisne. This had followed the first encounter of the BEF (British Expeditionary Force) with the Germans at Mons and the ensuing Battle of the Marne. His battalion was one of the elite units of the British Army with 1,000 of the finest soldiers the country could produce. It went to France in August 1914 with great optimism that the war would be over by Christmas. By the end of November, it had held the line during the First Battle of Ypres and, periodically reinforced, had suffered nearly 1,000 casualties. Thus began the stalemate and the horrors of the trenches, in which Wilfrid was to lead his men over the next six months until he died of wounds during the Battle of Festubert on 19 May 1915.

Had he survived that battle, contemporary accounts make it clear that he would likely have soon been promoted to brigadier general and given a brigade. His second-in-command, George Jeffreys, retired as a full general and his brigadier, Lord Cavan, rose to become a field marshal.

Wilfrid went to France aged 44, a father of three young children and a devoted and loving husband to Violet, granddaughter of Lord Raglan of the Crimea. A career soldier, educated at Eton and Sandhurst, he was the epitome of a Guards officer. He had enjoyed a privileged and comfortable life as the son of a wealthy banker. His soldiering had included the full range of ceremonial duties that would have been expected of a Grenadier, with the occasional foray into colonial wars and a stint in Sydney, as aide-de-camp to the Governor of New South Wales.

Wilfrid arrived in France to take over a battle-weary battalion under constant attack. His officers and men knew that they owed their surviving the retreat from Mons to his predecessor, who had been recalled home for retreating without orders, thereby saving the battalion from annihilation. Wilfrid quickly gained the deep respect of all who served under him.

In the midst of continuous fighting he managed to write to Violet most days, in the most challenging conditions. She compiled the volume of letters and diaries that form the core of this book. These were typewritten and bound by John & Edward Bumpus, Ltd in 1917. Although correspondence from the Western Front was heavily censored, Wilfrid was remarkably frank. He painted a vivid picture of the constant shelling and trench conditions through the winter of 1914–15. As a professional soldier, he carried out his orders to the best of his ability, but he was rarely complimentary about his high command. He respected his professional German adversary, but was disgusted at the way in which the Germans conducted their war. He despaired at the loss of the men under his command and of the many friends and relations who fell before he did.

There were some moments of light relief: the arrival of gifts, such as a cake from his children, or a pheasant from his sister-in-law, was always welcome in the mess. Visits by the Prince of Wales to the battalion were something to write home about, particularly when he managed to fire a shot at a German or was conveying a delighted German officer prisoner of war in the back of his car.

England was not far away. Wilfrid was able to get *The Times* the day after publication. As a soldier on the Western Front, he was interested in the other theatres of war. His increasing frustration with Churchill's ill-fated campaign in Gallipoli is clear. Developments on the Eastern Front were also closely followed.

Wilfrid chronicles a nine-month period during which the western world experienced fundamental change. The industrialisation of war saw the annihilation of Britain's professional army. Violet had to deal with the implications of this at home, and constantly worried about her husband. This was an age of nascent technology, which we now take for granted: the development of aerial and submarine warfare, the use of chemical warfare and the beginning of electronic communications. Cavalry charges and the sword became redundant and Britain found itself on the front line with the threat of attack by airship. The need for industrial-scale munitions production brought about labour unrest and helped bring down the British government.

Britain and the rest of Europe would never be the same again.

As a commanding officer, Wilfrid assumed responsibility for his nephew, Desmond Abel Smith, who later considered that he owed his survival through the war to his uncle. Wilfrid's letters describe how Desmond was sent out to his battalion in December 1914. He was transferred to another Guards regiment *en route* and Wilfrid describes how he fought hard with his high command to get him back. Desmond was swapped for another subaltern, who was dead within a month. His account of his uncle's death describes the loss he felt.

Wilfrid's letters to Violet do not convey the full horror of war, as he wrote them in a matter-of-fact way so as not to alarm her unduly. I have included letters that he wrote to fellow soldiers that describe the brutal reality of the front more vividly and complement his battalion diaries. His accounts of the First Battle of Ypres have been much quoted. He records his deep disapproval of the 1914 Christmas truces that were made on other sections of the line but not his. He experienced some of his most difficult trench combat over this period. I have incorporated quotes from historians of the war to complete the picture.

As would be expected of a commanding officer of the Grenadiers, Wilfrid had very high standards and was a strict disciplinarian. But his letters also show a deep sense of compassion for his men and a desire for their advancement. His leadership inspired a devoted following shown in the condolence letters that Violet received after his death.

Wilfrid was a devoted father and wrote regularly to his children. It was not easy carrying out the role of father from the front. His letters clearly mark the holidays that he missed with them. Wilfrid's understanding and support comes across strongly, no more so than when he writes to his eldest son, Ralph, about coming bottom of the class, when his younger brother, Lyulph, had done rather better. But he did not shy away from telling his sons what he expected of them and how they should support their mother over Christmas while he was away. Wilfrid's letters to his daughter, Sylvia, highlight the love that he felt for his children and for the family dog, an Airedale terrier called Jack. He treasured the letters he received from his children, the last of which was found in his pocket on the day he was fatally wounded. Ralph's account of being fired at with corks from a friend's anti-aircraft pom-pom gun must have lightened the mood in battalion HQ.

In transcribing Wilfrid's letters, I have sought to retain his punctuation and abbreviations, only amending them to make it easier for the contemporary reader to follow. His letters to Violet only contain the text that she had transcribed in 1917. His other letters have been transcribed in full.

I have got to know Wilfrid well. I wish I had known him in person. His letters remind us of the sacrifice that he and so many others made, and that we and future generations must never forget.

1

Wilfrid's Early Days

Wilfrid Robert Abel Smith was born at Goldings, near Hertford, on 13 September 1870, the eighth of twelve children and the third of five sons of Robert and Isabel Smith. Robert Smith was a successful banker descended from Thomas Smith of Nottingham, who founded the first English provincial bank in about 1658. Smith, Payne and Smith was well known in the City of London with premises at 1 Lombard Street. Robert was a God-fearing, philanthropic banker of the kind more often to be found in Victorian times than in the present day. Born in 1833, he had married Isabel Adeane in 1857, when she was only 18. The young couple lost no time in producing a large family. Their first child was born nine months and three days after their marriage. At the age of 30, Isabel found herself with eight children. Four more were to follow by 1879. There were six to nine years between each of the surviving four brothers, one having died at the age of 9, so it seems that none of them will have been at the same school together.

Wilfrid spent his infancy at the old house at Goldings in the village of Waterford near Hertford, where he had been born. When he was 6, the family moved into the enormous new Goldings built higher up the hill away from the damp of the river below. This house still stands but has been divided into apartments. It was designed by George Devey, one of the most successful but least-known domestic Victorian architects. It is described by Mark Girouard in *The Victorian Country House* as 'One of Devey's largest and most depressing houses'.[1]

Robert did not undertake this project until he had built Waterford's first parish church in 1872, where there is now a memorial to Wilfrid. He employed Morris & Co. to fit out the church's interior and it contains one of the finest collections of Pre-Raphaelite stained glass with windows designed by William Morris, Edward Burne-Jones and Ford Madox Brown.

Wilfrid followed his two elder brothers to school at Cheam, near Newbury (according to his mother, 'the only good private school then in existence'),[2] and then to Eton and the Royal Military College at Sandhurst. It was at Eton and Sandhurst that his ears apparently suffered from battering in the boxing ring, resulting in some deafness; it was a characteristic (the deafness, not the boxing) later possessed by his daughter Sylvia and her son. He was fond of music and took up the cello.

His taste for a soldiering career was almost certainly sparked by his father's younger brother, Philip Smith, a tall, finely built bachelor who had a distinguished career in the Grenadier Guards and retired as a lieutenant general. Philip was close to Robert and Isabel and would have seen much of the children. In 1882 he took the 2nd Battalion of the regiment (which Wilfrid was himself destined to command) to Egypt where, under Sir Garnet Wolseley, the expedition scored a startling victory at Tel el-Kebir over a far superior force of insurgents by a brilliant little battle lasting thirty-five minutes. One can well imagine the pride and delight of the 12-year-old nephew at the triumph of his uncle, who was rewarded with a CB (Companion of the Order of the Bath).

Wilfrid's Lent Term school report from Eton in 1885 gives little indication of the 14-year-old's true potential. Whilst he came first out of thirty-two, his

Wilfrid's Eton school report, Lent 1885, when he was 14. (Author's collection)

class was Division XVIII, so his peer group would have been amongst the least academic of his year group. His conduct report read, 'a terrible fidget: lacking in power of concentration: very fairly punctual', and his overall summary was, 'Deserves credit for steady industry, often against the grain. Is not a clever boy, and takes a long time in mastering new ideas, but retains them well when he has made them his own. Ought to make more effort to get the better of his flightiness.'

Wilfrid's exam results at Sandhurst suggest that he was not a candidate for the Sword of Honour (his marks placed him at the top of the bottom quartile for his year), but his riding prowess earned him a special certificate of proficiency. He was commissioned into the Grenadiers in 1890, joining the 1st Battalion in Dublin and moving the following year to London. He spent the following seven years in and around the capital. His adjutant (a 'head boy' role responsible for the young officers) was Charles Fergusson, a fierce and terrifying man later to reach great heights, who would have seen that Wilfrid behaved himself and learned his business swiftly and well. That apart, he must have had a wonderful time.

It was a good life for anyone fortunate enough to have been born into a prosperous family when the British Empire was at the height of its confidence and prestige, and never more so than when fashionably placed in society. Military duties were humdrum, largely confined to ceremonial, administration, sport and home-grown entertainment. From time to time, there were camps for rifle shooting (described as 'musketry') and marches and manoeuvres still conducted in scarlet tunics and bearskin caps. Leave for the officers was plentiful and could amount to several months of the year so long as it was spent in developing military virtues of courage and skill in the hunting field or killing pheasant and grouse. Dinners, balls, levées and parties of all kinds were numerous. Wilfrid returned to Goldings often and there were other fine houses to visit. His fun, however, will have been much marred by the death in 1894 of both his father Robert and his uncle Philip (his mother lived until 1913).

Curiously, though he used 'Abel' as part of his surname in bookplates and elsewhere, his military records invariably show him as W.R.A. Smith. His wife was always 'Violet Smith' or 'Mrs Wilfrid'. It was the succeeding generation that first adopted 'Abel' as a matter of course. His bookplate also identifies his chosen profession as a soldier with a bearskin and a sword in the bottom right-hand corner.

Wilfrid's first service abroad came in 1897, when the 1st Grenadiers went to Gibraltar. They were refused permission to take bearskin caps. Whilst the stay cut short Wilfrid's shooting season at home, it gave him the opportunity to go after different quarry from the usual fare of pheasant, partridge, hare and rabbits. His game book records a five-day shooting expedition to Seville and the River Guadalquivir in search of bustard and geese with two fellow officers, the Hon. Edward Loch and Edward Verschoyle. Wilfrid was to write to Loch's sister, Lady Bernard Gordon Lennox, seventeen years later following the death of her husband, Lord Bernard Gordon Lennox, during the First Battle of Ypres.

Wilfrid recorded at the end of the trip:

> The weather throughout was glorious, just like June, and we all enjoyed it enormously, the only blot being that Verschoyle never hit a thing the whole time. He was very seedy and had jaundice badly when we got back. We had to pay 1 Peseta for each bustard and 30 cents per goose to get them into Seville, and 10 pesetas to get them onto Gib. It was a great trouble, but they kept well and ate first rate. Total 57 Head.

The first real excitement arrived in 1898, when Wilfrid's battalion was given notice to join Kitchener's Sudan expedition, designed to bring an end to the persistent Dervish activity and to avenge the death of General Gordon in 1885. Kitchener achieved his purpose in decisive fashion. The 1st Grenadiers travelled up the Nile by rail and riverboat, arriving at Omdurman where, on 2 September, at derisory cost to the British and Egyptian force, over 10,000 Dervishes, mostly armed with primitive weapons, were mown down by rifle, machine gun and artillery fire without getting anywhere near the firing line. What part did Wilfrid play? In 1973 an account of Omdurman was published by Philip Ziegler, who asserted that, at an early point in the battle, there had been a messy and inglorious scuffle in front of the line between a Dervish and one of Kitchener's staff, 'Lt Smith of the Grenadiers'.[3] Not so. The offending officer was Smyth of the Queen's Bays, who was rewarded with the Victoria Cross. Wilfrid was in charge of the battalion transport and looking after mules in the rear. But it must have been exciting nonetheless. Press cuttings of the campaign, including several drawings, were collected at home and Wilfrid later pasted them into an album which survives.

The following extracts from a letter that he wrote to his mother on 5 September 1898, following the fall of Khartoum, give a flavour of his experiences on the expedition:

My dearest Mother,

So it's all over and our flag is once more over the Government House at
Khartoum side by side with the Egyptian flag. We had a desperate fight, it
lasted five hours, and is said to be the biggest fight ever fought in the Soudan.
I suppose you will want to know all about it, and as I have nothing to do and
time hangs rather heavily on our hands, I will tell you a certain amount …

At 6.45 by my watch the first shell went, and then for an hour and 50 minutes
we fought. Their first line came rather to the right of my Battn. led by the
Kalifa's son. As soon as they appeared the Artillery began. Their first shot went
too far, the second a little short, the 3rd got them exactly over the big banner
carried by the Kalifa's son. Down went the banner and Heaven knows how
many men. I saw all this beautifully through my glasses, and then I had to set
to work getting up ammunition, as the Battn. began to do a bit of execution.
At last they retired and we got ready to advance. They never came nearer to us
than 700 or 800 yards …

The Town stinks worse than any place I could imagine, and if we stay here
long I am afraid there will be a lot of sickness …

Not long after returning home, Wilfrid was given a plum appointment as
ADC (aide-de-camp: personal assistant) to the Governor of New South
Wales. This was the only time he served away from his regiment and it
had momentous consequences. The Governor, William Lygon, 7th Earl
Beauchamp, was, at 27, younger than his own ADC. A glittering political
future was forecast for him and he had been appointed to acquire some
experience of public service (as it happened, it was later discovered that he
was rather too fond of liveried footmen and his prospects collapsed in ruin).

How Wilfrid came by the appointment is not clear but such affairs
were often handled on a personal basis and he will certainly have known
Beauchamp's younger brother, Edward Lygon, a Grenadier who was fated to
be killed in South Africa in May 1900. Comfortably installed at Government
House in Sydney, Wilfrid was responsible for the Governor's personal and
social affairs. The seating plan for a large dinner in January 1900, written in
his own hand and including his own name, was on show to tourists in 2012.
His time in Australia involved travels across the continent and a visit to New
Zealand in March 1900. Here Wilfrid experienced the traditional welcome,
the Haka. He was also able to enjoy the novel experience of shooting godwits
at Onehunga, a port on the edge of Auckland.

A visitor arrived in the form of Violet Somerset, Beauchamp's cousin and the daughter of the 2nd Lord Raglan. In the beautiful gardens and Scottish baronial splendour of the Government House, she fell in love with the ADC and he with her. They were engaged on 17 September 1899. A handsome portrait was painted in Sydney of Wilfrid as a captain. Promotion could be very slow as it depended on vacancies being created by death or retirement.

Wilfrid returned home on 1 November 1900 and on 3 December he and Violet were married at Holy Trinity Church, Sloane Street, by the Reverend John Mansel-Pleydell, his brother-in-law. The honeymoon was spent at Goldings, at Longhills near Lincoln with his second brother Eustace and his family and at Normanton near Nottingham, one of the seats of the Earl of Ancaster, before they settled in London.

Violet's diary for 1901 is a delightful record of some of the joys and agonies of a young bride, as well as a few of the great events of the time: 22 January – 'Queen died at 6.30 pm. Wilfrid shot at Papplewick.' Wilfrid's game book recorded a bag of fifty-nine for the day. It was his last day of the season and his summary of it read: 'Did not get home from Australia till 1st Nov. and so got no shooting to speak of.'

Violet's husband's routine does not seem to have been more irksome than in earlier years, but when Wilfrid had to spend nights away on guard or in camp, she wrote, 'Oh how I miss him,' though he wrote to her every day and sometimes also sent a telegram. They lived quietly though many visits were made and returned and they enjoyed a variety of London entertainments. Wilfrid's younger brother, Bertram, was a frequent visitor and the two hunted together when in the country. Curiously, there is no mention of the tragic death of his eldest brother Reginald and his 13-year-old nephew Cyril (Reginald's son) in that year. There was cello in the evenings (Violet was a good pianist), piquet and even the new game 'bridge'.

He often went to work by bicycle, which did him credit in an era when an officer of the Guards was not supposed to be seen on a bus or carrying his own shopping. On occasion he would ride to Goldings while his wife travelled by train. The first evidence of their possessing a car comes in 1903, when Wilfrid's accounts show a new category of expenditure, 'Motor', starting with an entry of £179 12s paid to Locomobile Co., for the purchase of a car.

And despite the ominous news on 18 December, that 'Wilf was told that he is to take the next draft to S. Africa next month,' Violet's diary ends with, 'What a happy year 1901 has been,' followed by a memorandum, 'House-parlourmaid, Annie Smith, Bladon, £20 a year, 1/6 washing, no beer'.

On 16 January 1902, Wilfrid sailed from Southampton to South Africa to join the 3rd Battalion. The Boer War had already been running for over two years and both the 2nd and 3rd Battalions of the Grenadiers had been out for most of that time. But the battles of the early months, which had often proved more painful for the British than for the Boers, were long past and the war had become a matter of manning strongpoints, blockhouses and barbed-wire lines along the railways, and launching drives to round up the Boer guerrillas while their farms were burnt and their families moved into the now notorious concentration camps.

Wilfrid's company was responsible for a part of the railway line. It attracted little attention from the hard-pressed Boers, who made peace on 1 June. Wilfrid is recorded as having left for England on 27 June, which was fortunate as the main body of the battalion was not home until October, having been away for more than three years.

In July 1903, back with the 1st Battalion, Wilfrid was appointed Captain of the King's Company, traditionally containing the tallest men in the regiment. This was a coveted post that he held until the end of 1906 and would have been approved personally by the king. One of his albums records Wilfrid being received by the king on 27 June 1905 and presented with 'a pair of Sleeve Links bearing the Badge of the Company'. In fact, the only special role for the company was to find the bearer party at a monarch's funeral and thereby attract some little glory for its captain. Wilfrid would no doubt have reflected somewhat ruefully on the timing of his tenure, which lay squarely between the deaths of Victoria in 1901 and Edward VII in 1910, but he had the consolation of a coronation medal in 1911.

During this time the family started to arrive: Ralph in 1903, Lyulph in 1905 and Sylvia in 1908. At some point they moved to Upton Lea in Slough (telephone Slough 62).

On relinquishing the King's Company at the end of 1906, Wilfrid was promoted major and went again to the 3rd Battalion. Here he stayed for eight years, until the outbreak of war in August 1914. War clouds were gathering well before that time and training had taken on a new urgency. There were reforms in the army. Fitness and discipline were further improved. Long marches were frequent. Above all, the sharp lessons taught by the Boers were learnt and shooting skills reached a level that was probably never to be surpassed. They were to be needed in spades.

Wilfrid was a meticulous man and kept detailed accounts of his income and expenditure. His first account book is dated 1883 when, aged 13, he would have started at Eton. His banker father presumably encouraged him to account for his money from an early age. The 1883 accounts itemised the money he received throughout the year, mainly from his father, which totalled £19 10s. His later accounts provide an interesting insight into the lifestyle of a Guards officer of the day. In 1907, his net army pay as a major was £411 10s 10d, an amount comparable to what a major would earn in 2015. Out of this he had to cover regimental expenses of £137 12s. These included £2 2s for a wedding present to Lord Bernard Gordon Lennox (who was to die on 10 November 1914 in the First Battle of Ypres). The net balance of his army pay covered only a small proportion of his family's living expenses, which totalled £1,568 4s 6d. A Guards officer required a significant private income. Perhaps the most surprising significant category of expenditure was 'Subscriptions' which, at £162 18s 10d, accounted for over 10 per cent of the family budget. While this included subscriptions to a large number of regimental and sporting clubs, together with The Travellers Club, nearly £100 was paid out for life insurance. Wilfrid's accounts go into great detail, itemising, under 'Sundries', numerous purchases of dog biscuits, a dog collar and chain and even a drill book, which cost 3s.

2

Outbreak of War and Promotion

On 9 September 1914, Wilfrid was promoted lieutenant colonel and appointed to command the 2nd Battalion in France. At the time of his promotion, he was Senior Major (second-in-command) of the 3rd Battalion, where he will have been largely occupied in drawing in and training reservists. This battalion remained in London until the formation of the Guards Division in July 1915, though many of its members would by then have been sent to make up for the heavy casualties incurred by the other two battalions. The 2nd Battalion (known in the regiment as 'the Models') had been one of the first to go out in the BEF in August.

Michael Craster explains in *Fifteen Rounds a Minute* that:

> This was not quite an ordinary Battalion of course. The Brigade of Guards, the modern Household Division, did not have a monopoly of discipline, smartness and professionalism in the BEF, but as an élite they did believe in the highest standards in all three, believe in them, demand them and maintain them, whatever the cost. They might be matched, but never beaten ... Approbation was not given lightly, either within or without the Brigade, but when given it was well merited ...[1]

Formed in 1656, the Grenadiers are the most senior regiment of foot guards. They have a friendly rivalry with the Coldstream that goes back to the Restoration of Charles II. The Scots Guards, who trace their origins back to 1642, are the third regiment of the original guards trinity. The Irish Guards were still very new, having been formed in 1900 by order of Queen Victoria to commemorate the Irishmen who had fought for the British Empire in the Boer War. They had seen their first action at the Battle of Mons in August 1914.

Whatever their regiment, men of the Brigade of Guards felt a common bond as members of what was, in effect, a large family. The officers formed a close, tight-knit community and many could count numerous generations of service in their family. They knew each other well and were frequently related. Wilfrid's letters talk about his nephews, cousins and friends in the Grenadiers and other Guards regiments. Only guardsmen could command guardsmen and they would happily respond to orders of any officer in the Brigade. The Guards had a very strong tradition of welfare for their men, a concept not common at the time. Officers were trained to put the comfort of their men before their own personal needs.

Guardsmen came from a wide variety of backgrounds. Their minimum height restrictions and strong sense of discipline made them fearsome adversaries. Their effectiveness as soldiers was further enhanced by their loyalty to the regiment and an unrivalled pride in their conduct and appearance that went beyond simple discipline. By the beginning of the First World War, soldiers could sign up for three years of service followed by a commitment to serve for nine years in the reserves. Britain had a relatively small standing army of about 250,000 men at the beginning of the war but the reserves enabled battalions to be brought up to fighting strength very quickly in August 1914.

When war came to Britain on 4 August 1914, the 2nd Battalion was at Wellington Barracks. It was well trained and its equipment was all ready when mobilisation orders were received. By 6 August, nearly 3,000 Grenadier reservists had reported, been examined, clothed, armed and equipped, and joined their battalions.

Training was still being carried out and the king and queen came down to the gates of Buckingham Palace as the 2nd Battalion was returning to barracks from a route march. The men marched past in fours and saluted the king, their colonel-in-chief.

A Grenadier Guards private holding up his 1908 pattern webbing 'marching order'. This consisted of 150 rounds of .303 ammunition in the front pouches, water bottle, entrenching tool (on his right), haversack, bayonet and entrenching tool handle (on his left). The pack with great coat, ground sheet and personal items is in the centre. (Grenadier Guards)

The 2nd Battalion marching past Buckingham Palace, watched by the king and queen. (Grenadier Guards)

Lieutenant Colonel Corry leading 2nd Battalion out of Le Havre. (Grenadier Guards)

The battalion, then commanded by Lieutenant Colonel Noel Corry with twenty-nine officers and 1,000 men, crossed over to France on 12 August. It disembarked at Le Havre and marched out of the town to an overnight camp 5 miles away. The following day it entrained to begin the journey to the outskirts of Mons to meet the German threat.

The BEF, which went to France in August 1914, comprised about 86,000 men in two army corps, under the command of General Sir John French. The 2nd Battalion Grenadiers was placed in 4th (Guards) Brigade with three other battalions, 2nd and 3rd Coldstream and 1st Irish Guards. The 4th (Guards) Brigade was one of the three brigades of the 2nd Division under Major General Charles Monro. This division was one of two in I Corps, commanded by Lieutenant General Sir Douglas Haig.

Military Units during the First World War

Unit	Composition	Commander
Army	Two or more corps	General
Corps	Between two and five divisions with supporting arms and services	Lieutenant General
Division	Four brigades plus artillery, engineers and support services, totalling 12,000–20,000 men	Major General
Brigade	Four battalions, approximately 3,000–4,000 men	Brigadier General
Battalion	Building block of the army: four companies, 1,000 men at full strength	Lieutenant Colonel
Company	Subunit of a battalion, usually about 250 men	Major or Captain
Platoon	Subunit of an infantry company. Four sections of about sixteen men	Lieutenant or Second Lieutenant
Section	Subunit of an infantry platoon, usually about sixteen men	Corporal.

In the first few months of the war, the battalion took part in the confusion of the withdrawal from Mons, the 190-mile march to south of the Marne achieved in two weeks under the late August sun and the cautious pursuit of the German Army to the Aisne.

After the Marne, the battalion's commanding officer, Noel Corry, had been sent home. Judging correctly that his battalion had been told to hold an untenable position at Mons, and that he had a better understanding of the situation than his commanders further back, he had courageously defied his orders and withdrawn his men. Happily, he was later vindicated and given another command in 1915.

Philip Wright, the Grenadiers' Regimental Archivist, describes the patrolling on the Aisne:

Fighting on the steep heavily wooded slopes of the Aisne valley eventually congealed into trench warfare with the armies of both sides locked in the mud of their static positions. 'No man's land' between the trenches was covered in unburied bodies.

The trenches were gradually improved and deepened despite intense shelling from field guns and heavy howitzers. Rabbit netting was procured from the neighbouring woods and converted into wire entanglements. Raids were periodically made to stalk the enemy's snipers hidden in trees, haystacks and wood stacks, which had been hollowed out and loop-holed. The skill of the highly trained soldiers with the Lee Enfield .303 rifle – fifteen aimed rounds a minute minimum (the so-called 'mad minute') – was used to great effect, although the losses sustained by the battalion were also considerable.

Two patrols on the Aisne within a few days of each other illustrate both the effectiveness of this rapid firepower, which the Germans often mistook for machine guns, and the initiative and resourcefulness of the junior NCOs in command.

Lance Corporal P H McDonnell led a patrol with two men to reconnoitre a small wood a few hundred yards in front of the battalion lines. They discovered a large party of about thirty Germans in an advanced trench at the forward edge. The enemy thought they had captured the three men and began to walk forward to take them prisoner. At this point McDonnell gave a sharp order to fire and the resulting hail of bullets from the patrol caused a considerable number of casualties. Before the Germans could recover from the confusion the three Grenadiers had escaped. McDonnell was awarded the DCM. His citation read: 'On 27th September made a first class reconnaissance and discovered an unsuspected German trench.' He later transferred to the Welsh Guards (formed in 1915 largely from Grenadiers, Wales having been a regimental recruiting area) and was promoted to sergeant.

The citation for the DCM awarded to Lance Corporal W Thomas is more detailed: 'On 1st October went with three men through a wood to burn a wood stack from which sniping took place, and meeting a patrol of fifteen Germans fired at them and drove them off. After waiting they went on and successfully lighted the stack.' The battalion war diary records that two Germans were killed and that Thomas himself was badly hit. He was subsequently promoted to sergeant. On 3rd December, the King, accompanied by the Prince of Wales in Grenadier uniform, inspected 4th (Guards) Brigade at Méteren. It was his first visit to the front and he presented DCM medal ribbons to McDonnell and Thomas and five other members of the Battalion.

Thomas was killed in the trenches a few days later on Christmas Eve 1914 and is buried in the Guards' Cemetery, Windy Corner, Cuinchy. An extract from a letter sent to his sister by the men of 4 Platoon of 1 Company reads: 'He was killed instantly by a shot in the head on the afternoon of 24th December. It may be a relief to you to know that he died fighting to the last. The Germans were in our trenches and he barred the way shooting down every man that came his way. He saved many of us and we greatly sympathise with you in your loss.'

Wilfrid, as his Commanding Officer, wrote to Regimental Headquarters: 'You will be sorry to hear that Sergeant Thomas was killed the other day. He got the DCM for good work on the Aisne and never received the medal. He came out as a Private and has worked his way up to Acting Sergeant by sheer merit. He was a gallant man and a great loss to No. 1 Company.'[2]

In his letter of 10 December, Wilfrid sent Violet a copy of the battalion's diary for the first half of September before he took command.

DIARY

2nd BATTALION GRENADIER GUARDS
September 1st, 1914   To   September 18th, 1914
Sept 1st
Marched from Soucy 4 a.m., fighting rearguard action. Hotly engaged at Villers Cotteret, 4 Officers Missing, 2 N.C.O's [sic], and Men w., 122 Missing. Halted at midnight. Bivouacked in parts of Betz and La Villeneuve.
Sept 2nd
Marched at 2 a.m. Halted for breakfast at 9.30. Marched to Rolenter, near Meaux, and bivouacked.
Sept 3rd
March at 7 a.m. to Pierre Levée, and occupied position on Pierre Levée-Ligny Road.
Sept 4th
Marched at 9.30 a.m. Battalion engaged. Marched to La Bertrand, arriving at 11 p.m., and bivouacked.

Sept 5th

Marched at 5 a.m. to Fontenoy. Halted at 10 a.m. for 2 hours. Bivouacked at 3 p.m.

Sept 6th

Marched at 5.30 a.m. to Tonquin. Bivouacked at 8.30 p.m., and entrenched.

Sept 7th

Marched at 4 a.m. Halted at 9.30 a.m. to 2.30 p.m. Battalion joined Advanced Guard. Bivouacked at …

Sept 8th

Advanced at 8 a.m. Battalion engaged in wood fight. Stephen and 18 <u>w</u>. Bivouacked 8.30 p.m. near Les Peauliers.

Sept 9th

Ready to advance at 5 a.m. Moved at 9 a.m. about half a mile, and halted till 1.30 p.m.

Bivouacked at Domptier about 8 p.m.

Sept 10th

Ready to advance at 5.30 a.m. Moved at 7.30 a.m. Bivouacked 8 p.m. at Breuil.

Sept 11th

Ready at 5.30 a.m. Marched at 7.15 a.m. Very wet.

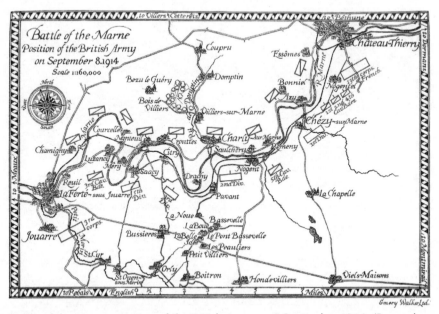

Battle of the Marne, position of the British Army on 8 September 1914. (Ponsonby, Vol. I, p. 46)

Sept 12th

Ready at 5 a.m. Marched at 9 a.m. Marched 3 miles and halted till 12 noon. Advanced and billetted at 8 p.m. Very wet.

Sept 13th

Ready at 5 a.m. Marched at 8.30 a.m. Attacked position after heavy Artillery fight. Advanced and billetted at 8 p.m. Very wet.

Sept 14th

Advanced at 5.30 a.m., and crossed the Aisne at Pont Arcy by pontoon bridge. Battalion took and held position near farm La Cour de Soupir, after a heavy fight. Entrenched and remained in position.

Des Voeux and Cunliffe k. Gosselin, Walker, Mackenzie, Stewart, Vernon, Welby w. 17 k. 67 w. 77 m.

Sept 15th

Remained in position – heavily shelled.

Sept 16th

Remained in position – heavily shelled.

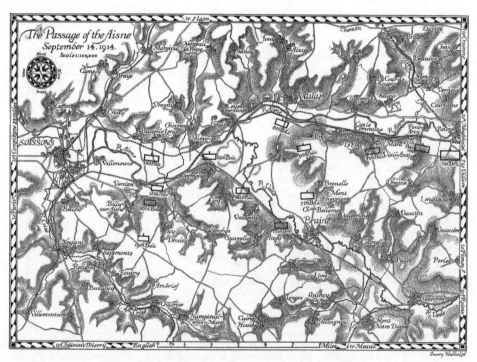

Passage of the Aisne, 14 September 1914. (Ponsonby, Vol. I, p. 58)

28

Sept 17th
Relieved by Oxford L.I. [Oxfordshire and Buckinghamshire Light Infantry], and billetted at Soupir.

Sept 18th
Relieved the 3rd Battalion Coldstream Guards at La Cour de Soupir farm at 4.30 a.m. Entrenched.

· BACKGROUND NARRATIVE ·

Wilfrid corresponded with his three children, Ralph (then aged 11), Lyulph (aged 9) and Sylvia (aged 5) throughout his time on the Western Front. In September, they went to stay in Deal. Ralph and Lyulph soon went to their boarding school, West Downs, near Winchester, and Sylvia stayed in Deal until December:

Sept 8th 1914
Sandown Road

My dear Father

We arrived about 6.00 yesterday. There is a cruiser and a gun boat guarding the coast here, and there is a hospital ship here too, we saw a wreck on the Goodwin Sands today, it had four masts, and we saw the coast of France too. We could see the light ship on the Goodwin Sands. We heard the guns at Dover, and saw the harbour. There are eleven thousand sailors outside Walmer Castle. It was very hot here yesterday, but it is much cooler here today. They say that they have not had much rain here since the first of August. There were wrecks here last month two of them were Spanish ships. There were three German ships here yesterday, but there is only one here today. Cargo ships are passing here all day going to Dover. There is a very big pier here. We went on the beach before breakfast for twenty minutes this morning. We are three minutes' walk from the sea here. Everybody thinks it is quite safe here, because of the Goodwin Sands. There is no sand here, but only big and small stones. It is very shallow water here, and seems quite safe for bathing, as people bathe all day here, and some at 5.00 in the morning. Lyulph and Sylvia send their love to Mummie and you.

Your loving son
Ralph

3

Wilfrid Takes Command of his Battalion

Wilfrid travelled to France with the Earl of Cavan, a Grenadier friend, who was taking command of the 4th (Guards) Brigade. Cavan, Viscount Kilcoursie, had joined the Grenadiers in 1885, after attending school at Eton. He served with the 2nd Battalion in South Africa and had no ambitions beyond a command in his own regiment. This he achieved in 1908, when he was given command of the battalion. He retired from the army in 1913 and became Master of Foxhounds for the Hertfordshire Hunt. He was recalled at the start of the war and was given command of the brigade succeeding Brigadier General Scott-Kerr, who was wounded on 1 September at Villers-Cotterêts.

As Henry Hanning explains in *The British Grenadiers*:

> it was the view of Sir Henry Wilson that [Cavan] 'doesn't see very far, but what he does see he sees very clear'. It was by no means a bad verdict, for nothing could have been more important than clarity of vision, particularly in the desperate days of autumn 1914 …
>
> In September 1915 he was appointed the first commander of the new Guards Division, though he did not approve of the concept. He was horrified to hear that all four Grenadier battalions were planned to be joined together in a single brigade and managed to persuade Kitchener against the idea. He also refused to allow the division to be put into another assault on the Somme in November 1916, saying, 'No one who has not visited the trenches can know the extent of exhaustion to which the men are reduced.'[1]

Cavan was promoted in 1916 to lead XIV Corps, which fought first in France and then on the Italian front. In 1922 he succeeded Sir Henry Wilson as Chief of the Imperial General Staff and was appointed field marshal later that year. He retired in 1926. His nickname 'Fatty' reflected, in good army tradition, the fact that his physique was very much the opposite.

On the Aisne, the 2nd Grenadiers had been led by their second-in-command, George Jeffreys, a man of outstanding capacity and determination. Jeffreys was the son of a rural landowner in Hampshire and descended from the brother of the notorious seventeenth-century judge of the same name. His nickname 'Ma' was derived from a Mrs Jeffreys, known as 'Ma', who had kept a house of ill repute in Kensington in the 1890s.

Educated at Eton, Jeffreys joined the Grenadiers in 1898 with whom he served at Omdurman and in the Boer War. He was commanding the Guards Depot in Caterham in August 1914 when he was sent across to France at short notice to replace Lord Loch, who had been posted to the Staff, as second-in-command of the 2nd Battalion. Jeffreys led the battalion for much of the retreat from Mons, the Marne and the Aisne before Wilfrid's arrival on 18 September. He took over command of the battalion in May 1915, following Wilfrid's death, and remained on the Western Front for the rest of the war, except for a period recovering from severe wounds in 1916. By 1918 he was a major general, commanding the 19th Division. He was general officer commanding (GOC) London District at the time of the General Strike in 1926 and was promoted to full general in 1935 as GOC-in-Chief Southern Command in India. He retired in 1938 and became MP for Petersfield in a 1941 wartime by-election. In 1952 he was created a baron and appointed Colonel of the Regiment, the first outside the Royal Family since the Duke of Wellington.

Jeffreys was a man of dauntless spirit. Hanning describes him as 'a fierce and austere man, with a dry sense of humour and an eagle eye for detail'.[2] It says much for Wilfrid's standing that on his arrival Jeffreys resumed his original role without the least resentment. On 19 September he wrote: 'Sorry to lose command, but glad to serve under such an old friend as Wilfrid.'[3] The two became known as a perfect combination. Craster wrote of Wilfrid that:

> He proved to be an outstanding Commanding Officer, who very quickly gained the deep respect and affection of all who served under him. The combination of Colonel Smith as Commanding Officer and Major Jeffreys as Senior Major gave the Grenadiers a partnership in command that was often considered to represent the ideal.[4]

Wilfrid's battalion had a full strength of 1,000 men in four companies of over 200 each, a machine gun section, a signalling section and administrative and support elements, including transport that was all horse-drawn. This was a large body to control, especially in confused conditions. The commanding officer was mounted but had to be on foot when in close contact with the enemy and going round his companies in the firing line, often a long and exhausting business conducted in the dark. The men were all serving regulars or reservists who had served their years with the colours, so had been ready for war with little training. Drafts of reinforcements would quickly bring battalions up to strength after a major engagement. The days of new volunteer armies and conscripts were yet to come. Wilfrid set sail for France on 12 September. He wrote his first letter to his wife, Violet, the next day:

Sept. 13th

<u>At Sea.</u> We did not get away from Southampton till 10 a.m. yesterday. We had to wait a long time for some horses which arrived late. We dined at the Local Club on Friday night, Cavan, Ardee, Brooke and myself, and had a nice quiet dinner, but indifferent food. The same can be said of the food on board, still it is better than nothing. We are eating the fresh food out of our hampers and keeping the things which will not go bad for the possibly long train journey. We ran into rather dirty weather in the afternoon, rain and a head wind, but this morning is better. The sun has come out, and the sea has gone down, though there is a good Atlantic roll.

Our ship is the 'Victorian', Leyland Line; she is really a cattle boat, and has just returned from taking a load of horses, so she is in a pretty filthy condition. The Captain says he has been at it day and night for six weeks, and has never had a chance to clean her. I wonder what news you are getting to-day. It seemed very good yesterday morning, and I do pray that we have got them on the run. We are going very slow, being stopped by head winds, and I doubt if we are going more than 8 knots. However, she behaves very well, and it is no use fussing for Time and Tide wait for no man.

Sept. 14th

We have had a good day on the whole, and it has become clearer and calmer. We are hoping to get in to-morrow morning, so I cannot tell when I shall get a chance of writing again. I believe it takes a long time to get up the river to Nantes, as they are dependent on the tide.

· BACKGROUND NARRATIVE ·

On his way to the front, Wilfrid met his cousin, Alan Tritton, who had been wounded on 1 September at Villers-Cotterêts. He would be killed on 26 December in the trenches near Béthune and is buried in Le Touret Military Cemetery with Wilfrid:

Sept. 15th

I have got a good way on my journey, as far as the Advanced Base. I hope to join the Battalion to-morrow. The trains are awful. We have taken 14 hours to do 120 miles.

We have seen a lot of wounded French and prisoners pass here. I saw Tritton in the Coldstream yesterday, shot through the hand. He hopes to be back in a fortnight.

I have just had a good bath, and a few hours' sleep, which is very refreshing, after a long journey, who knows when we shall get the next? It is very pleasant being so many together. I think there are 9 of us altogether for the same Brigade.

Sept. 17th

Just arrived at railhead. All well.

· BACKGROUND NARRATIVE ·

Wilfrid arrived at the front to find his battalion entrenched and battle-hardened from the heavy fighting of the previous few weeks. The German shelling was intense. He was given command of the 2nd Battalion on 9 September 1914. Wilfrid's reference in this and some of his later letters to the change in the battalion since Pirbright likely refers to his temporary command when it was in camp there:

Sept. 18th

Got to the Battalion this morning, which I find sadly changed from what it was six weeks ago at Pirbright. We are hung up by the Germans at present, who shell us from dawn till dark. It went on all day yesterday. We heard it ten miles off, and could not quite get up last night, but slept in a church a few miles off. It began again at dawn, and goes on all day. They appear to be trying to break us with shell-fire, and an occasional night attack. I find everybody very cheery, although they have never had a day's rest. Colston, Jeffreys, Pike, Gilbert Hamilton, and Bernard [Gordon Lennox] all well. Let their wives know if you can. I believe George Powell is all right, but I have not seen him. It has rained hard for two days, which makes it rather miserable, and we hardly ever see our kits, and have nothing except what we can carry. I am so glad to at last command the Battalion, and although it is a difficult job taking over a Battalion actually in the firing line, I must do my best, and hope all will go well, but there is no doubt that we have a tough job before us.

DIARY

Sept. 19th
Took over the Battalion in trenches at La Cour de Soupir Farm.

Commanding Companies:
1. Hamilton
2. Lennox
3. Symes-Thompson
4. Colston

Other officers were:
1. Stocks
2. Powell
3. Miller
4. Ridley

Bailey, Congleton, and Nesbitt came out with me.
We were shelled all day – lost 2 men k., 5 w.

· BACKGROUND NARRATIVE ·

The unprecedented nature of the war they were fighting was becoming increasingly apparent. Inkerman was a Crimean War battle in 1854, the last time the British Army had experienced a large number of casualties in a single battle.

Lord Francis Scott recovered from his injuries. He moved to Kenya after the war where he became a prominent farmer and politician:

Sept. 19th

My word, it does rain here. It poured in torrents all last night, and the trenches are in an awful state. Half the Battalion are in the trenches all the time, and shelled incessantly. How one survives this sort of thing is a marvel. In spite of it we have only lost one man slightly wounded in the last two days. We cannot advance till the French get on a bit. The Battalion had a great fight the day before I arrived, and lost more men than have been lost since Inkerman, including three Officers, Cecil, Des Voeux, and Welby. We get no news of any sort, and know nothing except what goes on in our Brigade.

Yesterday a shell stampeded about 50 horses, who galloped down the road – my pony tried to bolt, and I lost my cap. Extraordinary to relate, beyond being plastered with mud, it was hardly damaged. Poor Francis Scott, with whom I was riding, was not so lucky. He was knocked over and most of the horses were over him. I was much alarmed for him, as he did not get up, but I got back to him, and found he was only a bit knocked out. I got him to Head Quarters and a doctor, and think he is all right, but have not seen him since, as he is with the Irish Guards.

Thank Heaven it has stopped raining, and I hope we shall get dry, but these beastly guns are sure to bring on the rain again. I have had very little sleep since I landed; the train journey was awfully slow, noisy, and uncomfortable, but I am very well, and manage with odd hours of sleep, and odd hours of food. We are fed quite well at present, but rely almost entirely on rations.

DIARY

Sept. 20th

Very heavily shelled all the afternoon – lost 4 men w.

Sept. 20th

You must not expect letters like this in future. It is only because we are standing still, hanging on by our teeth while the French push on. If we were only stronger we could get on, and push them back. As it is we cannot, as our strength will only enable us to hang on. I write in a sort of cave, safe I hope, from those horrible shells. Yesterday we had an extra dose of them, I suppose just to show what they could do. They had been going all the morning as usual, but from 2 till 6 they fairly let fly. One of the Brigade Staff told me last night that they had been amusing themselves by counting them, and they averaged 50 a minute. It was like hell let loose, and the gunners calculated the afternoon's amusement must have cost them £35,000 in ammunition. In the evening they made a feeble attack, and we wiped them out. I was thankful the men have learnt at last to dig and burrow in like rabbits. I don't know what others lost, but we lost only 2 killed, and 4 wounded, entirely owing to good digging. It is a gruesome business burying the poor fellows at night, but somehow it seems better that it should be ended for them than that they should be badly wounded.

The men are splendid, and I think their bravery in disregarding danger is largely due to British stupidity. I don't think they realise their danger, which is a great blessing for them, and makes them stand like rocks, when the highly strung foreigner can't stick it; but the men are tired. I can see that. They have not had one day's rest since they started to refit and wash, etc., and the difficulty of keeping them awake at night is extreme – in fact the Officers (and I have only 10 Company Officers) have to keep at them all night to keep them awake. The Brigade has really done more than its share.

DIARY

Sept. 21st
Relieved by the Irish Guards in the early morning, and billetted in the town of Soupir. Went to see the line at Chavonne, which we had to take over the next day.

Draft arrived with Tufnell and Marshall.

Sept. 22nd
Marched to Chavonne about 5 a.m., relieved the Bays [2nd Dragoon Guards (Queen's Bays)] and 11th Hussars. Dug in. H.Q. at Chavonne and 2 Coys. [abbreviation for Company], 2 Coys. being in the trenches.

Sept. 22nd

We have changed our place in the line, and are a little more comfortable, though the same shelling goes on all day. We have to hold the Germans here while the French come round the right flank. Near here is one of the sad scenes of war which would do many people in England good to see. A charming

Château, somewhere about the size of Goldings. It is now a hospital. I went round it yesterday. The beautiful drawing-room is full of wounded lying on the floor, so incongruous with all the beautiful furniture shoved away anywhere. The dining-room is an operating room. Mattresses from all over the house lie in the passages, etc. The sheets have been torn up for bandages, and all this with tapestries and pictures on the walls, that ought to look at other scenes. Outside, the beautiful lawns have had hundreds of horses bivouacked on them, and are like a farmyard. The most lovely begonias (large beds of them) are trampled by horses. The lake supplies water for them, and is like a duck pond. The stables are full of wagons of all sorts; the boxes and stalls have been full of wounded, as also the coach-house. The nice little church is full of wounded prisoners, and shells have cut the kitchen garden to bits. In fact the place looks ruined, and if the Château had not had the Red Cross flying, I have no doubt it would have been burnt by now by shells.

When we took this ridge, ten days ago, there was a lovely farmhouse with thousands of pounds of stock and grain, a real prosperous place. To-day the house, which I am sorry to say was full of German wounded, and was shelled by the Germans and burnt, is a ruin. All the stacks have been set on fire by shells, and have been burning for days. The stock has mostly been shot, the cows and Germans all lying together in heaps. The farmer stood it for two days, and then offed it. Much of the corn has never been got in, and the whole place is entrenched. I am afraid many children [French] have been wounded. They can't always escape the shells, but they play about in the villages, and do not seem to realise it. The French about here are not very friendly, and we think many of them spies! I expect because they are more frightened of the Germans than of us.

The weather is now lovely, but very cold at night. It would all look so beautiful if it was not for this ghastly war. I have lost all count of days. I only know the dates by the messages I receive and send.

· BACKGROUND NARRATIVE ·

Wilfrid sent a short letter to his son Lyulph:

Sept 22 14

My dear Lyulph

I hope that you are well and happy at school. I often think of you all and wonder how you are getting on.

We are fighting every day and are having a very hard time, but I hope we are gradually pushing the Germans back.

It is very cold at night. We have nothing to sleep in except what we can carry, as we never see our transport and we are all very dirty. I am lucky if I can wash my face and hands once a day and a bath we never see.

I have no time for more.

My love to Ralph and remember me to [headmaster] Mr Helbert.

Your affectionate father

Wilfrid

DIARY

Sept. 23rd to Oct. 12th

Remained at Chavonne. Improved trenches till they were very strong. Got shelled most days. Lost 6k., 9 w. The weather was glorious all this time.

Sept. 24th

I got your first letter yesterday, so they take a long time coming. In this village are several of the Coldstream. Dick Sawle, Pryce Jones, etc. all very well. No news, same shelling. Glorious days and bitter nights. I heard a story yesterday which may comfort you and others. I saw a doctor who stayed with the wounded prisoners after our great fight during the retreat, and he says the wounded were wonderfully well cared for by the Germans. Of course, there are isolated cases of brutality, but otherwise they were treated very well, and had nothing to complain of.

It is wonderful how the Battalion got through the retreat; many Officers lost everything they possessed, and the stragglers have not all turned up yet. I really cannot write any more, the noise of the shelling is so great.

Sept. 26th

Such glorious weather, and a lovely view from the cottage I am writing from, only spoilt by the din of our guns, and the returning shells. Most of the glass has been shaken out of the windows, and one gets very weary of the noise. From morning till night, and during a great part of the night, it goes on, and this artillery duel has been going on for 12 days! My morning walk round the trenches is not all joy! I generally have difficulty in getting out and back – only half a mile away. We have all had some wonderful escapes from this shelling, but it is most unpleasant. The only advantage in stopping here is that we get mails and newspapers, which have been delayed for weeks. The men get no rest worth speaking of – day and night most of them are on duty. The base having been changed, I expect we shall get mails quicker.

Yours of the 27th arrived to-day. What we want more than anything is matches; they are unobtainable, the parcel post won't carry them. People are kind in sending tobacco, etc., but without matches they lose much of their value, as you can only light from a fire.

Sept. 28th

You will be quite spoilt having so many letters from me, but it will not go on once we get a move on, and when that will be, one cannot tell. We are told that everything is going on well, but really we know very little, except this, of the general situation. I cannot help thinking that our advance will be pretty slow in future, unless the French score some great success, as the Germans will fight as hard as they can. I do not think the shell fire has been quite as heavy to-day, whether that is, as we hope, that [*sic*] our guns have done some good, or whether they are merely devoting their attention to another part of the line, I do not know.

I am sorry to say I have lost Ted Colston, who has gone home with appendicitis. He is a great loss, and has done very well. I hope he will get home, and through it safely. I am glad to think of him safe at home with his people, to whom he is so much. His men ran down to his ambulance to say farewell to him, which I thought very nice of them, particularly as he has worked them very hard. They don't mind that, however, as long as the Captain is a good fellow.

A great luxury to-day: we got some butter, the first since we arrived. It is very hard to get anything of that sort, as the natives have not much for themselves.

I am terribly short of Officers – I wish more would come out.

For some reason they will not let us have our kits up, they are kept 5 miles away, and so we have nothing but what we stand in, and the constant dirt, when unnecessary, is annoying. I sleep in my boots every night, it saves trouble if there is an alarm, and except that the wet makes one's feet very sore, I don't really care a bit. If we may not mention names it makes it hard to write, though I have no doubt you know whereabouts we are.

Sept. 30th

The sort of food luxuries we want are such things as potted meats, small plum puddings, soup squares, possibly cakes, if they will travel, but they must be sent in small quantities – a huge parcel is no good, as we can't carry them. We get very good rations, heaps of jam, biscuit, and often bread, and when we can we buy butter, eggs, etc., but they are very difficult to get. You might order Fortnum & Mason to send me 2lbs. of coffee every week, if possible, to be ready for making. We never get it, and it is a capital thing in the early morning. One gets tired of perpetual tea. We used to have it as a ration in South Africa, but now only get tea.

I never get my clothes off, and very seldom my boots. If I ever take my boots off at night, there is sure to be an alarm, so I have given it up altogether.

We do not anticipate a big attack at present but the Germans make small attacks at night, which means a lot of shooting and noise, as you cannot see what is going on, but our movements will entirely depend on how the French get on. I only pray that we shall not go back again. I forget if I told you that Eben Pike is my Adjutant – he does very well, and there was no one else to take the job on.

A parson has just turned up, so I hope I shall have to conduct no more funerals. I dislike it extremely; it is such a distressing job.

Yesterday we got a goose, being Michaelmas Day, but we couldn't manage the stuffing, or the sauce! We get plenty of papers, but about ten days old as a rule.

Sept. 28 14

My dear Ralph

I wonder how you are getting on and Lyulph too his first term. I expect he likes football very much. We have had fine weather lately, but it is very cold at night and [there is] generally a thick fog in the morning which is very chilly when you do not have much breakfast! There is such a pretty château (country house) near here with pretty gardens, but they have all been spoilt and smashed to bits by the horses and guns and the German shells – and it looks more like a ruin than anything else. We got a certain amount to eat, but the Germans came over this country first and swept it clean of almost everything and so there is not much to get out of it now. Mummy tells me that you looked after her very well at Deal. You and Luff must write to her and cheer her up while you are at school. My love to Luff; look after him well and much love to you

from yr affect

Father

[Luff was a short form of Lyulph used by the family and also by friends all his life who could not pronounce or spell Lyulph correctly.]

Oct 2nd

Letters come oddly. I got yours of the 17th after the 20th! I heard yesterday officially that they hope the postal service will be better in future, and that letters will get home and return in five days each way. The kits coming up enables me to write on better paper. I know how hard you must find it to read, as I have to read so many messages in the course of the day, and I expect by the end of this show my eyes will have gone, but I expect you would rather have my scraps than nothing!

A parson arrived yesterday – Fleming by name – the first time a parson has seen the Battalion since the beginning of the war. We had a service this morning in the church here, lent by the French curé. Just a Communion Service. It was an odd experience, with shells backwards and forwards all the time. I was astonished at the number of men who turned up, particularly as they had been in the trenches all night, and I am glad to say several Officers came.

We are very comfortable in a small house, where we can get a fire to dry and warm ourselves, and I sleep on a bundle of straw, which makes the stone floor less hard! The men are in barns, etc., and as there is plenty of straw, they are fairly comfortable when they come in from the trenches – (all this sounds like the Crimea), but the eternal shelling makes sleep by day difficult. To-day we have had an unusually peaceful day.

I am afraid the weather has broken; to-day is wet and foggy, and looks very like winter, but we must be thankful for the wonderful sun of the last week, which has made things better for us. The health of the troops has been wonderful, but I am afraid, with the cold coming on, we cannot expect this to last.

We often see the aeroplanes returning from the German lines. It is most exciting to watch them. The Germans turn on their guns, and I have seen twenty shells burst near them at times – generally nowhere near them, but now and again most unpleasantly close. I do not think they have ever been hit. A German one came over two nights ago, and saw a bridge we were making. Sure enough, half an hour after, they sent four of their big shells plumb at it, and caught the gunners' horses watering. I happened to be riding over to see the Brigadier at the time, and you never saw such a mess. The accuracy of their guns is extraordinary. Prisoners though, complain of the accuracy of ours, so it appears to be mutual. I hope it is.

· BACKGROUND NARRATIVE ·

Reinforcements were gradually being sent out to the BEF. The Indian Expeditionary Force, with about 50,000 troops, had travelled slowly from India and landed in Marseilles at the end of September. It suffered further delays due to rearming and difficulties with supply trains, finally seeing action on the Western Front at La Bassée at the end of October. A fourth corps was sent to France from England in October under Sir Henry Rawlinson. This included 1st Battalion Grenadiers:

Oct. 3rd

Will you order me two stars and two crowns? I have got a private soldier's greatcoat, and want them for the shoulder-straps.

You will know by now (I see it in the papers) that we are just over the Aisne, a small river with a canal about a quarter mile behind it. Not a very nice position if we were forced back, which I hope there is no chance of, and we are about the centre of the British Line. The papers say we are steadily advancing. As a matter of fact we have not budged from the ground won on the 14th and 15th, when we lost nearly two hundred men. I arrived just after that to find a gloom set in after the heavy loss of Officers. You would hardly believe it, but it is a fact that there are only three Captains and one Subaltern left who were in the Battalion when I took it over at Pirbright! Most of the men are changed too. It is rumoured that we stay here till the arrival of the Indians and the 4th Army, but personally I believe we shall stay here till the French get on on the left, when we hope the Germans will bolt again. We certainly cannot take the hills to our immediate front without more strength than we have at present.

We hear the German bands at night, and sometimes in the morning. They seem to play to cheer up the men. The other night we put a couple of shells into their singing bivouac, and the music ceased abruptly.

· BACKGROUND NARRATIVE ·

The Fourth Army was not formed until early 1916.

Wilfrid wrote to his daughter Sylvia who was still staying at Deal, asking after Jack, the family's Airedale terrier who was to feature regularly in his letters to his daughter:

Oct 3 14

My dear Sylvia

I wonder how you are and how you like the sea. You ought to be a round, rosy little freckled thing by now. Have you been bathing in the sea, I wonder? I suppose you miss the boys now that they are at school. I see lots of little boys and girls out here, but they are not having a happy time that you are. They can hardly go out of their houses and have no school to go to and I am afraid that many of them cannot get too much to eat as they cannot go to the towns to buy things.

I wonder how Jack is. Give him my love. Do you call him about as much as ever? I expect you do, you little rascal!

I send you so much love; I often wish I could see you again. You will be such a big girl by the time I come home.

Yr affect

Father

Oct. 4th

One line in haste by Percy, who is just going home, to say I'm very well. I have written to you so often that I have nothing to say.

Oct. 6th

We are now getting letters in five days, and you are the same I believe. I sent a line by Percy the other day. He is one of the Press Bureau with French. As regards the situation here, we are much quieter. The shelling has been comparatively peaceful the last few days, just enough to let us know they are there. I believe they expected to shell us out of our position, and then get us into trouble crossing the river and canal at our backs. Now they find they have not been able to do so, they are quieter, and just waiting to be turned out of their very strong position. In '70 [during the Franco-Prussian War] they had a great battle here and drove the French into the Aisne. We know little here, and get odd and lying rumours, but I gather the great battle between the French and Germans, is going on in the north somewhere near Lille. We doubt anything much coming of it, and think the papers at home much too 'cockahoop'. Unless the Germans withdraw or are out-flanked, I do not see how we are going to turn them out of the strong position to our immediate front. From what I gather the people at home expect this to be a long war, and the Head Quarters out here expect it not to last long, if Russia can get on.

I think out here the Generals are inclined to be too sanguine. They never come near us or look at the German position. Cavan is the only General we ever see, and I do not even know the G.O.C. Division by sight: I think it would do the men a lot of good to see a General sometimes near the front.

Lately the weather has been warmer, but inclined to be wet, and that always makes one feel cold, particularly at night.

We are over strength now, and have two hundred men waiting at the Base. The days draw in, and I do not look forward to the long winter evenings. We have a service here every evening at 6.30, which draws the men well, I think largely for the sake of something to do in the evenings. It is strangely quiet there at night, after the noise of the day.

· BACKGROUND NARRATIVE ·

Wilfrid wrote to his brother-in-law, Lord Raglan, who was Lieutenant Governor of the Isle of Man from 1902 to 1919. He had joined the Grenadier Guards in 1870 and fought with them in the Second Anglo-Afghan War. He was Undersecretary of State for War from 1900 to 1902. Two of Lord Raglan's three sons, Wellesley and Nigel, had been wounded. They were both to survive the war, Nigel emerging with a DSO and MC.

The George Morris mentioned was the first commanding officer to lead an Irish Guards battalion into battle. He was killed on 1 September during the retreat from Mons, near Villers-Cotterêts:

Oct 7 14

My dear FitzRoy

I am sure you will like to have a few lines about the 2nd Battalion. First of all I am so sorry about your two boys, but much relieved to hear that they might be worse. I hope they will both make a good recovery. I got here and took over the Battalion the morning after the Battle of the Aisne. We were doing Advanced Guard that morning, and apparently the same old order was given that 'the Pursuit would continue'. The country was v. wooded and we found the Germans entrenched just beyond the wood and also occupying the wood in some force. The result was a big fight in which I gather the Brigade got pretty well mixed up. And eventually by night we gained the crest of the hill beyond the wood. Our casualties were v. heavy. In the 2 days fighting on the Aisne we lost nearly 200 men, which I suppose is the largest casualty list in the Regiment since Inkerman. We have been holding the crest ever since, though as fast as we get well dug in in one place, we are shifted to another and begin digging again. Having got the crest, we found the Germans had a v. strong position in front of us and for days they tried to shell us out. Days and days they rained shells on us from dawn till dark without ceasing. I never thought such shelling was possible or that any Army Supply would stand it. The noise has been deafening, some of their big shells bursting with a terrific row and making enormous holes in the ground. One reason for our large casualties when taking the hill was that one of these shells burst among our men and the Connaughts, when 72 men were killed and wounded of which 40 were ours. They have shelled us daily, ever since, but it has decreased considerably the last week. I think they found at last that it was a waste of ammunition. The only time it is safe to go about is after dark or early in the morning. The German guns do not appear to be early risers! We get sniped a bit, but I think we have won at that game. The men are splendid and they are utterly indifferent to the shells and take messages about as if they were going down Piccadilly. I gather that the retreat was a terrible business and between you and me was very much like a rout. I am told we were far better than anybody else, and I have been told by outsiders that our discipline was wonderful. I do not think, though, that Grenadiers were quite satisfied with it! The Irish Guards are the devil. Their discipline is nil. And it is apt to demoralise. I gather that poor George Morris was killed because he was up in the firing line trying to do what his rotten officers couldn't do. But that is between you and me. We have lost a lot of officers. In fact, there are only 4 officers left who were in the Battalion when I first took them over at Pirbright before the war. We have been busy during this comparative lull, re-fitting and pulling the men together and I think now we are hoping to move again soon. I do not think it will be long before we do. Sitting still and being shelled is no fun. When moving about one does not bother about it so much and it is such a rotten way of losing good men, lying like rabbits underground.

I hope you are all well at home. I have good account of V, who has been wonderfully plucky all through. I am indeed lucky to have such a wife, when one knows how hard some wives have made it for their husbands. But it is a bad job for them at best, poor things. Out here the idea is that we have got through the worst of it, provided always that the Russians are successful, but the French are v. uncertain. They cannot hang on to what they win, but run away and then have to do the job all over again. Love to you all

Yr affect

Wilfrid

· BACKGROUND NARRATIVE ·

The Russians had invaded East Prussia in August with a force of 800,000 men, but were heavily defeated by the Germans at the Battle of Tannenberg at the end of August and pushed out of East Prussia during the first half of September in the Battle of the Masurian Lakes. They staged a counter-attack at the Battle of the Niemen from 25 to 28 September, during which they forced a German retreat back to the border and recaptured much of the ground they had lost two weeks earlier:

Oct. 8th

I had hardly finished my last letter to you when we were subjected to a terrific bombardment for three hours. I was in mortal fear this village would get on fire, which with so many men in it (half a Battalion Coldstream and half us) would be very serious. However, after an anxious afternoon the darkness came on and it ceased, and except for the loss of three horses, and one man wounded, nothing happened except a few houses knocked about. We have had a good bit of shelling to-day, with a deafening noise. They have been trying to find our guns, but I trust have not succeeded.

The news of the Russian victory in East Prussia, which reached us to-day, has been hailed with joy. It seems marvellous, but we get the 'Daily Mail' from Paris sometimes now. Sometimes it is a day or so old, but occasionally we get it the same day! In fact the latest joke is to grouse at the hardships of war when the daily newspaper is late!

The weather lately has been glorious, but very frosty at night.

If my letters suddenly cease, you will know we are moving. I have no idea whether we shall or not, but I should not be surprised if we did now at any time. I should not be altogether sorry – one gets sick of this eternal noise, though I suppose it will be only changing one noisy place for another. How one wishes the whole thing could be over and done with, but that won't be for many a long day, I fear. One hears of some good fellow gone every day, which is very depressing, but one cannot help feeling some good will come of it for those who remain.

· BACKGROUND NARRATIVE ·

Wilfrid was concerned about the events unfolding in Antwerp, a major target for the Germans. It had been under formal siege since 28 September. The British government was fearful that once the city and its forts had been captured, German forces would advance quickly towards the Channel ports, possibly threatening Britain itself. On 1 October, the British decided to redeploy a division of troops that had originally been intended for the BEF. On 2 October, the Germans penetrated two of the city's forts. Winston Churchill, First Lord of the Admiralty, was sent to report on the situation. Leaving London that night, he spent three days in the trenches and forts around Antwerp. He reported back to Lord Kitchener, the Secretary of State for War, that Belgian morale was low and their resistance was weakening. In response to a request from the Belgian government, the British despatched 6,000 Royal Navy troops who landed at Dunkirk on 3 and 4 October, arriving in Antwerp on 6 October. But they were too late. The Belgian government had already left the city. The order to evacuate was given for the next day, 7 October, and was carried out over the following two days. The Germans moved in to occupy the city, which formally surrendered on 10 October:

> Oct. 10th
>
> Things look bad in Antwerp. I gather that the Belgians are losing heart, and it is hoped we may be able to push through Belgium and clear the country of Germans. It is odd how the main battlefields keep changing, and owing to the modern use of railways, which is a feature of this war. I believe the Indians are not yet up, which is a great pity as they are badly wanted. They are most extraordinarily leisurely in sending up reinforcements to the front. I fancy the French don't help much, as they want their lines to feed their own men and take the wounded away.
>
> It is very cold and raw to-day. I wrote to FitzRoy the other day when we could hardly put our heads out on account of shelling.
>
> Some days we get no post or papers, and the days are sometimes long in consequence. If we could only go for a walk in this country, it would be charming, but in the first place it is not safe, and also if one does go out, somebody is sure to want something.

Oct. 12th

Thanks for the soups. We put everything into the common fund. Our mess is the Head Quarters mess, consisting of myself, Jeffreys, and the Adjutant, Doctor, Transport Officer, etc., and the Companies all run their own messes. They have taken away our kits again, so I expect we are on the move again shortly, and my letters will probably suffer in consequence. I can't carry much when on the move, without our kits, but I cram up my second horse as much as I can.

We hear that Antwerp has fallen. The Germans were cheering all the afternoon two or three days ago, and that was the reason I suppose. We heard that the 7th Division was going there, but I don't suppose that was true. I don't expect much of this fight in the north – it looks like a stalemate affair, but we hope and pray that the Russians will have a great success at Cracow.

We had a bitter night last night, with a hard frost. I go round the trenches every morning soon after 5, and it was as white as snow. Although sleeping under cover, it was jolly cold, but I manage alright. December will be jolly though, won't it? The leaves are falling fast, and it looks very wintry.

4

13 October to
22 November 1914
– First Battle of Ypres

By the end of September, it had become clear to the Allied commanders that the fighting on the Aisne had become bogged down. They embarked on a series of manoeuvres to the north designed to outflank the Germans. The Allied line was lengthening to the left. The position of the BEF in the centre was causing supply difficulties as the British line of communication cut right across the French communications. A position in Flanders would automatically shorten the train movements between the Channel ports and the British Army. It was therefore agreed that the BEF should be replaced by the French Territorials on the Aisne and moved up to Flanders. This operation had begun on the night of 1–2 October with units moving in great secrecy and the enemy was unaware that they had gone. It was completed on 19 October when I Corps, of which Wilfrid's battalion was part, finished detraining at Hazebrouck. Two days later, the corps was in position near Ypres.

After the loss of Antwerp, Ypres was the only Belgian town still in the hands of its own people, a fact that gave it enormous emotional significance far in excess of its military importance. The First Battle of Ypres was the first really enormous encounter of the war, though it would tragically be succeeded by others on the same scale or even greater in the succeeding four years. It was absolutely unprecedented in size and duration. Its impact on the British after a whole century of peace can hardly be imagined. Waterloo had been settled in a day: First Ypres took four weeks of unrelenting struggle between huge forces. Wilfrid's battalion suffered 714 casualties between the beginning of October and 18 November, while the BEF suffered overall casualties of nearly 55,000 during this period.

The Germans had two great strengths: powerful and numerous artillery and vast numbers of men whom they threw into battle in the most prodigal manner. The British opposing them were heavily outnumbered, but quickly learned to dig fast and deep, and they were highly skilled in shooting, trained to fire fifteen aimed rounds per minute. So devastating was the effect that the enemy were convinced that they were facing machine guns, of which each battalion had only two on establishment at the time. On 15 November, one company alone of the 2nd Battalion fired 24,000 rounds. The enemy were sometimes in such numbers, and so close (often less than 100 yards away), that the difficulty was to shoot them quickly enough. Whatever the difficulties of supply, there always seemed to be enough ammunition.

Most of the British casualties were caused by shells, of which the Germans fired prodigious numbers. There was no time to dig comprehensive trench lines, with deep dugouts and some overhead protection, such as would later cover the Western Front. Holes were dug for three or four men only. Communication between them was always risky and, in woods such as the 2nd Battalion Grenadiers occupied during their time at Ypres, shells bursting in the trees above, rather than on the ground, brought shrapnel and splinters of wood raining down from above and many felled trees, impeding movement.

There were, of course, no radios and little opportunity to lay telephone lines, even if they would had survived the shelling. Flag and hand signals were of very limited use. Orders and reports were therefore largely conveyed by messages scribbled in pencil and carried by runners, who often had the most dangerous job of all. The Germans had fully expected to reach Paris in six weeks, as they had done in 1870, and were humiliated and nettled at being halted and driven back on the Marne and Aisne. They *had* to prevail at Ypres. The Order of the Day issued by the German General Staff on 29 October conveys more than a hint of desperation:

> The breakthrough will be of decisive importance. We must and therefore will conquer, settle for ever the centuries-long struggle, end the war and strike the decisive blow against our most detested enemy. We will finish with the British, Indians, Canadians, Moroccans and other trash, feeble adversaries who surrender in mass if they are attacked with vigour.[1]

As it happened, Wilfrid's old 1st Battalion, just arrived in Belgium, was the first to be engaged, and close to where the 2nd Battalion would soon fight. They were thrown into a confused battle, in turn defending and counter-attacking, and after a few days were withdrawn having lost three-quarters of their strength. Among the officers killed were Wilfrid's nephew, Sydney Walter, Violet's nephew, Norman Somerset, and her cousin, Lord Richard Wellesley. It was an exceptionally savage fate for a battalion that did not even have the few weeks' fighting experience acquired by the 2nd Battalion.

It was usual for a battalion showing particular gallantry to be recognised by the award of a decoration to its commander. Later in the war this was in most cases the Distinguished Service Order (DSO) but in 1914 the DSO was also awarded to junior officers, there being no other decoration for gallantry besides the Victoria Cross (VC). Thus the DSO hardly satisfied the exceptional achievement of a battalion at Ypres. Several officers commanding battalions, including Wilfrid, were therefore awarded the Companion of the Order of St Michael and St George (CMG), originally a diplomatic decoration but now brought into use for the military also. At the end of 1914, the Military Cross (MC) was introduced as a gallantry decoration for junior officers and thereafter the DSO became the usual award for distinction in battalion command and the CMG for a brigadier general similarly deserving.

DIARY

Oct. 13th

Relieved by French about 2 a.m., and marched to Perles: arrived at 5 a.m., and billetted at a farm. Very lucky to get away without being shelled. Extraordinarily quiet after the shelling of the past three weeks.

Oct. 14th

Marched at 4 a.m. to Fismes, entrained and left at 7 a.m. Passed Paris, Amiens, Abbeville, Calais.

Oct. 14th

I am writing in a very shaky train, I don't know whether you will be able to read it. We are just outside Paris. How different from the last time I was there with you! And how little we then thought of all this; and we are travelling to a place not many hours from you. We got away from our entrenchments two

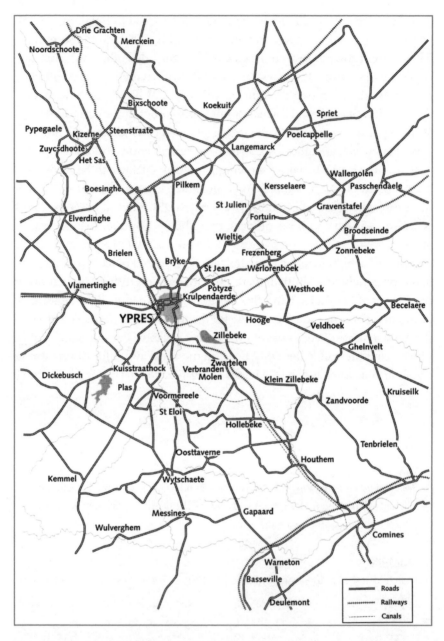

Ypres and the surrounding area, where the First Battle of Ypres was fought, October and November 1914. (Scale: approx. 1 cm : 1 mile)

nights ago in the dark, and I breathed a sigh of relief when we got safely and quietly five miles off without being shelled, in the stillness of a glorious frosty night. We had watched for many days every corner that is regularly shelled, and all along our road were huge holes made by the German 'Black Maria' [British slang for large-calibre German shells which gave off black smoke] shells! I was very glad to get the Battalion safely away. In the early dawn we reached a small village (Perles), where we billetted in the barns, etc., away at last from the eternal noise of guns, which we only heard faintly during the day. It was a bitter night and freezing hard, but quite still, like December. During the ten minutes [*sic*] hourly halts, one got chilled to the bone, which did not improve a cold I got a few days ago. However, I am all right again, thanks to my medicine chest which contains plenty of quinine! By the way, we have a charming doctor, who looks after me like a baby. We are lucky to have such a nice man.

We got to bed at 6 a.m, being twenty-five hours since I last had a lie down, and then we had breakfast at 1 p.m., and luncheon at 6 p.m., going to bed about 8 p.m. I got a real bed, at a farm house, to lie down on, which was very comfortable. Except to have a sort of bath three times, I have not had my breeches off since I left the ship!

We moved again at 3 a.m. to the train, and now we are moving wearily along at about fifteen miles an hour, and likely to do so till the small hours of to-morrow. However, it is resting to see civilisation without guns. It seems so odd to be fighting in this sort of country; we have always associated war with the tropics in the past. It has turned much warmer again.

I wonder what the result of the fall of Antwerp will be. I think they had to take this as they failed at Paris. How odd all the outskirts of Paris look – all the trees cut down to prepare for its defence, and yet everything going on apparently as usual. We have just left, having stopped there for twenty minutes – all the people waving frantically at the men – and well they may, for we saved Paris.

DIARY

Oct. 15th

Detrained at Hazebrouck at 8 a.m., and billeted in the town.

Oct. 16th

Hazebrouck.

Oct. 17th

Marched at 7 a.m. to Boescheppe and billetted.

Oct. 18th

Boescheppe, had a bath, first time for a month.

Oct. 18th

We sleep in odd places every night, but generally under cover. I am glad to hear 5 Officers are arriving to-day. I was done out of my Church to-day, being too busy, but one cannot expect much Church out here. Everybody well and cheery here; the weather keeps up, thank goodness, but it is raw, and sometimes very foggy.

Oct 19 14

My dear Lyulph

I hope you are getting on well at school and like the football and your games. I am sure you are glad to get out of the nursery and be a school boy.

It is getting very cold out here and the nights are very damp and foggy. How would you like to see all the soldiers out here? There are thousands and thousands both English and French. But they do not look much like what they do at home, for their clothes are old and dirty and they don't often get a wash. And there are thousands of horses of all sorts, but I am afraid they have suffered very much, for the work is very heavy and many get killed. We spend the nights in villages, whenever we can and we sleep in some funny places, and try to get straw to lie on to keep warm. Wherever the Germans have been, we do not find much left, because they take all the cattle, horses and food. We always have to pay for everything we get, but I hope, if we get into Germany, we shall not pay them a penny, but take what we want. The Germans are very cruel to the poor people, and I have seen individuals who have been driven from their homes. Don't you pity them? Some photographs were taken the other day of some of my men, in their trenches – I hope you will see the pictures when they are put in the papers. Give my love to Ralph. I hope he is quite well again. I have had your nice letters in my pocket since I got them, but they are getting very black and dirty now!

Good bye, my dear boys – work hard and then enjoy your games as much as possible.

Yr Affect

Father

Oct 19 14

My dear little Sylvia

I wonder where you are and whether you have gone back home yet to see poor Blu who must miss you so much. I am sure you must be tired of the sea by now? or do you like the sea very much? I saw 2 aeroplanes fighting in the air about a week ago. An English and German one. The English got away alright, but the German came down so quickly that I think he was badly damaged. I watched them through my telescope, as they were high up, and it was like watching two large birds. They both seemed to be trying to get above one another and then suddenly something happened and the German came gliding down, while ours went sailing away towards home shot by the German big guns, and there were little puffs of smoke following it for a long time, till it got out of range. Germans seemed to be shooting very close to it.

Goodbye, my dear, I wish I could see you and give you a hug.

Yr affect

Father

DIARY

Oct. 19th

Boescheppe. Maitland, Cavendish, Rose and Hughes joined.

Oct. 20th

Left Boescheppe at 6 a.m., and marched through Ypres to St. Jean. Here we dug in with two companies, and billetted in farms. Later in the evening I had to send up another Company to fill up a gap caused by the Coldstream having moved to meet an attack on the right of the line. Heavy firing in front. Battalion as follows:-

1. Hamilton, Symes-Thompson, Hughes, Bailey
2. Lennox, Miller, Rose
3. Powell, Cavendish, Congleton, Marshall
4. Maitland, Ridley, Nesbitt, Stocks

H.Q. Jeffreys, Pike, Howell, Tufnell, Cunninghame

· BACKGROUND NARRATIVE ·

Wilfrid's HQ team comprised Jeffreys, his second-in-command; Pike, adjutant; Howell, battalion doctor; Tufnell, machine gun officer; and Cunninghame, transport officer.

DIARY

Oct. 21st

Marched at 6 a.m. by Wiettge to position of assembly near Hannebeck Brook about 2 miles W. of Zonnebeke. Advanced about 1½ miles towards Paschendaal, meeting with some opposition – eventually entrenched the line of the road. 3rd Battalion Coldstream Guards on the left: 2nd Battalion Coldstream Guards on the right of us.

The Hon. W. Bailey and A.K.S. Cunninghame. (Grenadier Guards)

Irish Guards in reserve. Strong counter-attack by Germans at dusk, who came on saying 'Don't fire, we are Coldstream!' Unfortunately for them, they hit off Ivor Rose, and were repulsed with heavy loss.

There was a great deal of shelling on both sides all the afternoon, and the fires at night (farms and ricks) lighted up the country for miles; lost 6 <u>w</u>.

Oct. 22nd

Remained in trenches with 2 Companies. Had 2 Companies dug in in root-fields in rear, and moved Head Quarters back to a farm about 600 yards back.

Oct. 22nd

The Flying men tell me the French Flyers have done no good at all, and are useless. So much for saying we were behind them! Our Flyers are wonderful, and if they had faster machines could drive the Germans off altogether, as a German now will not let them come near them if they can help it.

We had a battle yesterday, but did not get on very far. Our line is so long that one part cannot get too far ahead of another, and some are very sticky: we got on further than anyone else but it is all rot saying we have nothing in front of us. There are heaps of Germans, and as an army, they are very good, and their gunners are perfect. The Belgians have never done any good I am told. They will not stand the shelling, no more will any but highly trained and disciplined troops.

The French and Belgians who are not far from us are most unreliable. I expect our advance will be very slow, unless something unexpected happens. No doubt we will kill heaps of Germans, but there are always heaps more. We got a lot last night after dark. The Germans attacked one of my platoons shouting 'We are Coldstream', but we let them have it, and picked up 100 this morning. They are up to every dirty trick. It was all over in two minutes. I have the greatest faith in the men at night, if they are well dug in. (and they do dig now, like rabbits!) They shoot so well that all I have to see to is that they have plenty of ammunition, and no German will ever reach the trenches.

The crowds of refugees are the saddest sights imaginable, miles and miles of them, and the Germans like to get among them, and come with them, but we are up to most of their tricks now. The Germans have burnt all the houses for miles. Last night the sky was all lighted up, and it looked like an inferno. They do it, I suppose, to prevent us attacking, but it is very foolish of them, as they attack us, and we give them toko. If we advance we shall find no houses to sleep in. There is not a soul left in the country. All the farms are deserted, and the cows and pigs wander about aimlessly. The men milk them in the interval of shelling! The crops are splendid but wasted; it is as if a plague has passed over the land.

I haven't had my boots off at all for three days and nights, and wet socks make one very cold and sore, but I see no immediate prospect of a peaceful day or night. The battle is raging round us, for the moment we are comparatively peaceful. How long it will last, goodness knows. We have just heard officially of a great victory in Russia. Please God it is true, it will help us more than anything. And now I must stop.

DIARY

Oct. 23rd

Remained in trenches. French attacked with 2 Divisions and some Cavalry, but did not get far. Miller <u>k</u>. Maitland and 16 men <u>w</u>. Several wounded this day by premature explosions of our guns, which were constant and most unpleasant. German shelling heavy all day. We were relieved by the French this night. I was left with the Battalion as escort to the guns. The whole Brigade was relieved and marched off, but the French who were to relieve us never turned up. After a long and anxious wait, during which an attack was made on the French, we eventually got away at 2 a.m., and moved to a farm a mile back.

Oct. 24th

Ordered to move at 5, but found guns could not get relieved by the French till 12. Moved to another farm and just got settled to sleep, when we were ordered to move at once and join the rest of the Brigade. Moved in ¼ hour, and joined the Brigade near Hooge, and marched to Ekaternest, where I was told to join the 6th Brigade. Saw the G.O.C. (Fanshawe), who told me to be in Reserve at Ekaternest. Got a comfortable place, ate and slept till dark, when we joined our Brigade which was at the same place.

· BACKGROUND NARRATIVE ·

Two of Wilfrid's nephews, Norman Somerset, son of Violet's brother Arthur, and Sydney Walter, son of Wilfrid's sister Edith, were killed with 1st Battalion Grenadiers on 23 and 24 October respectively:

Oct. 24th

I got two or three letters from you yesterday, and several others. They arrived when we were having a poor time in the afternoon – shells and bullets all over the place, and it was quite comical that at such a moment I got a message that thirty bags of mail are arrived (the accumulation of a fortnight), and if they were not fetched away they would be left on the ground. We got them, and one of the many problems I had to solve that afternoon was how to carry them. However, we did manage it somehow. The battle has been raging now for three days and nights – it is quite appalling at times. We lost a good boy, Miller, yesterday, and several men. We were badly shelled, and had a wretched afternoon and night. We have had no sleep to speak of for some nights – fought and marched without ceasing – an anxious day is followed by an anxious night, and then another anxious day follows. However, however bad it is, it might be worse, but it is very unpleasant at times. The Germans are doing all they can to drive us into the sea, and whatever rot people may talk, they are a tough nut to crack, and very good at this game of war. Poor Tony Markham was badly wounded yesterday, and is only just alive. His optic nerve is out.

The 3rd Battalion Coldstream caught it again two days ago. They are very unlucky, and have been all through. They are a jolly good Battalion.

I've just heard about Norman and Sydney; you will understand my sorrow – I really can't write about it. Please God the Kaiser shall pay for it in this world or the next. It is awful how the only sons have caught it – one after another have gone. Thank God it is in a good cause. Such a noise going on!

I did not get a lie down till three this morning, and got up at 4.45 a.m., and this continual noise is very trying. Our guns nearly drive me mad sometimes, and they always are near us and get shelled back, so the noise is awful. I believe they do very well, but we want more of them.

The plum pudding was excellent, and much appreciated by the Head Quarter's Mess. I'm writing in a very cramped position behind a farm house, so I can hardly write legibly. I see no end to this battle. They say all is going well, but we don't know much of what is going on. I can't write more to-day. I am so sad, poor Edith and Arthur. Everything round is dead or dying. Horses, cows, pigs, men; the chickens always seem to escape shells and bullets! And now I must try and get a few minutes [*sic*] sleep, if I can in this noise.

DIARY

Oct. 25th

Marched at 8 a.m. to a position of readiness near Polygone Wood [*sic*]. Informed by Brigadier that an attack was to be made on Reutel the next day, after we had heavily shelled the enemy's position. Meanwhile we must reconnoitre position. Ardee and I with Jeffreys, Bernard [Gordon Lennox], Rose, Francis Scott, and Alexander went off, and spent a long time looking round. We went to the top of the Château, where we got a good view of the Germans, and thought it a tough undertaking. Just as we were leaving the Château, the shells began to come, and we scattered. Ardee and I went together, and got back to our Battalions, who we found marching out to do the attack! Fresh orders had been given. We were shelled as we advanced, and made the attack through the wood. On emerging from the wood No. 2 (Bernard Lennox) got under heavy fire, and maxim fire – it was getting dark, and we could get no further. The companies were all mixed up in the wood. The Irish Guards had got some way on our left, and suffered considerably. Eventually we took up a line at the edge of the wood with 1 and 2. 3 and 4 I collected and kept in reserve. We were within 150 yards of the Germans strongly entrenched, and it was hopeless trying to get on, unless we could outflank them, which was impossible. Found ourselves next to the Scots Fusiliers, 7th Division, who were very shaky, and we had to occupy some of their trenches during the night. 3 <u>k</u>., 4 <u>w</u>., very lucky to get off so cheap.

Oct. 26th

Remained in same position, and heavily shelled. Any thought of an advance was now given up. 1 <u>k</u>., 6 <u>w</u>.

Oct. 27th

Remained in same position, and heavily shelled. 2 <u>k</u>., 1 <u>w</u>. The Château was heavily shelled at times. We were relieved during the night by the Camerons and Black Watch, and retired to a farm a mile back, which we reached about dawn.

Oct. 28th

Moved at 7.30 a.m. to support the attack of the 5th and 6th Brigades on Beccalaere. Eventually dug in and remained in reserve on N. edge of Polygone Wood, where we remained at night. 1 <u>w</u>.

· BACKGROUND NARRATIVE ·

Ashley Ponsonby, stepson of Wilfrid's sister, Hilda, had been injured whilst fighting with the Ox. L.I. not far from Wilfrid's battalion. Though he survived this injury, he was to be killed in action in September 1915:

Oct. 28th

I can't write much to-day. I am too busy. We march and fight and dig – dig, march, and fight, and get on little by little, but not very fast. We hope the Russian victory will relieve the pressure here.

I'm afraid my last letter was rather a low one, for which I am sorry. We had had a wearing time, and then came the news of the losses in the 1st Battalion, and I was depressed, but I am all right again, though it is depressing at times, and one gets harassed [sic].

I am in a little farm house with scarcely any light on, as we don't want the lights to show, so I can hardly see what I am writing, so you must excuse a scrawl.

Continued later. I was called away and so continue now late at night. I have just come in, such a glorious night with a lovely moon, and everything so quiet and peaceful after the din of the day. The country very like home, when you cannot see the destruction of war – and then, out of the glorious night comes the furious noise of rifles, and one stops and wonders how the men are getting on. Sometimes the shooting is for nothing at all, but it is so difficult to stop, once it starts, at night, and sometimes it is an attack and one has to wait and wait for the result. Provided we have had time to dig properly, I have no fear at night, unless a shaky Regiment is on my flank, which sometimes happens. Some Regiments have suffered fearfully, and I am sure that the reason is partly that they will not dig properly – luckily we have strong men who can dig, tired or not.

I relieved the Oxford Light Infantry the other day, and was sorry to hear that Ashley was wounded, but they said he was not bad. And now no more for to-night. You are probably thinking of bed, thank God, and I am going to wander about for some hours before I lie down on some straw – but we all have much, very much, to be thankful for, every day of our lives out here – one does realise that, and I feel it more every day.

DIARY

Oct. 29th

Moved to S. edge of Polygone Wood and entrenched. No. 4 Company was sent early in the morning to help the Camerons. They dug in and had a bad time, as they were badly shelled, and it rained hard. No. 1 and Machine Guns were sent at the same time to dig in near the Château, as the Germans were attacking the 1st Brigade very heavily. 2 k.,7 w.

Oct. 29th

Same positions in the morning. Moved in the afternoon.

Oct. 29th

A most glorious October day to-day, a rare day for partridge driving. A furious battle is raging not far off – the Germans have made a desperate attack this morning. We have a mass of guns turned on them, so I hope all is going well. Meanwhile, I am fairly quiet with only one Company gone on, so I seize the opportunity to write. This I always do, and so get through my letters, though I often have to write in a beastly cold clay trench, or a still colder unlived-in cottage, which has often been inhabited by the pigs and calves left behind by the unfortunate people of the country. These we clean up and sleep in at night when we can, and get clean straw to sleep on. The men, as there are so few houses left standing that we cannot billet them, dig deep holes for themselves and put straw at the bottom, so they are fairly safe from shells during the night, at any rate as safe as we are in houses. If it rains, however, the trenches get full of water, and they have a miserable time. Heavens: what is the world like without big guns? Yesterday we were surrounded by them, French and English, while we lay in a wood waiting to get on. We started at seven in the morning, and got 200 yards, where we stayed all day. Luckily, it was to us a day of rest, which we wanted badly, as we had been up all night, and after digging in as usual in the wood, the men go to sleep – but sleep is difficult, unless you are dog-tired, with the awful noise round you. Luckily the German guns did not pay us much attention yesterday, though there were a good many bullets flying about.

I had a good sleep last night and wanted it. Generally when I want a good sleep messages come in every two hours, and orders have to be given, which disturbs one's rest.

The noise of the guns and shells has become positively boring. Of course, one is semi-conscious of the danger, but the feeling of boredom is uppermost. One would like to get away for a few days from the never ceasing din. I can't see how these battles are to end. It becomes a question of stalemate. With a line of this length you can't get ahead anywhere (or else you get in a dangerous position) unless the whole line can get on, and you can't get on because there are no flanks, and you cannot therefore get round them. As soon as you outflank, an aeroplane gives away the show, and the enemy meet it, and vice versa with us, so it is a never ending business. You get to within a few hundred yards of each other and dig, and there you stop, sniping all day and shooting all night at imaginary or real night attacks. Relieving trenches under these conditions is a most difficult job. The Black Watch relieved me the other night, and it took the greater part of the night. You cannot do it by day, and the moment any movement is detected at night, an attack is expected and shooting begins, so you have to wait till all is quiet again. You generally lose a few men at these difficult games in the dark, and I am always relieved when the Companies get back safely.

I haven't seen my baggage for three weeks, so I am filthy – except to shave and wash my face and hands, I have not had a chance of doing anything else. Now I have written a long yarn in this infernal din, so I will stop, and eat a biscuit.

· BACKGROUND NARRATIVE ·

At the end of October the area east of Ypres, which came to be known as the Ypres Salient, was in imminent danger of falling to the Germans. The first half of November was to see some of the fiercest fighting of the opening months of the war, the British Army desperate to prevent the enemy from breaking through the line at Ypres.

Everard Wyrall, in the first volume of *The History of the Second Division, 1914–1918*, states that the Klein Zillebeke part of the line, which was defended by Lord Cavan's 4th (Guards) Brigade during this period, 'was considered by the German Higher Command to be next in importance to the possession of the Ypres–Menin road, which would open the way to the town itself'.[2] Klein Zillebeke marked the southern edge of the Ypres Salient and it had to be kept from the enemy at all costs.

Few positions were firmly entrenched and some places, such as a wood that came to be called Shrewsbury Wood, were at risk of being lost because the British had failed to establish themselves there when they were unoccupied. On 2 November, the Northamptons had been driven back by the Germans.

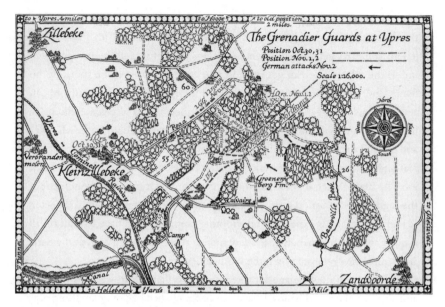

The Grenadier Guards at Ypres. (Ponsonby, Vol. I, p. 142)

Cavan ordered Wilfrid's battalion to leave their packs and go straight through the wood with their bayonets. A contemporary account by Ernest Hamilton describes the scene:

> These Ypres woods have all the appearance of an English copse wood, that is to say, they are formed of some six year's growth of hazel and ash, with standard oaks dotted about here and there. Incidentally they were at this time full of pheasants, destined to be shot in normal times by the Lords of the Chateaux of Hooge, Gheluvelt and Heronhage. Precisely in the manner of a line of beaters driving game, the Grenadiers now pushed through the thick undergrowth, and while the pheasants rose before the advancing line, so did the Germans run. By 4.30 the wood was cleared and the morning line restored.[3]

The Germans' retreat enabled the Northamptons to reoccupy their trenches.

Wilfrid's diary and letters over the next three weeks describe vividly the fierce and often confused fighting during this period and the heavy losses that he suffered in holding the line. Sergeant George Thomas was awarded a DCM, 'For conspicuous gallantry on 6 November in holding on to his trenches under very heavy shell and rifle fire (after being twice buried by shell explosives) until he had only two men left and the enemy were in rear of his flank.'[4]

Maxims were machine guns named after their inventor, Sir Hiram Stevens Maxim, who invented the first recoil-operated machine gun in 1883.

DIARY – REPORT

SECOND BATTALION GRENADIER GUARDS
October 30th, 1914 to November 21st, 1914.

On the afternoon of October 30th, the Grenadiers and Irish Guards, and the Oxford Light Infantry were sent under Lord Cavan, from the Polygone de Zonnebeke Wood, to help the line which the Germans were forcing back somewhere between Zandvoorde and Klein Zillebeke. The 2nd Battalion were told to go and reinforce the Cavalry, who were holding a line very lightly somewhere north of Château de Hollebeke. It was just dusk when we arrived at Z. of Klein Zillebeke. I went forward to see what the Cavalry were holding, and found they were holding a long line very lightly on a forward slope which appeared to me to be an untenable position. After a considerable delay, owing to the darkness, I arranged with the Cavalry to hold their present line, while I dug in in rear of them. My right was on the railway, my left on the Klein Zillebeke Road in the following order:- from right to left. No. 2, No. 1, No. 3 and 1 platoon No. 4; the rest of the Battalion and Head Quarters being N. W. of the wood between the railway and Z. of Klein Zillebeke. We got up teas and supplies, ammunition, etc., and were well dug in by about 1 a.m., when the Cavalry withdrew and went to the rear. The Irish Guards were continuing the line North of Klein Zillebeke Road. On the 31st the French were ordered to attack through my Battalion – the Irish Guards were told to join in, and I was ordered not to leave my trenches. The French advanced at dawn, and immediately very heavy shelling commenced. The French never got beyond the line of my trenches. Some of them got into my trenches, some dug new trenches in front of and behind my line. Many wandered back through the wood where the shelling was so terrific that I had to move my H.Q. back, and dig in again behind a hedge about 300 yards from the wood. About mid-day the Germans appeared to be going to attack us, but they all eventually moved northwards. The shelling continued throughout the whole day till just after sunset, and was simply terrific. Early in the afternoon, I got a message from the Brigadier to say that the Germans had broken through the line on the left of the Irish Guards. Another message came shortly afterwards, as far as I can remember in these words:-

'The situation is extremely critical: you are to hold your ground at all costs. Sir D. Haig relies on the Grenadiers to save the First Corps, and possibly the Army.'

I had been suffering casualties from shell fire, and No. 3 particularly had been having a bad time, and I had already had to support them with one platoon. On the receipt of the Brigadier's message I took up the remainder of my supports, and every available rifle, to the line of the trenches, the supports remaining about 400 yards in rear of No. 3. It was then about 3.30. I informed the Brigadier what I was doing and I got the following back, sent at 2.20 p.m, 31st:-

'Splendid, hang on like grim death. You may save the Army.'

Meanwhile the Germans had broken through as far as the 'Brown Road', later on I got a message from the Brigadier to the effect that the situation was easier, and that the Oxford Light Infantry were coming up on the left of the Irish Guards. Shortly after dark the shelling ceased and I went round the line. It was an extraordinary sight; a farm in the middle of my line was blazing, the hedges were all torn to bits, and the whole place was ploughed up with shells. I found everybody quite happy, though very tired, and I found my casualties were extraordinarily small. This I venture to put down entirely to the good digging of the men, and to the fact that our position was rather concealed, owing to the nature of the ground. Rose had been buried by a shell, but was dug up again. Otherwise, my casualties were only about 40 N.C.O's [sic] and men.

During this day I had been very anxious about my right. My right rested on a high railway embankment beyond which was a small wood and it was very difficult to keep up communication. There were a few British Cavalry there, and I was told that the French were coming up to help them, as the Germans were said to be attacking towards the Canal Bridge. (The Canal was dry). I do not think the French ever arrived, and I was very anxious all the latter part of the afternoon. However, the German attack never developed, and all was well by dark. During the night 31st to 1st November, we were relieved by the French, and withdrew about 4 a.m., into reserve in rear of the village near Z. of Zwartelean. We had not been in reserve many hours before we heard that the Germans had broken the line again, and I was ordered to go and report to General Bulfin, who I found in a wood near contour 60 [which came to be known as Hill 60 and was much fought over throughout the war], ¾ of a mile S.W. of H. of Herenthage. By the time I got the Battalion there, General B. had been wounded, and it was difficult to find out what the situation was, and what I was required to do. Eventually Lord Cavan took over the command, and ordered me to clear the wood, S.E. of the Brown Road, with the bayonet. I was ordered to leave my kits at the farm in rear of the wood. (Eventually, when I got back the kits that night, many of them had been looted). I launched the Battalion into the wood, which was very thick, and I was very much afraid I should get the Battalion hopelessly lost. We found the Germans were not in the wood, but they evidently had been, as there were many dead lying about. Near the far edge of the wood I managed to find three Companies out of the four, and eventually found No. 2 who had reached the front edge of the wood. One platoon of No. 1 had gone beyond the wood, and suffered severely from Maxims. I found No. 1 had touch with the Oxford Light Infantry on the right, and No. 2 had touch with the same regiment on the left. No. 3 was filling up the gap between 1 and 2. I cannot say enough about the good leading of the Captains on this day. We were launched into the wood in a great hurry; the wood was very thick with very few rides, but somehow the Captains had their companies altogether at the far edge of the wood. No. 4 was with me in support of the Battalion: as soon as it was dark, the Germans did their best to set the wood on fire. Thank goodness they did not succeed, although there were one or two fires blazing not far from us.

I went round the line and arranged where we were to dig in. The position was a very nasty one, and very difficult to hold, and the Germans were very close to us. We dug in and got food, etc. About 10 at night I was ordered to take over with my reserve company the line held by the Gordons on the left of the Oxford Light Infantry. I had a look at this line and found no trenches worth speaking of, and the line very lightly held. I took No. 4 over there, and we dug in just in rear of where the Gordons had been.

On the night of November 2nd this Company was very heavily attacked. It was shortly after dark, Jeffreys and I were going round the companies to see how they had fared during the day. We had hardly reached No. 4 when very heavy firing broke out on the line held by No. 4, and the Oxford Light Infantry on their right. The Germans attacked with the beating of drums and the blowing of small horns. A curious thing happened during this attack. At one time firing almost died down, and it was passed down the line 'Don't fire, the Northamptons are going to charge', (the Northamptons were on our left). We shouted to the men to go on firing; fire was at once taken up, and went on until the attack died away. I tried next day to find out where the order started from, but could never ascertain anything. I have not a doubt in my mind that it was started by the Germans, some of whom got within a few yards of the line. This part of the line was taken over by the Oxford L. I. during this night. The next morning they reported to me they had counted 300 dead in front of this Company. During the next day or two the Germans moved across our front several times towards the Irish Guards. On each occasion we took heavy toll with rifle fire, and once with machine guns.

On November 6th it was reported that the Germans were moving in large numbers towards the right, i.e., the Irish Guards and French, who were on their right. Some time early in the afternoon I got a message from the Irish Guards that the French on their right had been driven in. Almost at the same moment I had a message from Hamilton that the Irish Guards had also been driven in, and that his right was in the air. He also informed me that he had sent a platoon to block the Brown Road on the right, where it entered our wood. Shortly afterwards I heard the Germans had reached the Brown Road on my right, and some were advancing round my right rear. At the first alarm I had posted Tufnell with one machine gun on the Brown Road to guard a ride through the wood, across which the Germans would have had to come to get behind my line of trenches. I also sent Congleton with one platoon to stop the Germans getting through 'the gap' in my right rear. For some reason, that I have never been able to get an explanation of, Tufnell took his machine gun with Congleton's platoon. I believe the machine gun had one good target, but Tufnell was unfortunately hit at this time, and I never found out exactly what did occur. After a very anxious afternoon, about dusk the Household Cavalry arrived, made a most gallant charge with the bayonet, and drove the Germans back about the Brown Road about the word Zwartelean [sic]. For some hours during the afternoon, the right of No. 2 had been absolutely in the air. The men of No. 1, who were on their right, had been practically all killed or wounded by shell fire shortly after the Irish Guards withdrew. Sergeant Thomas, who commanded the right platoon of No. 1., remained at his post after the Irish Guards had gone till he had only three men left. During this time this N.C.O. was twice buried by shells and had three rifles broken in his hand, he then withdrew with his three men to the Brown Road. It was during this time that Sergeant Digby was very severely, and I believe, mortally wounded. He was never seen again. As soon as it was dark I sent Captain Powell with a part of No. 3 to get in touch with No. 2. This was eventually done to my great relief, and the line was once more safe. During this very anxious afternoon Colonel Davies, who commanded the Oxford L.I., helped enormously on my right with the few men he happened to have in reserve. I went to see the Brigadier, as soon as I knew the line was safe, to find out what line he wished us to hold under the circumstances. He ordered me to throw back my right towards the Brown Road. (I omitted to say that a Company of the Sussex was sent to help me during the afternoon, and they largely helped to save the situation on my right).

I went back and let the men have their teas before digging the new line. About this time Congleton appeared and told me he had successfully stopped a lot of Germans getting through the gap. He reported he was holding the gap between the Sussex and, I think, the Cavalry. He had lost several men, but said he had collected several Irish Guardsmen, with his platoon, who, however, had no rifles or ammunition. He collected rifles from casualties, and carried them himself, with an orderly who carried ammunition, back to arm these Irish Guardsmen. He held this gap during the night, and withdrew in the morning. The intelligent way in which this Officer handled his platoon during this afternoon was admirable, and I sent in his name specially to the Brigadier. We arranged the new line about midnight, and I left the men to dig about 1 a.m. When I returned at 4 a.m. I found the men splendidly dug in, in spite of the trees and the pitch darkness of the night. I considered this a fine performance as the men were very tired, had suffered heavy losses, and the Companies (1 and 3) were much disorganised.

On the 10th of November we had a terrible shelling, and owing to my right being thrown back, we were badly enfiladed by the German guns [enfilade is fire directed from a flank down the length of an enemy trench or position]. The shelling continued throughout the whole day all over the wood, many trenches were blown to pieces, many men were buried, and the trees fell in dozens. During this day Lennox and Stocks were killed by shells, Congleton was shot through the heart, Tudway was hit by a shell on the head and died a few days afterwards. Powell was buried by a shell, was dug up and brought to my dug-out by two gallant men under very heavy shell fire, and he was in a very bad way. That night the wood was in an awful state. Fallen trees made it almost impossible to get about, and I had great difficulty in getting away my wounded, none of whom could be got away during the day.

That night we went into Corps Reserve for four days. Three nights out of the four we were marching about all night. Each day we were moved in support of various parts of the line, and were considerably shelled every day. On the 15th we returned to Lord Cavan and held a part of our old line, and also 'the gap' and the wood W. of 'the gap'. On the 17th we were heavily attacked about 'the gap' and repulsed the Germans with very great loss. Our casualties were small, but we lost Symes-Thompson, and Lee Steere killed, and C.S.M. Gillette severely wounded. On the night of the 19th we were relieved by the 3rd Battalion Coldstream, and on the 21st we went to Meteren to rest and re-fit.

During the 20 days, 31st Oct. to 19th Nov., the Battalion lost 12 Officers and 466 men. At the end of this period I had 6 Company Officers and about 350 rifles. I had also lost a great many horses.

(Signed). W. A. Smith.

Lt. Col.

2nd Battn. Grenadier Guards

Nov. 3rd

All well here, but we have been having a desperate time lately. I haven't had any of my clothes off for three weeks for a wash, and I have not had a wash for three days. We had an awful afternoon two days ago, but Fatty told me afterwards we saved the situation, which I was proud of, but it was an awful episode. However, I am still alive and very well, but terribly sleepy, as all of us are – we have had no sleep for four nights. Hope to write again soon.

Later. I wrote hurriedly this early morning, not knowing what the day would bring forth, but if the Germans will give us a little peace, I will write more. We have had a strenuous time of late, and been in many nasty positions. The Germans have been trying desperately to break through the last week. We have had one trying day after another, no rest at night, and many anxious hours. We have marched from one place to another, where the Germans break through, and driven them back, or dug and held them. We had a terrible day three days ago. We had got to a place late the previous evening, and had to dig all night. The next day we went through the most appalling day I have ever known, we were shelled with great big shells from daylight till the last moment of night. I was terribly afraid we were going to share the sad fate of the 1st Battalion. Nothing but the mercy of Providence saved us from terrible losses. Shells, and enormous ones, burst continually all day all round us. Things were not going well that day, and I was told that the 1st Corps relied on the Grenadier and Irish Guards, who were side by side (the Coldstream being elsewhere) to save the Corps and perhaps the Army. I took up every available man to the trenches, and at last the shades of night fell and the din ceased. We wondered to find ourselves alive, and our losses were extraordinarily small, thanks to good digging. The men were splendid, never gave an inch and took messages about with the utmost indifference. But the scene that night was one to be remembered, two farms in our lines were blazing, the hedges all torn to bits, the roads and lanes with enormous pits made by shells. The trees in the woods looked as if an earthquake had taken place, desolation and destruction everywhere. And then broke out the glorious moon of a brilliant night – a different world to the day – and perfect peace and silence.

We were relieved by the French that night, and got away by 4 a.m., fed the men and went into Reserve. In three hours though we were hurried off again to another place a few miles off to do the same thing, and we had a nasty wood fight to clear the wood of Germans who had broken through. We got to the far edge of the wood, after great anxiety on my part that I should lose the Battalion in the wood, and again we dug like fury. We have now been here for thirty-six hours, and were attacked heavily all night, and most of yesterday, but have managed to repel every attack, and the Germans are now digging in in front of us, so I hope we have got the better of them. But everybody is dog tired, and we want a rest badly. It has been a most critical week, and our losses are very heavy. The Irish Guards suffered heavily the day we were mercifully preserved. Some Battalions are reduced to 200 men and no Officers. They say the Emperor has been here in person urging on his men, and my word, they are brave. We have killed hundreds the last few days, and these woods are full of them, poor things. It has been a most trying time for nerves. I had one man went mad the other day for a bit, but he pulled himself together after a time.

Rose had a great escape – a shell landed in his trench and buried him – he was dug up, and is fairly well, but very deaf, and has only been in hospital two days.

I am very well, but find it hard to think after all this, but please God we shall have a rest soon. All the above came on the top of three very hard weeks. I am very proud of my Battalion, and hope I shall do them justice, but I get very anxious at times.

· BACKGROUND NARRATIVE ·

Another of Wilfrid's cousins, Henry Adeane, a nephew of his mother, had gone missing. He was killed in action near Ypres on 2 November but his body was never found. His name is commemorated on the Menin Gate at Ypres:

Nov. 5th

I was so sorry to hear last night that poor Harry Adeane (Coldstream Guards) has gone, whether killed or a prisoner, I do not know. I lost 30 men yesterday and several horses. We had a dreadful shelling again all day, and it looks as if we are in for another to-day. It is a curious life one leads here at times – rather like a rabbit. Here we are in a wood, the front edge of which is entrenched and held by us, with the Germans entrenched about 400 or 500 yards off. We live in a hole further back in the wood, i.e., myself and Head Quarters and odds and ends. We are dug in deep with a good cover, so unless a shell lands practically in our 'dug-out', we have a good chance. When this shelling goes on, we go to ground just like rabbits, and don't come out unless some duty has to be performed. Yesterday we were in from ten till dark, and we have just gone to ground again to-day. The noise, as usual, is deafening, and very tiring to the head. The men all dig in well, and know how to protect themselves, but in spite of this I lost 30 yesterday. The four previous days I lost nearly 150 –

many valuable losses. We have killed hundreds of Germans in this wood, and the wounded are difficult to find. One poor fellow has just been brought in who must have been lying out for two days, and as it rained all last night, he must have had an awful time.

The winter is on us, and the leaf is falling fast, and we shall have sickness if we have to sit in this wet clay wood for long. I never hated a wood before, but I shall never forget this one; it has been a constant anxiety since I entered it, and a shell trap too, as they take it off the map and search it with shells, which is unpleasant.

We all want to sleep for twenty-four hours, I don't know when I last had more than three or four hours in a night, and you cannot sleep by day in this noise. Also messages are sure to come if I close my eyes by day. We badly want a few days off, our boots have been wet for days, and my feet, and I suppose others', are very sore from having had them on so long without a chance of taking then off. I am side by side with the Oxford Light Infantry, Ashley's Battalion – a jolly good one – and their Commanding Officer is Joey Davies' brother [Henry Davies], we are great friends. No more for to-day.

What a shock it must have been about the poor 1st Battalion; I mourn for Stucs [Humphrey Stucley] and many others.

Nov. 7th

Just a line to say I am well. We are having a very anxious time, and I am anxious day and night. We are still in the same place and see no chance of a rest, but we must hope for the best. I trust the Battalion will do well, but it is only with difficulty we can keep them awake, and I have not one man to spare for rest day or night. We hope some reinforcements will soon come.

· BACKGROUND NARRATIVE ·

Turkey commenced hostilities against Russia on 29 October and Russia formally declared war on Turkey on 2 November. Great Britain and France followed suit, formally declaring war three days later, on 5 November.

Reports were coming through from the Eastern Front that the Russian Army in East Prussia was successfully pushing back Austrian and German forces:[5]

Nov. 8th

Possibly time for a little longer letter to-day. To-day I am told it is Sunday, and like many recent Sundays, it is being spent being shelled all day. We are still in this beastly wood, and have been here now for a week. It was last Sunday when we came here. I see it is in the papers, so I can say it is not far from Ypres. Since then we have fighting day and night, and I have lost nearly 300 men since we got into the wood. Shells fly all day and bullets all night, and it is anxious work.

It has been very cold, particularly at night but we have managed to feed the men well, and they are splendid, though terribly sleepy. I lost poor Tufnell two days ago, which nearly broke my heart. He was such a good boy, and so keen with his Machine Gun: he is a great loss to me. The great mercy has been that, except for one wet miserable night, it has not rained, though the fog has been almost as wet. I cannot write much in this noise, and now firing has begun again I must stop.

Later. During a lull I will add a little, but it will probably be disjointed on account of the din going on. The Household Cavalry did a fine charge (on foot) the other day, but lost several Officers: they were most gallant.

Tell Jack Robarts that Norman Orr Ewing has done grandly with the Irish Guards. He and Jack Trefusis are about all that is left with them now, and Jack has done wonders.

I hear Turkey has come in. Well!, she will repent it before she has done. Good news from Russia last night: cheered us much.

We have taken considerable toll of the Germans here, but their beastly guns are what cause the casualties. They go on all day, and though they waste heaps of ammunition, some must take toll. The only small comfort is that every shell costs them heaps of money, which will, I hope, help to bleed them to death. The Infantry is beneath contempt compared to ours. They are brave enough, jolly brave, but at night it is too much like shooting a flock of sheep, poor things. They have discipline and do what they are told, but their attacks at night in this wood develop into the poor devils wandering rather aimlessly about, under our terrific rifle fire. The Germans are fighting this war with guns and machine guns, and jolly good they are. They require skill and experience to avoid them even to such a small extent as one can avoid them, but I'm afraid new troops will pay a heavy price to them.

We have now been fighting every day since October 15th, and these days and nights of anxiety do try one, but I am very well in health, and though one longs for rest, I know we have much to be thankful for, (and none know it better than we do) and some day rest will come – all that matters is that the

Battalion should do well. I wonder if you will be able to read this? What a way to spend Sunday this is!

Nov. 9th

All well to-day. We have not had such a bad day as usual. I have no time for more to-night.

· BACKGROUND NARRATIVE ·

Wilfrid wrote to an old friend, Freddy Hervey-Bathurst, who was serving with the Staff. They joined the Grenadiers at about the same time and served together in the Sudan campaign and Boer War:

Nov. 9th, 1914

My dear Freddy

How nice to see your writing again. We've had the devil of a time. We have been fighting every day since Oct 15th and such a curious form of fighting, utterly unlike anything one ever expected. The shelling is appalling. Not only are the shells so huge and various, but the number that have been launched at us daily now for weeks must amount to millions. We have had some awful days. Saturday 31st we had dug in during the night and then had 12 hours of the big Marias without a check. The men stuck it grandly although many were buried and dugout. I had 4 that day within 20 yards and thousands of shrapnel and high explosive. But we were well dug in and survived it. The Irish Guards lost heavily that day on our left. The next day (1st) we moved to a wood to retake the line which had been broken. We had to clear a wood of Germans, which we did. I thought I should never see my battalion again, but we turned up at the far end of the wood and entrenched. Since then we have remained in this beastly wood being shelled like the devil all day, and at first attacked many times at night.

The first night I happened to be with one company when they were attacked. The Germans beat a drum and blew a curious little horn all the time rather like the horn a keeper blows to start the beaters. We had a good shoot. 300 dead were lying next morning within 100 yards of the line – some only 20 yards off. We have accounted for a vast number since we entered the wood.

On the other hand I have lost 290 men in the same time, chiefly from shells. These shells smash the trees like match wood and fall on the men in the trenches. It is marvellous the way they stick it. I have had many anxious moments here and elsewhere. It is a great responsibility commanding a battalion out here. Nothing but the mercy of Providence has saved us time and again.

The German infantry are beneath contempt – but their guns and maxims are splendid and their snipers a great nuisance. The poor 1st Battalion have practically ceased to exist. The Irish Guards have 200 men and 3 officers left. I could tell many stories of that regiment. I believe the 1st Battalion Coldstream and the 1st and 2nd Kiddies [the nickname of the Scots Guards, which originated in 1686 when the Scots Guards were brigaded for the first time with the Grenadier and Coldstream Guards] are in much the same state. The 'Ins' [Inniskilling Fusiliers] did a grand charge the other day, on foot, but lost 4 officers killed.

We want a rest badly. I have not had my boots off for nearly a month and never washed except hands and face. It is very cold in the wood, buried underground like a rabbit, and one can hardly move out during the shelling by day. We have no sleep. The noise of our guns and the shelling stops it by day, and the night is full of alarms. I am very fit, thank God, but very tired and sometimes very anxious. But I suppose it will last some months yet.

It would be a joy to get away from the noise for a few days. Except for 36 hours in the train it has been continuous since I came out. We had some bad shelling on the Aisne, but that was paradise compared to this. One gets sick of seeing nothing but dead men and animals – perhaps some day we shall get home and I shall have many a yarn to tell you and I think you would be satisfied with the old regiment. The London Scottish are next to me in this wood. Only came last night. I hope they will stick it. It is awful being next to people who run away and I have had a lot of that.

Glad to hear Peter is well. I expect the Missus has no time to write to you. She is busy with wives and widows. What a sad time it is for all at home. Let the Missus know your address. I lost 2 nephews in the 1st Battalion, poor boys. Good luck, old boy, write to me again.

Yours

Wilfrid A Smith

Nov. 10th

I've had a terribly sad day to-day. We've had an awful shelling, I'm afraid of saying how many thousand shells have been hurled at us in this wretched wood to-day. And alas! I've lost five Officers, and God knows how many men. Tell Mrs. Powell as soon as you can that George is all right. He was buried in his trench and dug out, but beyond a shaking and possible concussion, he is not hurt. Tell her also that he has done awfully well, and I can never thank him enough for his good work. Poor Bernard [Gordon Lennox] gone also – an excellent boy – Congleton gone too, and Stocks, and Tudway wounded. One of the saddest days of my life. I have lost over 300 men in this wood, and we have been at it for ten days, day and night. I am now waiting (10 p.m.) for a relief that is coming. I really do not think even this Battalion could stand another twenty-four hours of it. The men have been wonderful. Many are buried by the shells, and I have no idea how many I have lost to-day. But I am sad to-night, and must write no more.

· BACKGROUND NARRATIVE ·

Wilfrid's battalion now went into Corps Reserve, bivouacking in dugouts. In *The Grenadier Guards in the Great War 1914–1918 Volume I*, Sir Frederic Ponsonby records that:

> Lord Cavan in writing an account of the day's fighting, said 'The 2nd Battalion Grenadiers made a wonderful stand to-day against enfilade fire of the worst description. They stuck it out magnificently.' ...
>
> Having been placed in Corps reserve for four days, officers and men of the Battalion were under the impression that they were going to have a quiet time for that period, sleeping in peace at night and resting during the day. But they were mistaken. In reality, they spent three of the nights marching about the whole time, and each day they were moved up in support of this or that part of the line, to the invariable accompaniment of considerable shelling ...
>
> The worst of it was that those placed in reserve were at the beck and call of any General who wanted reinforcements. At one time the Battalion was placed under four Generals, and received different orders from each, which came about because the units in front got hopelessly mixed, and the battalions were constantly changed from one brigade to another.[6]

Wilfrid described his experiences during this period. The 'Woolly Bears' he refers to were German shrapnel shells.

DIARY – REPORT

A few days in Corps Reserve

On the night of Nov. 10th we were relieved by the Welsh Regiment and the Munsters, who took over our line at Klein Zillebeke Wood. It took most of the night to relieve and get away, and it was about 5 a.m. when we reached Bellewaarde Farm, north of Hooge, where the Battalion went into 'dug-outs' in the wood and Head Quarters into the Farm House.

About 7.30 a.m. I rode over to the Head Quarters 2nd Division to report to General Monro. He was very kind, congratulated the Battalion on the good work it had done, sympathised with our losses, gave me breakfast, and said that we were to rest that day, and that the next day he would come over and say a few words to the Battalion. I rode back to Head Quarters and looked forward to a wash and a good sleep. When I got back I found that the Battalion had been ordered to be ready to move at a moment's notice, and very shortly afterwards I was ordered to move to a wood north east of Hooge Château. I was told that the line had been broken and that we were to be ready to help. I was told to put the Battalion in the wood, but I found some guns hard at work there, which of course meant that we should be shelled. I put one company in the Wood, and the remainder of the Battalion were scattered about the grounds of the Château in comparative safety from shrapnel. We were shelled pretty well all day, chiefly by shrapnel and 'Woolly Bears' and we had a few casualties. About 3.45 I was told an attack was to take place to retake the trenches the Prussian Guard had captured in the morning, and that the Battalion was to support the attack. The Sussex, Oxford Light Infantry, Irish Guards, and Gloucesters were taking part in the attack. The trenches the Prussian Guards had captured were south west of Polygone Wood, close to our old Brigade Head Quarters. We 'blobbed' across the open ground towards the wood east of Hooge Château. The G.O.C. 5th Brigade insisted on my going forward at once to see General FitzClarence (1st Guards Brigade) whose Head Quarters I was told were at the south corner of the wood. The result was that I was hustled off without being able to give proper orders to the Captains. Never, if I can possibly help it, will I allow any General to make me do such a thing again. I went on to the corner of the wood where I expected to find General FitzClarence, but he was not there, and I sent Jeffreys on to see if he could find him. Meanwhile it was getting dusk, no attack seemed to be going on, and I halted the leading Company. I got another message to go and see General FitzClarence, and at the same time I got information from a Subaltern in the 15th Hussars exactly where he was. About this time they began shelling us with shrapnel. I got safely to a 'dug-out' in the wood where I found Jeffreys and Corkran (Brigade Major). He told me he had never heard anything about the proposed attack, that he had no idea we were anywhere near, and that General FitzClarence had gone off somewhere and he could not get hold of him. He asked me to wait till the General returned. It was then getting dark and began to rain hard. I sent Jeffreys back to collect the Battalion. Shortly after he had gone the shelling was rather heavy, and I was wondering whether he had got back safely when some Officer came into the 'dug-out' and said 'Your Battalion has rather caught it from shrapnel'. I said 'Did Jeffreys get back all right'? 'Yes', he said, 'but the Officer with him was hit'. My heart sank as I knew that must be Pike, and so it turned out. I found afterwards we had lost about thirty men crossing that field. Trefusis turned up about this time with the Irish Guards, and he and I waited in the 'dug-out' while Corkran went to find his General. Time passed and nothing happened, so I went to see what had happened to the Battalion. I found Jeffreys had managed somehow to get them together in the dark. It was a pitch dark night and pouring with rain. I went back to the 'dug-out', and getting tired of waiting, I went to a house close by where I was told Head Quarter 1st Brigade was. There I found General FitzClarence who told me that the Oxford Light Infantry were to take the German trenches; if they did not succeed, my Battalion and the Irish Guards were to take them. I asked if I might feed my Battalion first, and eventually was allowed to, and ordered to be back at 2 a.m. He told me his general intentions. I must say I did not like it a bit. We none of us knew exactly where the trenches were, nor had we seen the country by daylight. The men were dead tired, it was pouring with rain, and the mud was awful. However, there was nothing for it. I went back to the Battalion, and after a great delay, owing to the dark, we got back to the Château grounds, and I sent on for the cookers to come up. The Château grounds I found full of gunners, sappers, and all sorts of oddments. We were all wet through and you couldn't see your hand in front of your face. With the greatest difficulty we got the Battalion more or less together, and after a long delay the cookers arrived. We gave the men food, and Bailey (whom I had appointed Adjutant) arranged hot food for the Officers in the Château. Meanwhile a thunderstorm came on and it rained harder than ever, after which it cleared up. We had some hot food in the Château, and got about an hour's sleep.

We paraded at 12.30 a.m., and marched back to the Head Quarters of the 1st Brigade. The slush and mud were awful. I had gone forward with the Adjutant, and General FitzClarence explained his plan. He had not heard whether the Oxford Light Infantry had succeeded or not, but we were to move at 3 a.m. The Irish Guards leading in fours, followed by the 2nd Battalion Grenadier Guards. On arriving at

Wilfrid's sketch of the plan of attack on 11 November 1914. (Author's collection)

Polygone Wood, the Irish Guards were to halt on the west side of the wood in fours facing south east, and the Grenadiers were to be in the same formation just beyond (i.e. west of) the Irish Guards. At 4 a.m. the Grenadiers were to advance and go straight for the German trench taking it in flank. The Irish Guards were to follow the Battalion. (See rough sketch)

It appeared to me at the time that it was odd to embark on this enterprise without waiting to get any report from the Oxford Light Infantry. However, about 3 a.m. we started, the General and his Staff leading at the head of the Irish Guards. We wallowed down the muddiest lane I have ever been down, and kept the Battalion pretty well together. After going about a quarter of a mile some shots were fired, they came both from the Germans and also from the Connaught Rangers, who were lining the west edge of Polygone Wood, facing south west. (It is only fair to the Connaught Rangers to say that I afterwards heard they had not been warned of this advance. All the same it ought to have been obvious to them that we were not Germans, as we were inside the British line). As soon as the shooting began, a number of Irish Guards turned and bolted straight back to the Grenadiers. Jeffreys and I who were leading the Battalion spent our energies in warning the Battalion to stand fast and in trying to stop the Irishmen. The Grenadiers never moved, though the Irishmen got among the ranks of some companies and created a certain amount of confusion in the dark. We halted, and waited to see what was going to happen. All the time a certain amount of bullets were flying about, and after a short time we advanced again and got to the west edge of the wood, Corkran having returned and told me where to go. We got into a ditch on the edge of the wood, and Corkran went to try and find General FitzClarence. He had hardly left me when Bailey told me the General had been hit badly, close to us. The next thing I heard was that the General was dead. After a few minutes I saw some men approaching us, who turned out to be the Oxford Light Infantry. I recognised the Commanding Officer, Colonel Davies, and called to him. I asked him if he had attacked the Germans, and what had happened. He said, 'No, I haven't, and I'm not going to'. He then told me he had carefully reconnoitred the position, that the Germans were well wired in front, that another trench in rear was full of Germans, and most probably machine guns, and that in his opinion the job was a hopeless one. I said that was exactly what I had expected to be the case, that the General had been killed, and we had better consult as to what was to be done. He asked my opinion and I said I thought the best thing would be to get the Battalions back behind the wood (i.e. west of Bosschen Wood) before it got daylight, and that we had not much time to spare. This we eventually decided to do, and we gave the necessary orders to our Battalions and went to see the G.O.C. 5th Brigade, who was at a farm not far off. As far as I remember I never saw the Irish Guards at this time. The G.O.C. 5th Brigade (Colonel Westmacott) agreed that the attack must be off, and arranged to hold a new line a few hundred yards further off (i.e. west) from the trench the Germans had taken. This is what had seemed to all of us the obvious thing to have done the previous evening.

I went back to the old 1st Brigade Head Quarters where I found Corkran, who had sent for Colonel MacEwen, O.C. Camerons, to take over the command of the Brigade. The Gloucesters had been told to dig, during the night, the line it was now settled to hold, but they were not strong enough to hold it, and I had to find a Company to help them. This Company (No. 4) under Captain Ridley, found the trenches had not been dug, and had to dig them. Tired as they were, they dug for their lives and got well dug in by about 6.30 a.m. or 7 a.m.. I was told to take the rest of the Battalion back to the Château grounds, where we had been the previous day. This I did, sending Jeffreys to see No. 4 had all they wanted. We got back to the Château, much to my relief, and so ended one of the worst nights, if not the worst, I have ever spent in my life. I now found that I had lost one Platoon of No. 1, and the whole of my Head Quarters. They had got lost in the dark, and goodness only knows where they had got to. I was then nearly driven off my head. Within an hour I was put under four Generals and received orders from all of them. G.O.C. 1st Brigade, G.O.C. Cavalry, G.O.C. 5th Brigade, and finally the G.O.C. 1st Division. The last (General Landon) came to me personally and told me to take the Battalion and the Irish Guards to the wood on the Menin Road, a quarter of a mile east of B.5, where we were to remain in 'dug-outs' and counter-attack the Germans, if they got through the line again. Off we went again, and eventually we were put under another Commander, Colonel Cunliffe-Owen, who was given command of that section of the line. Of course we had to dig in again more or less, and then I think the men slept soundly most of the day, in spite of considerable shelling. We made our Head Quarters with five other Regiments, who were holding this portion of the line with Battalions of very much reduced strength, and we stayed there the whole of the 12th and 13th. This wood we were in was shelled continually during this day, but except for the noise, which prevented any sleep, we came to no harm. On the evening of the 13th I was ordered to move the Battalion to some 'dug-outs' about half a mile back (west), my company in the trenches was relieved, and we moved off after we had had food about 10 p.m. When we arrived at our destination, and had just settled where to put the Companies, a staff officer appeared, and said we were to go to another wood, where we could rest in peace. They called this wood 'Sanctuary Wood', because it had never been shelled. After some delay we reached this wood three quarters of a mile off, and at last got to sleep about 3 a.m.

About 6 a.m. I had a look round, and saw some guns just in rear of us, so I wandered down to see what they were. They turned out to be some Howitzers, and the Officer told me they had been shelled out of every place they had been to, by guns with a range of fourteen miles!, and so they had come to this place.

Sanctuary Wood or not, I knew we were in for another shelling, and it began fairly early and went on all day. Gilbert Hamilton left us on this morning, his 'dug-out' having fallen in on him. About 2 p.m. on the 14th I got orders to be ready to move at once as the line had been broken. Thank goodness nothing came of it, and we were left in peace, and at night shelling ceased. I got orders about 5 p.m. to move back to the 4th Brigade that night. Although this meant another march all night, it was hailed with joy by all ranks, nobody wanting any more 'Corps Reserve'. We started about 8 p.m., and got back to our old Brigade Head Quarters about 1 a.m., took over a part of our old line, and got settled about 3 a.m. on the 15th. During our 'Rest' we had marched about during three nights out of four, and been shelled properly every day.

Nov. 13th

Still having a poor time. I got away from my wood only to get to a worse place after but four hours [sic] rest. For two days we had perfect misery, wandering about all night wet to the skin, and finally fetched up in a horrible place where we can get no water or anything. I haven't had a wash of any sort or description for three days: it rains on and off continually. We are close to the Germans, so we can show no lights except in our 'dug-outs', and the mud is awful. I can only describe our condition as being weary beyond words, and I really cannot read the papers, which give such rosy accounts of our so called progress anymore. Although they may be justified by the general situation, in our little bit we see no progress and constant losses. I have lost my Adjutant, (wounded): Sergeant-major (sick), 8 Officers and 370 men in ten days.

I have been sent to another Brigade to fill in a gap, and we are mixed up with all sorts of Regiments, and so we are generally very uncomfortable. Well I suppose it can't last for ever, and I must be patient, but sometimes one is indeed weary. But I am very well, for which I am thankful. If only I could get twenty-four hours [sic] sleep I should be all right: a long sleep would be a great relief.

Eben [Pike, Wilfrid's adjutant] is a great loss to me, and entails much extra work at a time when I have had great losses, and the Battalion is alas no longer what it was a fortnight ago. We are, however, better off than Line Battalions who are reduced to 150 and 200 men, and sometimes one or two Officers.

My love to the boys, I have meant to write to them for days, but have had no time. I luckily got off my letters to the bereaved parents just in time the other day when I had half an hour to spare. It is a sad heartbreaking work writing to them, but it is all one can do for them. I feel these poor boys' deaths dreadfully, but we live with constant death round us, and must accept it.

When I think of poor Bernard's utter weariness some days ago (I left him in his trench in the early morning, and wished I could take his place, he was so done) and alas! never saw him again. I think of him now at peace, away from all this noise and misery, and though it is terrible for her, poor thing, it can't be bad for him, and must comfort her to feel he can rest at last. I can't bear seeing my friends go day after day, and when Eben was hit, my heart sank, but I must face the difficulties and hope for the best. If I didn't put my trust in God, I couldn't have lasted as long as I have, and I feel I shall be helped as difficulties arise, but the difficulties have been so many, and coming so quick one after another, that I have felt overwhelmed at times lately. Just got a message from Douglas Haig about the work of the 1st Corps lately. Perhaps we have done a big thing after all!

· BACKGROUND NARRATIVE ·

Lamenting the lack of relief troops, Wilfrid makes reference to Lord Roberts, one of the most successful commanders of the nineteenth century. He had led the British Army during the Boer War and been commander-in-chief of the British Army from 1901 to 1904. In retirement he had been a keen advocate of introducing conscription in Britain to prepare for a great European war.

The small but highly trained regular and reserve army of the BEF was reinforced by Territorial regiments, known as Terriers, which in peacetime were composed of part-time volunteers.

Tom Brand, Viscount Hampden, was a contemporary of Wilfrid from Hertfordshire. He had preceded him as ADC to the Governor of New South Wales in 1898 and had commanded the 1st Battalion Hertfordshire Regiment since early 1913. He went on to command brigades at Gallipoli and back in France:

Nov. 15th

Such a jolly day – nearly dark and snowing most of the morning, and a white frost early. We were wandering about all last night, and came back, to my disgust, to my wood, but I hope not for long. This is the twenty-sixth consecutive day we have been under this infernal shell fire. For the first time in my life I feel not quite so young as I did! Another blow fell yesterday when Gilbert (Hamilton) had an accident and had to go sick, so I have lost three out of my four Captains in a few days, as well as my Adjutant. This makes things very difficult and has made me rather depressed. The weather has been wet and cold, and it is now just a month since I had my boots off or a wash all over. We are hoping to be relieved any day, but we have been promised so often and it has never come, that we no longer believe it. If the country had only listened to Lord Roberts some years ago, we should have been able to relieve us tired troops with fresh ones, and I believe the war would be nearly over. As it is, it drags on in a not altogether satisfactory way, and one can see no end to it. The newspapers at home are by no means accurate.

I want a refill for my electric light, the nights are long, and the woods are dark, so one wants it a good deal. It is a capital light, and has saved me from a broken neck many a time. The shell holes after dark are most dangerous, and every road is full of them.

There is a rumour that Austria is sueing [*sic*] for peace: if this is true it would help Russia considerably, and I see no hope except in Russia. I have never yet seen the French do anything, though I admit I have seen mostly French Territorials.

The Hertford Terriers have just come and joined our Brigade, commanded by Tom Brand. I have not seen them yet. How the Terriers will stand this shelling, I can't think. This is a horrible, ugly country, nothing pleases one's eye. I have not seen a civilian for 3 weeks, they have all cleared out, and there is not an unsmashed house in the country. Young Bailey is my Adjutant, a good boy, but has not the knowledge of Eben.

It's too cold to write more, and I am very weary, though not so bad as a day or two ago, as I got 3 hours sleep last night, which has bucked me up.

Nov. 16th

I have had bad luck with horses – had 2 shot and one stolen, with a good part of my kit, which is a bore. You have no idea what a daily inferno I live in. I can't see to write well, it is so dark in my 'dug-out', deep down in the cold clay – the only chance of life at times. We are beginning to understand what it meant to our forefathers to campaign in Flanders. The slush is awful, well over one's ankles, and the darkness at night in these woods is pitch. I am sorry people are disappointed with our 'mentions' in despatches. I'm afraid the public do largely judge by them, which is wrong, where all do well it is difficult to select. But I was sorry they did not put in all I recommended. I have just sent in another lot, and I trust they will get mentioned. If I could mention everybody who deserved it, I should have a long, long list. I can only pick out representatives of all ranks. The list that I send in has to pass through many hands, and gets mauled sometimes on the way. A hurried scrawl in the dark. I wonder when I shall be able to write peacefully. This is like a 30 days [*sic*] Waterloo!

Lord Cavan sent Wilfrid the following message on 17 November by messenger:

2 G.G.

Well done. Hope you have got my memo re calling on 1st Coldstream at once if necessary – now in the wood alongside of you – and you must use them to help both yourself and Irish Guards – When used up. Let me know – am turning all Artillery on to wood in your front.

Cavan B/G.

1.15pm 17 Nov. 14

I have no means of communication left except orderlies.

Nov. 19th

We left our trenches and the accursed wood in the early hours of this morning, and marched about 6 miles back. It froze hard all night, and has snowed all to-day. We have got back to a farmhouse, and the men are in farm buildings, (not safe from shells yet, but some way back) for the first time since October 20th.

Facsimile of a field service message written by Lord Cavan during the fighting on 17 November 1914. (Grenadier Guards)

So for 29 consecutive days we have been under shell fire – generally all day and sometimes all night – in heat, cold, slush, snow, rain, and wind; with constant anxieties, and in many critical positions. We hope to move on to-morrow, or the next day, to rest; but it is by no means certain, as the French say now that they cannot relieve us. I have lost 2 more Officers, Symes-Thompson and Lee Steere (only 20), and am reduced to 6 Company Officers. My fine Battalion of 1,030 men on October 20th has been reduced to 480, in spite of drafts. Two companies practically gone out of four. And so for one day at least we retire out of the firing line, and I am writing at a table. I have never said much about the general situation as I was never sure of being able to post letters. From our point of view the situation is by no means good, and has not been for weeks. We have made no ground for certainly a fortnight, and we have lost it inch by inch. This has been caused by the terrific shell fire of the Germans. Battalions have lost most of their Officers, and the men have been kept under the strain much too long, the result being that in many instances they have bolted. That means that the ground has been tried to be regained, always with loss and very often failure, and a new line has been taken up a few hundred yards back. The whole line the English have held has been much too long for their numbers, and the result is that we have been weak everywhere, and we have been hanging on by our teeth for weeks. We have stopped every advance of the Germans with great slaughter; only in many instances, to be shelled out of our trenches next morning. (I speak of the Army, not the Grenadiers; so far we have never lost a yard). The strain has been terrific. Battalions have been reduced to 150 men with 2 subalterns, and so the line which should have been held with one Battalion properly organised, has been held by six, seven or eight Battalions all doing their best, but unorganised, shaken, and with no faith in others a few yards off.

The German guns improve in shooting every week, and they can, and do, hit anything they like, and nothing they hit lives, except by luck. Our guns are splendid as far as they go, and have undoubtedly done splendid work, but we have not enough lyddite, and no guns of long range, or telephones, balloons, etc., all of which the Germans have absolutely perfect, and so we sit all day in a perfect inferno, without guns powerless to help us. If we had guns which could silence the German ones (which have a range of 14 miles) we would romp home, for we can always take on their infantry.

The awful episode I mentioned, was that one day the French near us ran away, followed by the Irish Guards, who were nearest to me. It was an awful afternoon. The Germans got right round my right flank. One of my Companies was practically blown to pieces in their trenches and had to fall back. Thank

God the others stood like rocks all the afternoon, but it was dark before I dared get in touch with them again, and re-establish the line. An enterprising enemy would never have allowed it. Splendid work was done by some of my boys, particularly by Congleton, and we stopped the Germans till the Household Cavalry came up and did a splendid charge with great loss to them. But they stopped the Germans and drove then back a bit, but we never get back to the old line. That afternoon cost me 80 casualties, and we laboured all night to get things straight again. But the line was never a good one again, and subjected to awful enfilade fire, which cost us many lives.

The French I have seen are hopeless. There are thousands doing nothing miles in rear, while we have been just hanging on. When they have attacked, they have walked about as far as our trenches, showing themselves as much as possible, then they go back, think better of it, and go forward again, often stopping at our trenches and either getting into them, or digging new ones in front and behind ours. The result is that we hate it when we hear the French are attacking, for it means that we are shelled all day. They will never combine with us and attack the same day, so we do our little attack, and next day the French do theirs. The result is no headway and great losses. If we are not there the French invariably get pushed back. I see no chance of getting forward under such conditions. The general situation is, I believe good, but it is still critical, and we on the spot see very little daylight. If we had 2 or 3 more Army Corps we should push them back to the Meuse any time we like. The French have them and won't use them.

My loss of my kit was sad. I had a fourth horse hit yesterday. I have managed to make up a few things from one source or another, and actually managed to get somebody to buy a Gillette razor for me at Ypres, which is smashed to pieces. But my great loss is my long boots, which were on my horse when he was stolen. I feel the cold awfully. I have not thick enough clothes and do not see how to get them at present – a thick woolly might help, but the difficulty is to get one's coat over it. One really wants a very much bigger jacket, and so be able to put lots underneath. I hope, if we rest, to get back to my kit, where I have some thick things. I have never been able to get at them since it turned cold. My boots are always wet through, and at night my feet get so cold that I can hardly feel them. We shall never be able to sleep in houses within 10 miles of the Germans. They simply smash every house to bits, so the old-fashioned Winter Quarters are impossible, and living underground is cold work.

I believe my Sylvia's birthday is soon, and so I am enclosing a line to her. I am hoping to get some sleep to-night, this is the first day for a month I haven't been on the strain all day, and sometimes all night. I hear nothing but the guns and rifles, which are like a huge orchestra, the roar changing according to the number of guns and rifles, or the rate of shooting. I have often listened, and seemed to hear them playing a tune, always the same weary metallic time, and to-day we have heard nothing, but it would take weeks to get it out of my head, and long before that, we shall be at it again!

Nov 19 14

My dear Ralph

I was glad to hear from Mummy that she has been to see you and that you are both well. The weather has been very bad lately. It rains most days and then freezes very hard at night, which is very unpleasant. We were walking about all last night in many degrees of frost, and the ground was quite white with frost which made our noses very cold. This is a very ugly country, where many of the greatest battles in the world have been fought. The mud is dreadful. In places it is almost up to your knees. Most of the roads have disappeared into a mass of mud, owing to traffic and the many shells which have exploded on them. And very often you cannot tell the roads from the ploughed fields. The country is all in a dreadful state. There is not a single house which has not been smashed to bits and nobody will be able to live here after the war for years. The Germans seem to like to smash everything for the fun of it, even when it can do them no good at all – but it is very sad to see the country in such a state. I have no more time today. Give the enclosed to Lyulph.

With much love from

Yr Affect
Father

West Downs
Winchester

My dear Mummie

I am just writing you a line, that I had a letter from father, dated Nov 19th saying that he was quite well, and that they had had very cold weather lately and it rains most days and very hard at night all Nov 18. There were many degrees of frost. That was all.

Your loving son
Ralph

Nov 19 14

My dearest little Sylvia

I believe it is nearly your birthday and so I am writing to wish you many happy returns of the day. I hope you will have a happy birthday and a nice cake with how many candles on it? Is it 6? I cannot remember. I am glad you like Deal. You will turn into a sailor if you stay at the sea much longer and that would never do. I suppose you know all the ships by now and their names? Give Jack my love and a kiss. I hope he has been a good dog and that he looks after you well. Won't you be glad when the boys come home for Xmas, which will not be long now.

It is snowing hard today and it looks as if it would go on doing so. Many kisses and much love from

Your most affect

Father

· BACKGROUND NARRATIVE ·

One of Wilfrid's responsibilities as commanding officer was to write letters of condolence to the next of kin of officers in his battalion who had died. This must have been a particularly distressing task during the middle of November 1914 when he lost six officers, all of whom were buried in the cemetery at Zillebeke church. On 11 November he wrote to Bernard Gordon Lennox's widow:

Nov. 11. 14

Dear Lady Bernard

I send my sincerest sympathy to you in your great loss. You know well how fond we all were of Bernard, but you cannot know what he has been to me during many anxious days within the last few weeks. He always did the right thing and inspired me with the utmost confidence, and I shall miss him as a soldier more than I can say. He was slightly wounded by a shell on the aft. of the 10th and was leaving his trench to get his wound dressed when he was hit again and died without doubt instantaneously. Douglas will tell you where we have laid him to rest and I can only once more assure you of our heartfelt sympathy.

Yrs Sincerely

Wilfrid A Smith

· BACKGROUND NARRATIVE ·

A week later, Wilfrid wrote to the parents of Lieutenant Lee Steere, who had been killed on 17 November:

> Poor boy! He was killed during a strong infantry attack by the Germans which his company repulsed with considerable slaughter. You will be glad to hear that owing to the steadiness of No. 2 Coy and of No. 1 on the right, the Germans failed to break our line, though at least one German got through and had to be shot behind the trenches. The ground in front of the Grenadier trenches was covered with fallen Germans. No. 1 Coy could count 80 in the first 50 yards. They could not see further owing to the wood. No.2 must have killed at least as many: and we think the two companies (about 180 rifles) must have killed about 300 Germans.
>
> … astoundingly well during the short time he has been with us, and was rapidly making a valuable officer. He was always happy and cheerful under the most trying conditions … He was buried last night in the small village churchyard of Zillebeke where I am sorry to say six Grenadier officers lie side-by-side. I hope it may help you to bear your loss to know that your boy was hit during doing his duty and doing it well in the presence of a dangerous and heavy German infantry attack.

· BACKGROUND NARRATIVE ·

On 20 November, Lord Cavan wrote a letter to Colonel Streatfeild, OC Grenadier Guards, a copy of which Wilfrid sent to Violet with his letter of 18 December:

> The 2nd Battalion move back tonight about 18 miles with the rest of the Brigade to refit, reorganise and rest.
>
> They leave the line intact, and in spite of great loss and untold sufferings and hardship, they fought the battle of Nov. 17 with as good a nerve as the battle of the Aisne. They have, perhaps, had the hardest time of any of the four Battalions, as their rest days in Corps reserve were entirely taken up with marching and making counterstrokes at various parts of the line. I can never express what I think of the great courage and endurance shown by officers and men during the defence before Ypres, and I should like to put on the

Regimental Records not only my sense of pride at being their Brigadier, but my debt to the Battalion for their great devotion to their duty.

They have kept up a respectable appearance which has been an example, considering that it has been absolutely impossible to change clothing for four weeks.

It is hoped that some Officers may be able to get home for a few days [sic] complete rest and change.

(signed) Cavan

Brigadier, Commanding 4th Guards Brigade

The Duke of Connaught, the Colonel of the Regiment, wrote to Colonel Streatfeild:

... I am appalled with the losses of Officers, N.C.O's [sic] and men in the 1st and 2nd Battalions, and I cannot tell you how deep is my sympathy with their families. If it is any consolation to them I hope they will recognise how nobly all have sacrificed their lives for King and Country. I am filled with pride at being the Colonel of a Regiment that has done so splendidly on service, and of all who have so nobly upheld the honour of the 1st Regiment of Guards.

In his letter to Violet of 20 December, Wilfrid enclosed a copy of Sir John French's Special Order of the Day dated 22 November 1914:

1. The sphere of operations over which the British Army in France has been operating is now much contracted and rendered more compact. Since the 21st instant it has been possible to keep a considerable force in general reserve.

   For several days past the enemy's activities against our front have been sensibly slackened, and it is quite possible that we may have entered upon the last stage of the great battle in which we have been engaged since October 11th.

2. At this moment I am anxious to address a few words to the splendid troops I have the great honour to command.

   In view of the magnificent way in which the troops of the British Army have fought, the hardships they have had to endure, and the heavy losses they have suffered, it is right that all ranks, collectively and individually, should form a just and reasonable conception of the general situation and the object which we are endeavouring to attain.

3. It is necessary for this purpose to realise in the first place the true limits of the theatre of war as a whole, and then to take a comprehensive view of the entire course of operations as they have proceeded up to the present moment, in order to estimate the value of the results attained.

4. It must be clearly understood that the operations in which we have been engaged embrace nearly all the Continent of Central Europe from East to West. The combined French, Belgian, and British Armies in the West, and the Russian Army in the East are opposed to the united forces of Germany and Austria acting as a combined army between us.

   Our enemies elected at the outset of the war to throw the weight of their forces against the armies in the West, and to detach only a comparatively weak force, composed of very few first-line troops, and several corps of the second and third line, to stem the Russian advance till the Western Forces could be completely defeated and overwhelmed.

5. The strength of our enemies enabled them from the outset to throw greatly superior forces against us in the West. This precluded the possibility of our taking a vigorous offensive, except when the miscalculations and mistakes made by their Commanders opened up special opportunities for a successful attack and pursuit.

   The Battle of the Marne was an example of this, as was also our advance from St. Omer and Hazebrouck to the line of the Lys at the commencement of this Battle. The role which our armies in the West have consequently been called upon to fulfil has been to occupy strong defensive positions, holding the ground gained and inviting the enemy's attack; to throw these attacks back, causing the enemy heavy losses in his retreat and following him up with powerful and successful counter-attacks to complete his discomfiture.

6. While we have been thus engaged the Russian Armies in the East, numbering some three to four millions of men, have had time to mobilise and concentrate their immense forces scattered over all parts of their vast Empire. Our Eastern Allies have already inflicted a series of crushing defeats on the Austro-German Forces, and are now rapidly advancing on East Prussia and Silesia in great strength.

7. The value and significance of the splendid role fulfilled since the commencement of hostilities by the Allied forces in the West lies in the fact that at the moment when the Eastern Provinces of Germany are about to be over-run by the numerous and powerful armies of Russia, nearly the whole of the active army of Germany is tied down to a line of trenches extending from the Fortress of Verdun on the Alsatian Frontier round to the

sea at Nieuport, east of Dunkirk (a distance of 260 miles), where they are held, much reduced in numbers and morale by the successful action of our troops in the West.

8. What the enemy will now do we cannot tell. Should they attempt to withdraw their troops to strengthen their weakened forces in the East, we must follow them up and harass their retreat to the utmost of our power. If they make further futile attempt to break through our line, they must be again thrown back with greater and greater loss.

The Armies of Russia are at their eastern gates, and will very soon be devastating their country and overthrowing their Armies.

The great fight which you have so splendidly maintained against superior numbers in the western theatre will be decided and completed by our brave Allies in the East, and I think that we on this side have reason to hope that we have completed the most severe and arduous part of our task.

We must, however, be prepared for all eventualities, and I feel sure no effort will be relaxed to meet with the same undaunted front any situations, however unexpected, which may arise.

9. I have made many calls upon you, and the answers you have made to them have covered you, your regiments, and the Army to which you belong with honour and glory.

Your fighting qualities, courage and endurance have been subjected to the most trying and severe tests, and you have proved yourselves worthy descendants of the British soldiers of the past who have built up the magnificent traditions of the regiments to which you belong.

You have not only maintained those traditions, but you have materially added to their lustre.

It is impossible for me to find words in which to express my appreciation of the splendid services you have performed.

(Signed) J.D.P. French, (Field Marshal),

Commander-In-Chief, The British Army in the Field

Nov. 21st

At last we are having our rest. We walked all last night and got well away from shells, and can now only hear them in the distance. What a comfort it is, I cannot describe. I shall get a good sleep at last. You will, probably, get this to-morrow night, as Jeffreys is taking it for me. He is going home on leave for a few days. They are allowing a certain proportion to go. If all goes well, I hope I may get away when he returns, but you must not put too much faith in it, as it entirely depends on the Germans, and we may have to go back to the trenches any day, but I may get home next Saturday evening for a few days, though I am afraid it is too good to be true. It is extraordinary how one can get on without sleep. I walked 16 miles last night, had one hour's sleep when I got in, and have been busy all day, but I am not over-tired. I expect I shall be much more tired when I have had a few nights' sleep.

The Prince of Wales is out with French, and is coming to see us to-morrow. It is odd to be in a house again and have a fire. We are going to do ourselves well, the boys will be all the better for it. The weather is like Christmas, snow and frost. I marched all last night with two woollies on and a great coat, and only just got warm. It must have been awful in the trenches.

We are a very small party now with a few gone on leave, and I miss our departed friends sadly. We left six in one churchyard. It was so sad passing them last night for ever.

Nov. 23rd

A few lines by somebody who goes home to-night. I am afraid you must not count too much on my getting home. I cannot believe the Germans will allow it, but if I do come, I ought to arrive at Victoria at 8.15 p.m. on Saturday night. I may want my British Warm coat. I am going to see what the fur coats they propose giving us (for £4.) are like, and I hope to know by the end of the week. I have got a little more used to the intense cold. I don't know how much frost there has been, but I should imagine 10 to 15 degrees day and night. I had a glorious sleep last night, and never moved for nearly 10 hours. I shall get as much sleep as I can this week. I am very busy re-fitting the Battalion. They look very dirty and unwashed, and it is so cold that I am afraid we all refrain from washing more than necessary! I had my first bath two days ago since the 18th October. I quite missed my boots. We have a very comfortable house here (Meteren) and a stove is very pleasant. I hope it won't make us too soft. Goodbye for to-day: I hope you will get this to-morrow.

· BACKGROUND NARRATIVE ·

Wilfrid left for a week's leave on 28 November. His diary records the battalion's casualties over the previous four months, which totalled nearly 1,000 men:

Telegram dated 28 November 1914 from Wilfrid to Violet, advising of arrival at Victoria. (Author's collection)

Casualties

2nd Battalion Grenadier Guards

Officers

DATE	KILLED	WOUNDED	MISSING
Aug.	2nd Lt Vereker		
Sept.	Lt and Adjutant McDougall Capt Stephen Lt Hon J. Manners Lt Hon W. Cecil Lt Welby Lt Des Voeux Lt Cunliffe	Capt Gosselin Capt Ridley Lt Needham Lt Walker Lt Stewart Lt Mackenzie Lt Vernon	Lt G. Cecil
Oct.	Lt Miller	Capt Maitland Lt Rose Lt Nesbitt	
Nov. 6th	Lt Tufnell	Lt Dowling	
Nov. 10th	Major Lord B. Gordon Lennox Lt M. Stocks Lt Lord Congleton	Capt Powell Capt Ridley Lt Tudway	

Nov. 11th		Capt and Adjutant E. Pike	
Nov. 17th	Capt Symes–Thompson Lt Lee Steere		
Total	15	15	1

NCOs and Men

DATE	KILLED	WOUNDED	MISSING
Aug.	1	6	
Sept.	50	152	8
Oct.	25	115	8
Nov. 1st	10	29	8
Nov. 2nd	4	12	1
Nov. 4th	4	26	
Nov. 5th	3	5	
Nov. 6th	26	114	3
Nov. 8th	1	2	
Nov. 9th	1	5	
Nov. 10th	21	37	16
Nov. 11th	1	28	1
Nov. 12th	1	12	3
Nov. 13th		1	3
Nov. 15th	1	4	1
Nov. 16th		1	5
Nov. 17th	10	7	
Nov. 18th	3	22	
Total	162	578	191

The volume of Wilfrid's letters and diaries contains a poem by the writer and poet Beatrix Brice, published in *The Times* on 2 November 1916. Brice was one of the first women to become a Red Cross VAD 'Lady Helper' on the Western Front. She wrote the poem in memory of the first soldiers who went to fight in France in 1914:

To the first seven divisions, the fallen, the prisoners, the disabled and those
still fighting.

Oh! Little mighty Force that stood for England!
That with your bodies for a living shield,
Guarded her slow awaking, that defied
The sudden challenge of enormous odds
And fought the rushing legions to a stand –
Then stark in grim endurance held the line.
Oh! little Force that in your agony
Stood fast while England girt her armour on,
Held high our honour in your wounded hands,
Carried our honour safe with bleeding feet –
We have no glory great enough for you.
The very soul of Britain keeps your day:
Procession? – Marches forth a Race in arms;
And, for the thunder of the crowd's applause,
Crash upon crash the voice of monstrous guns
Fed by the sweat, served by the life of England,
Shouting your battle cry across the world.
Oh! Little mighty Force, your way is ours,
This land inviolate your monument.

5

December 1914 – Rest, Refit and Christmas in the Trenches

It had become clear to everyone that the war on the Western Front was now deadlocked. Both sides were now entrenched along a front that stretched from the Channel to the Swiss border. It was to change only in detail over the next four years.

Wilfrid arrived back home in London on Saturday 28 November for a week's leave, returning to the front on 5 December. He was only to return to England once more, from 25 February to 2 March 1915. It was a busy few days that included a visit on the Sunday to his sons at their school near Winchester, and later in the week to his house, Upton Lea, near Slough, to see his daughter. His short period of leave coincided with his fourteenth wedding anniversary, for which he gave Violet a six-volume leather-bound set of the writings of the poet Walter Swinburne, each book inscribed with, 'My dearest V from Wilfrid Dec: 3.1914 Our Wedding Day'.

The king inspected the 4th (Guards) Brigade the same day, bringing with him the Prince of Wales (who would briefly be King Edward VIII) as a Grenadier. The prince was to be a frequent visitor to the battalion over the next few months.

The battalion's period of rest in Méteren provided an opportunity to hold Committees of Adjustment in accordance with the Regimental Debts Act 1893 to report on the assets and liabilities of the dead. Major Jeffreys was president and Captain Cavendish and Lieutenant Gerard served as members. Wilfrid forwarded the proceedings of seventeen officers to the brigade major on 18 December.

The First Battle of Ypres had severely depleted the BEF. It was not until the middle of 1915 that the first divisions of Kitchener's New Army of volunteers arrived in France. In the meantime, replacement battalions of Territorial forces were being rapidly re-kitted, brought up to full readiness and shipped over to bolster the fragile front line. Additional reserves were being created by mobilising older retired soldiers and reservists. Home-based battalions and part-trained reservists were pressed into action. Conscription was a hotly debated political subject in Britain and the army had to rely on volunteers at home and across the Empire until it was introduced in January 1916.

On 21 December, Wilfrid's battalion was ordered to transfer to a section of the line near Béthune in France, where the hard-pressed Indian Corps had lost some trenches. The Indian soldiers were poorly equipped to deal with the cold and wet they were facing. On the evening of 23 December, after two days of marching, the battalion took over the line at rue de Cailloux from the Royal Sussex Regiment after dark. This part of the line was located in a waterlogged valley.

Ponsonby described the grim scene:

These trenches were very bad, and had been hastily improvised from dykes, when the Germans succeeded in capturing our front-line trenches a few days before. The water was always knee-deep, in some places waist-deep, in mud and water, and as the enemy's trench was within twenty-five yards, his snipers, who were always enterprising, had plenty of opportunities of shooting.[1]

While some sections of the line indulged in informal Christmas truces, there was no let up in the fighting on Wilfrid's section over Christmas. Ponsonby recounted that:

The early morning [of 24 December] began with considerable sniping and bombardment with trench mortars. It was bitterly cold, and the water in the trenches made communication almost impossible. It seemed madness to attempt to hold such a line of trenches, and yet there was no alternative.

Notes of warning arrived from General Headquarters:

'It is thought possible that the enemy may be contemplating an attack during Christmas or New Year. Special vigilance will be maintained during these periods.

Please note that when the enemy is active with Minenwerfer [German short-range mortars], it is generally the prelude to an attack.'

The enemy had the advantage of the ground, for not only did his trenches drain into ours, but he was able to overlook our whole line. In addition to this he was amply supplied with trench mortars and hand grenades, so that we were fighting under very great difficulties. He mined within ten yards of our trench, and blew in the end of [Company] No. 2's trench, after which he attacked in great force, but was unable to do more than just reach our line …

In the evening Lt Col Smith came to the conclusion that fighting under such conditions was only courting disaster, and that it would be clearly better to dig a new line of trenches during the night, but it was absolutely necessary to finish the new line before daylight – otherwise it would be useless. Accordingly he gave orders for a new line to be dug, and the men, soaked and stiff with cold as they were, set to work at once. Rockets and fireballs gave the enemy's snipers their opportunity, and the freezing water and hard ground made the work difficult. There was, however, no artillery fire, though the Minenwerfer were nearly as bad, and threw large shells into our trenches. The new line was just completed as dawn broke on Christmas morning.

The sniping continued steadily the next day with great accuracy, and the slightest movement drew a shot at once. Captain E.G. Spencer Churchill was wounded in the head in this way, the bullet making a groove in his skull. The new trenches, however, threatened to become as wet as the old ones, although in the worst places they were built with a high parapet and a shallow trench. No. 3 Company, under Captain Cavendish, in particular succeeded in erecting an elevated trench of this nature, in spite of the incessant sniping which was carried on during the night.

Lord Cavan sent a message:

'Hearty congratulations on good night's work. Thank Captain Cavendish and his Company. Am absolutely satisfied with arrangements. Report when and how you manoeuvre the little stream.'

It being Christmas Day, plum puddings and other luxuries were distributed, and Princess Mary's present of a box, containing a pipe, tobacco, and cigarettes, was much appreciated.

In the evening the Battalion was relieved by the 3rd Battalion Coldstream, and marched back to Le Touret …'[2]

On the Eastern Front, the Germans had attacked the Russians near the Polish city of Lodz in mid-November with the eventual aim of taking Warsaw.

German forces of about 250,000 faced a Russian army twice its size. Almost a month of fighting culminated in the German occupation of Lodz on 6 December but the results of this battle were inconclusive. The Russians repulsed the Germans, saving Warsaw, while the Germans caused the Russians to abandon their offensive into Silesia.

Arriving in London on leave, Wilfrid had an unusual parcel to send to Bernard Gordon Lennox's widow:

4 Eaton Terrace
London S.W.

Dec: 1. 14

Dear Lady Bernard

The other day I found a rifle which dear Bernard had been keeping to bring home, and I thought you might like to have it. He took it from a german [*sic*] after the fight at Soupir on the Aisne about Sept 14th. I hope you have received the things I gave to Douglas last week.

I am so sorry to hear of your boy's illness. I trust he is going on well.

With so much sympathy

Yrs sincerely

Wilfrid A Smith

· BACKGROUND NARRATIVE ·

Wilfrid had already travelled down to Winchester to see his two sons at school, where they had given him a present to keep him warm during the winter:

Dec: 2. 14

4 Eaton Terrace
S.W.

My dear Ralph

It was very nice seeing you both on Sunday and to find you both so well. I am sure you will work hard. You did not have a fair chance owing to your going back so late, and I hope you will get on in the holidays and make up for lost time. I am sure that you will do your best.

Will you tell Mr Helbert that I had no time to pay the car on Sunday night and I told the man to put it down to my account?

I hope to go to Upton Lea to-morrow for the night and see Sylvia. On Saturday I go back to France.

Give my love to Lyulph.

Bless you both

    Yr Affect

    Father

Dec: 5. 14

4 Eaton Terrace
S.W.

My dear Lyulph

Thank you so much for your letter and for the nice scarf you have made me. I do think it kind of you to have taken so much trouble about it, and shall always think of you when I wear it in the cold weather.

Thank Ralph for his letter and tell him I am so glad that he was so nearly top. If the other boy had not had the cheek to get 1 more mark, he would have been top. I am sure you are glad that the exams are over and I am glad you have both done well.

Now I hope you will enjoy your holidays as much as you can – and look after Mummy for me while I am away. You must both help to cheer her up.

I was going today, but last night I heard that I could stay this Sunday, so I am going after church.

Goodbye, my dear boys. Bless you both.

    Yr Affect

    Father

Dec. 7th

Meteren. I got back safely last night, most luxuriously, I got a lift in a car from Boulogne to St. Omer, dined there, and came on in a shut Daimler, and landed here by 10.15 p.m. Not a bad crossing at all. Found everything here much as usual. Pouring with rain, and mud up to your neck. A few more Officers than when I went away, and a great deal to do. I believe we move on Wednesday, but have not heard yet for certain. I am uncomfortably hot in all my warm things, but I have no doubt that will change when we get outside again. I have hours of writing before me to pick up the threads, so I must not write more to-day.

I hear prospects of an altogether easier time in future, but that must depend on the Germans largely.

Dec. 9th

The rain and slush continue, I think this is the worst climate in the world, far worse than England. We have not yet moved, and I expect now we shall not go till Saturday. Things seem fairly quiet in the front.

The reports from Russia, as far as I can make out, are good; the Germans having got Lodz is not half as bad as it sounds. We have got so many people now in our small mess, that one can hardly write for noise. When we got here we were such a small party and rather down on our luck, that we agreed to mess together, and now we are too many.

The King came to see the Battalion last week, and was very nice. He gave medals to eight of my men who got the Distinguished Conduct Medal. I must try and get some more for them, there are many who deserve it, but I can't recommend them all. I wish my boys could get a D.S.O. or two.

A kiss to Sylvia who I suppose is with you in London.

Dec. 10th

It has turned very cold and miserable and wet here. We have not yet moved, but I expect we shall to-morrow or Sunday. I went yesterday to see the 1st Battalion about twelve miles from here, and got a good ducking on the way back. The whole country is as flat as a pancake, rather like the fens of Lincolnshire. The dykes are all full of water, and there is nowhere for the water to run to, and the filth and the mud I cannot describe. I found the 1st Battalion very well – saw Bobby [Lygon] looking extraordinary clean! The Old Friend [Laurence Fisher-Rowe] very well, but he has not been out of a house yet for a night, and has lived in a house all day, so they have not been having a bad time. I saw Sydney Clive yesterday for the first time during the war. He was very well, but is very hard worked. Most of what he told us was not for publication. They all seem quite happy about Russia, and say that the German losses have been enormous.

Kitchener says the war is going on for two years, but they think he does not realise what it would mean to every country but England, who as yet has not been touched by the War. In other countries all trade is practically at a standstill, and it is impossible to believe that this world can stand such a thing for two years.

I have copied the diary of the Battalion, before I joined, which may be of interest some day.

· BACKGROUND NARRATIVE ·

Wilfrid had strong views about church parades:

Dec. 13th

I hoped to have got a letter from you to-day, but it is astonishing how long letters can take to come from London. I went to church this morning, a fine large church, but very gaudy inside, and it was chock full of men, entirely voluntary. It bears out my theory that a good parson will get as many men to church as they get now compulsorily. I think that it speaks well for the French R.C's that they almost always allow us to use their churches, and I believe it is a thing that the R.C's are very particular about. We had a good organ this morning, which was a great pleasure. I have been busy all the week with many and varied things. I hope you will have received my Diary all right, and that it will interest you. It took me a long time to write, but it is a good thing to do so, while every day is indelibly impressed on one's mind.

I have at last got over my want of sleep, and get up like a bird every morning, but these dark mornings are horrible.

The Prince came again last night. Poor boy, he is very miserable at Head Quarters with nobody of his own age, and no special job to do.

We have no orders to move yet, but it cannot be far off now. We shall never get the war over if we sit here doing nothing all the time.

HRH the Prince of Wales.
(Grenadier Guards)

Dec. 14th

We are in the reserve to-day, waiting to move at any moment, whether the order will come to-day or to-night, goodness knows. I am sending a list of killed and wounded in November for you to keep with my diary. You will see that there is hardly a day on which we had no casualty. I think it is pretty certain that we shall be moving to-night or to-morrow morning, and so my letters may suffer, but I won't stop unless I am obliged to. I am hoping to get some more Officers any day now.

· BACKGROUND NARRATIVE ·

The Prince of Wales visited again having finally seen some action of a sort:

Dec. 15th

It dawned on me in the night that Christmas is jolly close.

The Prince arrived here late last night in high glee. He had seen a fight, (at a fairly safe distance) and had got a prisoner in his car! I never saw a boy so happy. The prisoner was in his car, guarded by his 'bear leader', while he talked to us in our house. Eventually he left his prisoner, (a Lieutenant) looking very comfortable, and having the time of his life, being driven by H.R.H. himself. He always drives himself in an ordinary car, with a hood and tremendous headlights.

Just got another letter from you. I'm glad Sylvia likes London. How like a woman to like shops! Well I suppose you will get this a day or two before Christmas.

We shall never beat the Germans unless we get on with it. We are, however, doing something, though I mustn't say what. The weather is so bad, no weather for fighting.

The Prince of Wales' car with his driver, Green, photographed by Lord Claud Hamilton, personal ADC to HRH, and possibly the 'bear leader' referred to in Wilfrid's letter of 15 December 1914. (Grenadier Guards)

· BACKGROUND NARRATIVE ·

The approach of Christmas brought a new set of challenges. Wilfrid also took the opportunity to express his frustration at the loss of life caused by the inflexibility of his commanders in contrast to the pragmatism of the Russian commanders at Lodz. In his absence, Violet and the children were going to spend Christmas with her Lygon cousins at their house at Madresfield on which Evelyn Waugh based his book *Brideshead Revisited*:

Dec. 18th

I am thinking of you all at home to-day, with the boys back from school, no doubt in the highest spirits. Everything seems to be hung up just now for all the Christmas parcels, which are becoming a positive nuisance. I am told that the rations of the Army are to be held up for twenty-four hours to enable the Princess Mary's presents to come up, and I have had reams of orders as to their distribution. I don't know what I am not responsible for in connection with this present. It was the longest order I have had since I have been out, and it seems rather ridiculous to make such a tremendous business of it when, after all, our first business is to beat the Germans. Our enemy thinks of War, and nothing else, while we must mix it up with Plum Puddings!

This is my last sheet of paper, so I must go on on anything I can beg, borrow, or steal. Paper seems rather scarce just now.

Dobson, who got a V.C. is a Coldstreamer – I am delighted he got it. He brought in two wounded men on the Aisne, under the continuous fire of the Germans, and they refused a V.C. for some quibble. However, he has got it at last, but they might just as well have done it at first.

The Russians at Lodz, dealt with a situation we have often had here on a smaller scale, in a sensible manner. Here, if you get into an impossible position, they won't let you fall back, because they are afraid they will be held to have lost ground. I have often implored to be allowed to move a few hundred yards back to hold a decent position, instead of a horrible one, but it has always been 'No', with the result of a horrible time for some days. The Russians dealt with it at once, thereby, saving many lives, and preventing any further set back.

I am sending you a copy of Fatty's letter to keep for me. I got Stretty [Streatfeild] to send some out for the men to see, as I thought it would please them.

Our weather continues [to be] horrible, and we really cannot do much good while it lasts. You cannot attack when you can hardly get your feet out of

Letter from Merwyn (?), aged 7, to the Grenadier Guards, enclosing a Christmas present. (Author's collection)

48, Abonmore Road,
Kensington, W.

Dear Grenadier Guards
I have saved all my
pennies to buy you a
Christmas present.
With much love from —
Your loving "Merwyn"
aged 7

the mud. The Germans are much stronger than we are, and we know what we did with them last month, when they tried to attack us, when we were so miserably weak. I can't make out how we are going to kick them out of Belgium yet, the papers all talk gaily of 'kicking them out', but it is a very difficult military problem. If Italy would come in now, it would probably be comparatively easy. I shall send this to Madresfield, as it will probably get to you quicker than London.

I hope you will all enjoy yourselves. I expect the boys will be very happy.

With our best wishes for
Christmas 1914
May God protect you and
bring you home safe
Mary R   George R.I.

Christmas card from the king and queen. (Author's collection)

Dec. 19th

I have been bothered for some days with toothache, which is annoying. I rode to-day to Hazebrouck to see if I could get a Dentist, and found a man who said what I thought, that it was the cold which had got into it, so I hope it will soon be better. Your iodine will come in useful for it after all.

I got two letters from you to-day, the 8th and 10th, the 9th having arrived yesterday. Such are the vagaries of the post.

We have not moved yet, though we are still ready to move at very short notice. The fact of the matter is that we have not done much good lately, and things are rather at a stale-mate. We hear Germany is trying to make terms with France and Russia – of course with a view to smashing us – very kind of them.

· BACKGROUND NARRATIVE ·

Wilfrid wrote a Christmas letter to his older brother, Eustace, who lived at Longhills in Lincolnshire. England was in a state of shock after the shelling of the Yorkshire seaside towns of Scarborough, Whitby and Hartlepool by German warships on 16 December. One hundred and seven men, women and children were killed and over 500 wounded. Wilfrid hoped that this would stir the nation into wholehearted support of the war effort:

Dec 19 14

My dear Eustace

Just a line to wish you all at Longhills a happy time at Xmas. At least as happy as it is possible to be this year. I'm afraid for many people all the world over it will be a miserable time.

We are not doing much at present. The weather is so bad and the mud so awful that it is very difficult to know how to get on. And the Germans are still very strong, though many of their big guns seem to have gone, possibly to Russia. Still we must get on soon, though it is a difficult nut to crack. From the headlines in the papers, one would imagine no war was going on outside England. I am sorry for the people who were knocked over, but 2 hours [sic] shelling will probably do more good than all the talking in the world. It will make people realise what England would be like if the shelling went on for months.

My Battalion is up to strength again except for 8 officers, so I have something respectable to look after. But the old gaps can never be filled, and one misses daily one's old friends and trusted comrades. However, that is War.

I have no time for more. Best love to you all.

    Yr affect. brother

    Wilfrid

                                    Dec 19 14

My dear little Sylvia

I hope you are having a happy Xmas and enjoying yourself. You must be glad to get the boys home again. What a big boy Lyulph must seem to you now. Will you tell Mummy that I have got the good raisins she sent to me, and also the nail cleaner, which will do very well. I wonder how you are getting on with your dinner every day now that I am not there to look after you? Anyhow I expect you will be able to eat your Xmas dinner of good turkey and plum pudding. Give my love to Mummy and tell her that I have not time to write to her today. I hope you are being a good girl and looking after Mummy for me. My best love to you. And give Jack a kiss for me and wish him a good bone for Xmas

    Yr affect

    Father

                                    Dec. 20th

I wonder whether you have been looking at the wonderful sunset to-night from our little garden. It was most glorious and wintry, and I imagined you and the boys admiring it. I am so glad you have them back, it will make a great difference to you.

We have been waiting to move at two hours' notice all the week, and so have had an easy time. I don't know how long it is going on for, but we are sure to move soon, I think. The progress is extremely slow, and will be, till somebody solves the riddle of how to get through the line.

I am sending you the order French issued at the end of November. It is very well put and clear.

I read an article in the 'Daily News' the other day, saying that this War was a triumph for Voluntary Service! Can you conceive it? How little people who talk like this realise the situation. If we had had any form of compulsory service, there would probably have been no War; there would certainly have been no retreat, and we should now be sitting on the Rhine.

I heard an interesting thing the other day on good authority. The Germans had always arranged that if they failed in the dash for Paris, they would fall back to the Aisne, but we drove them so fast that they got beyond the position they meant to hold and annihilate us, and we crossed the River where they did not expect us to. Had we been able to push the least bit more, they would have had to fall back to their position on the Meuse! No more to-day.

DIARY

Dec. 22nd

Parade at 7 a.m. at Meteren, and marched by Merville to Bethune, which we reached at 6.30 p.m. and billetted. We halted for hours about midday for dinner. As we left Meteren, we saw a fire raging in a farm which had been occupied by No.3. It was a beautiful farm, and I'm afraid much damage was done. I never discovered how it happened, all the usual precautions appear to have been taken, and the fire did not break out till the Company had been gone for nearly an hour. In all the many barns and billets we have occupied, it is the only fire we have had, which is wonderful considering the amount of inflammable straw, etc. in these farms. It was a bitterly cold day, snowing at times, and I walked most of the way. The Prince joined us a few miles out of Meteren and marched at the head of the Battalion with me all the way. The men were tired as they were carrying a great weight.

Dec. 23rd

Left Bethune at 7 a.m. Halted in a field near Le Touret at 9.30 in readiness to support the 2nd Brigade. It snowed hard and was very cold. The Prince came with us and left about mid-day.

Moved about 3.30 p.m. and took over trenches from the Royal Sussex Regiment near the Rue de Cailloux. We met the representatives of the Sussex Regiment at the Rue de L'Epinette, and the Companies went straight on to the trenches. It was a nasty bulletty walk. The snow and sleet and slush was appalling, far worse than anything we have had before. There was one communication trench for the whole of my line, and for a part of the Coldstream line, and this trench was thick mud up to the men's knees, and in places higher. The relief began at 6.30 p.m., and did not complete till 6.30 a.m. Poor men got stuck in the trench, and it took 4 hours to dig them out, during which time the trench was blocked, and they then had to be conveyed back to the dressing station in a state of collapse. Some of the trenches were up to the men's waists in water (particularly No. 1) and to get to their trenches it was even deeper.

Dec. 24th

From right to left No. 1., No.2., No.3., and No. 4 in reserve at Head Quarters. The Munsters (3rd Brigade) were on our right, and Coldstream (2nd Battalion) on the left. As soon as the relief was completed, Jeffreys began to go round the line, while I tried to get communication, etc. arranged. It was very difficult on account of the wet and mud. The signallers had been out all night laying wires in spite of a continual fusillade, and much to their credit, had got some sort of communication, but it was not good.

We cleaned up the house at Head Quarters and tried to drain and get the place less wet, but with no success whatever.

Jeffreys returned after being away about 3 hours, and said he had only been able to get round No. 1 Company, the wet and mud was awful. I got a message about this time from No. 1 that the Germans had sapped up very close to them, but as Jeffreys had just come back and reported that all was well as far as he could see, except for the wet, I did not think much of it. I left Jeffreys to dry and carry on at Head Quarters while I went round the rest of the line. It took me nearly an hour to get down the communication trench, and I found the trenches like Hampton Court Maze. They were all over the place, all full of mud or water or both, and once in, you could not tell where you were. The men were wet through, miserably cold, and in spite of hard work could make no progress with the work. They were being constantly shot at with Minenverfers [sic], which was a new experience to us. I saw one shell burst as I went down the communication trench. It burst just like a 'Black Maria', and though I did not think much of it at the time, I noticed just after a lot of earth fly into the air apparently for no reason. I afterwards found out it was a mine exploding.

I got along No. 2 trenches, and then a short way along I found a great block of men, who said they had orders to retire! I stopped them and tried to find out from whom the order had come. Eventually I found Marshall, who said there was nothing wrong, and that he knew nothing about retiring. As I couldn't move forward on account of the block of men, I told him to get things straightened out, and I went back to try and get to No. 3 another way. The only other way I could find was blocked with Coldstream, so I gave it up, hoping to get round later, if the water went down a bit. I got back to Head Quarters pretty wet through. I had not been back long before I got a message saying that the Germans were in No. I's trench, and that the Captain had been killed. At the same time a lot of men from 2 and 3 arrived at Head Quarters saying they had been told to retire. I sent Jeffreys down at once to see what was the matter, while I collected the odds and ends at Head Quarters to form a reserve. I found I had got about one Platoon from No. 2, and one from No. 3. What had happened was that No. 3 had withdrawn to close up with the Coldstream, which had been previously arranged should be done, as soon as some necessary digging was finished. About this time a shell had burst (which I saw) in No. 2., and a mine been exploded. The parapet was knocked down and Clive withdrew to a trench in rear. Being new to the game he did not realise that this left No. I's flank in the air. The two Platoons which arrived at Head Quarters were sent back as there was no room for them in the trenches occupied in rear of the former ones, but in the confusion no message was sent to explain this. Meanwhile No. 1 found the Germans swarming into their trench on the left, which they thought was occupied by No. 2, and the Germans also attacked them in front; the result was they had to fall back too, with considerable loss.

The new line was in all respects better than the old one, which ought never to have been handed over to me in the state it was. By about 1 p.m. all was straight again, except that I could not hear of two Platoons of No. 1, which was cut off from the rest of the Company by water, and as I found out afterwards, were rather thrown back from the rest of the Company, and had never been attacked. I never found them till the next morning. Cholmeley and Nevill killed. Goschen wounded and missing, Williams wounded, 15 k̲., 29 w̲. 5 w̲. and m̲., 4 m̲.

I went to Head Quarters after dark to arrange about the new line. It was a lovely starlight night [*sic*], and freezing hard, which with the previous wet, made it miserable for the men.

Dec. 24th

I have had no time to write lately, and cannot write much to-night, for I must try to get some sleep. Another bad day. We have lost poor Monty [Cholmeley], to my great sorrow, and two boys and many men, with very little to show for it. We are in a beastly place. We took over the Indian trenches last night. It is all slush and water, in some places up to your waist. Tonight it is freezing hard, to make it worse. As I rode back to-night from Brigade Head Quarters, in the bright starlight and white frost, and plenty of bullets flying about, I thought of you all at Madresfield. They are shooting now hard, and there is no peace day or night. What a cold, wretched, miserable Christmas, and now to rest.

DIARY

Dec. 25th

We dug a new line during the night under very difficult conditions. The Germans shot hard all night, and sent up flares, which lighted up like day. Marvellous to relate we only had two men hit while digging. Towards morning we finished the new line, and eventually found the two lost Platoons of No. 1., very cold and hungry, but all right. Heavy sniping all day. Relieved at 7 p.m. by the 3rd Battalion Coldstream Guards, and marched to Le Touret and billetted. The men very stiff and tired. Churchill w̲. 3 k̲. 19 w̲.,2 m̲. 55 cases of frost-bite, almost all in No. 1.

Dec. 26th
Le Touret in reserve.

· BACKGROUND NARRATIVE ·

George Goschen was the second son of Sir Edward Goschen, British ambassador to Germany from 1908 to 1914. He had been an attaché at the embassy in Berlin when war broke out. Wounded, he was taken prisoner of war on 26 December but was released in June 1916.

John Buchanan was one of a number of officers in Wilfrid's battalion who had been a first class cricketer before the war, playing for Cambridge University and the MCC. He was to win the MC and DSO. He continued his cricketing career after the war playing for the Free Foresters and Buckinghamshire.

Edward Spencer-Churchill recovered from his injuries. A cousin of Winston Churchill, in 1912 he had inherited Northwick Park, Gloucestershire, to which Winston was a frequent visitor. He became a leading oriental art collector. He wrote of Ma Jeffreys' *sang froid*, 'Perhaps my most vivid of many recollections of him is when – as Second in Command to Colonel Wilfrid Smith – in December 1914, he visited my unpleasant trench – a recent target for the Hun minenwerfer – and Captain Monty Cholmeley and others had just been killed near by. He was just as if on an ordinary parade, regarding these things as obvious occupational hazards, though I knew his real feelings well enough.'[3]

Dec. 26th

Thank the children for their letters, Sylvia particularly. Ralph's was beautifully written, I hope he will stick to it and continue to try and write well. I am quite overwhelmed with letters, my own and many for the Battalion. Such a quantity of Christmas things for the Battalion, which have to be thanked for, but I shall get through it in time. Having to dish out all these things has been a great burden, and came at a somewhat harassing time.

I wrote my last letter hurriedly in the middle of the night. We went into the trenches on Wednesday night, and had a real bad time – most cruel luck for these poor boys to have the first time they have been shot at, the result was, of course, trouble and anxiety. The country about here is dead flat, the most horrible country you can imagine. We took over the most horrible trenches, they were so wet and muddy, and you cannot approach them without being shot at, so all communication has to be by trenches, which are sodden and mostly under water. On our way there four men sank in up to their hips. It took nearly four hours to dig them out, and they all fainted several times from cold. Eventually we got the line taken over, but it took eight hours; the going was so awful. Poor Monty's Company were in a trench with water above their knees, and to get to it they had to wade up to their middles.

In the morning we were in trouble, the Germans were in many places up to ten to twenty yards of us, which we had never been told when we took over in the dark. They threw bombs at us, and shot a horrible explosive bomb, which was nearly as bad as a shell. The shelling was very slight, and our guns are splendid and improving every month, as they get more ammunition and bigger guns. To make a long story short, the beggars got into our trenches. The whole place was trenches and inside was like a maze, some trenches full of water and some not so bad, and what I saw of it was like a lot of rabbits running about with a ferret after them. We took up a line about a hundred yards back, which was a much better one, in fact the first line was untenable when we took it over, and had I had my old and trusted Captains, this would have been recognised at once in the dark, and we should have never tried to stop where we were.

Meanwhile, poor Monty's Company, No. 1 (Gilbert's [Hamilton] Old Company) did their best and were splendid, but the water hampered them and they had to give way to keep in line with the others. Alas! poor Monty was shot, also Nevill and Goschen (reported missing, but feared dead) – the last only joined a week and a nice boy – I believe the son of the Ambassador, but I must make sure before I write to him.

At night we had eventually to dig a new part of the line, which took all night, as it was dug under constant sniping and rockets, and we had no time to finish it, so two Platoons under a splendid young fellow, Buchanan, (just out) had to remain in the water all that night and next day till after dark, when we all got away for forty-eight hours, after which we go back again. The whole business cost me about ninety casualties, and a lot of Officers, three killed, as I told you – Churchill badly wounded, Williams hit in the foot, but still going and I hope will be all right, Eyre, a little boy just out, has had to go sick.

I have fifty-five to-day suffering from frost-bite, and two Officers rather shaky from the same cause, but sticking to it. The second night it froze hard, and I was very anxious for the men in the water, (who were cut off from the others by a ditch with water up to their middles, and who were up to their knees themselves) as to whether they would not be killed by cold, but they came out all right, stiff, cold and hungry, for they had very little for forty-eight hours, (I couldn't get it to them) but chattering and talking quite happily as they hobbled along, splendid fellows that they are. I had had a hot meal ready for them afterwards and they will, I hope, be mostly right to-morrow, but my Battalion is not what it was three days ago, Alas! And it is the first time the Battalion has given up a trench to the Germans, which is very sad.

I hope you will be able to read this, my candle gives a miserable light. I have been horribly cold, I got so wet going round the trenches and had no means of drying. To-night I have a good fire in the house we are resting in, and it is nice to be warm again, my poor feet are very chilblainy, they were dead for hours: I couldn't get them warm, and my hands get so cold too. However, I am very well and have painted my feet with Iodine to help the chilblains. I had a bit of sleep last night after two nights up, and am as right as rain.

Percy came to-day and said everybody at Head Quarters was very happy, and the general position excellent; that is good news, and helps you when you are up to your knees in water!

I am sending home my Christmas card, and shall send my Christmas present from Princess Mary! Bless her – she has been a nuisance! The cigars turned up to-day – taken a fortnight!

DIARY

Dec. 27th

Took over trenches from 3rd Battalion Coldstream Guards at 7 p.m. Water very deep in places.

Dec. 28th

A most boisterous night. Thunderstorm and heavy rain and hail, and a terrific wind. The cold was very severe. Trenches were falling in badly on account of the rain, and we were constantly at work rebuilding them with sandbags, etc. The mud, if possible, worse than ever. 1 w.

Dec. 28th

The frost has gone, and the rain and wet has returned. It is much warmer, but the constant wet makes one feel cold and chilly, and I have to shove in a good deal of quinine to help me through. We are on a beastly line and the work is very heavy, I have had such a lot to do, that I have only had a real sleep one night out of the last five. I must get some to-night, as I am shaky. My head gets so tired with the appalling amount of thinking one has to do by day and night, and I want Eben badly to take some of it off me – the boy is excellent, but young.

Heavens! my trenches are wet. When I went round to-day, I came back caked with mud over my knees, and of course it makes me chilly. I have an appalling amount of Christmas correspondence, thanking the many kind people who have sent things to the Battalion. I got through most of it during last night, when I had to sit up most of the time.

Poor Alan Tritton (Coldstream) was killed here yesterday.

DIARY

Dec. 29th
Began making breastworks instead of trenches. A few shells and constant sniping. 1 k., 3 w. Went into billets at Le Touret, when relieved by the 3rd Battalion Coldstream Guards at 7 p.m.

Dec. 30th
In billets at Le Touret.

Dec. 30th

It is odd to think of you all so peaceful at Madresfield. Christmas Day was anything but peaceful here. We were shot at from morn till night. At present we have been shelled very little, but the bullets fly all day and most of the night. Personally, I think it shows nervousness on the part of the Germans, and I think we ought to try and push a bit to get out of all the wet and slush. I believe they are holding all this wet line very lightly, though doubtless there are plenty behind. I doubt if we should lose more men getting on, than we do sitting still in the wet, and getting frost-bite and rheumatism. The matter is being much discussed by the high authorities.

My tooth has got well again, and except for a cold and cough I am very well, though beastly stiff from wet. The water yesterday was over our knees in the trenches, and though I try to get dry after going round, one can never get quite dry till one changes one's clothes. We have at present 48 hours in and 48 hours out of the trenches. When we are out we go back a mile or two and get into some houses, which is a great comfort, though the time out seems precious short, there is so much to do.

My cake from Goldings has just arrived, and I am just going to have a piece with my tea. Had tea, and the cake was good. I am too busy to write much to-day. I have had such a heap of letters to write lately, what with Christmas and my unfortunate casualties, and with my new and inexperienced Officers, and a foul line to hold, I have had a good deal extra to do. I never seem to get five minutes all day without a message or somebody asking a question. Some of these fellows want mothering badly.

I am horrified to hear that young Goschen had only joined the Regiment six weeks! He had no previous experience of soldiering. I have been disturbed 100 times while writing this.

DIARY

Dec. 31st
Took over trenches from 3rd Battalion Coldstream Guards at 7 p.m.

6

January 1915 – A Miserable New Year

It was a miserable New Year for Wilfrid and his battalion. The wet conditions made life very difficult, as Ponsonby describes:

> The water, however, was the greatest difficulty our men had to contend with: it made the communication trenches impassable, and accounted for more men than the enemy's bullets. It ate away the parapet, rotted the men's clothing, rusted and jammed the rifles, retarded the food supply, and generally made the life of the men in the trenches hideous; but in spite of all this discomfort the men remained cheerful and in good spirits.[1]

Ponsonby goes on to describe the work of the battalion during the first week of January:

> The line now taken over was near Rue du Bois, and the Battalion Headquarters were at Rue des Berceaux. Two companies were in the firing line, with two platoons in the front trench and the other two in support; the remainder of the Battalion formed the reserve.
>
> The rain continued in torrents, and the trench line became a sort of lake. The companies, not in the front trench, were engaged in digging second-line trenches, and a trench that was dug by Nos. 2 and 4 Companies was known for two years after as the Guards' trench. It was considered a model of what a good trench should be.
>
> The usual routine was to relieve the men in the trenches every twelve hours, and bring them back to be dried, rubbed, and cleaned; and there was

not much sickness, although several men were crippled with rheumatism, and would have found great difficulty in marching any distance. The gruesome task of removing the dead was effected by floating the bodies down the communication trenches.[2]

After spending January on the section of the line near Richebourg Saint-Vaast and Rue de Bois, the battalion marched from Les Choqueaux to Béthune. Ponsonby describes the battalion in transit:

> It was only during marches of this length that the whole Battalion assembled together, and saw itself as a Battalion, instead of in isolated companies. It presented an extraordinary appearance. Hung round like a Christmas tree, wearing fur waist-coats, gum-boots, and carrying long French loaves, braziers, charcoal, spades, and sandbags, it looked more like a body of irregular troops from the Balkans than a battalion of Guards.[3]

Reflecting the strict social order of the period, Ponsonby's regimental history was written entirely for officers. The arrival, departure and fate of every single one are recorded. Soldiers of other ranks are only named when performing some outstanding feat. One of the unusual features of Wilfrid's letters is the concern that he shows for the welfare and advancement of his NCOs as well as his officers. This concern was shared by Violet. She served on the committee of the Families Relief Fund set up by the regiment, which involved the ladies concerned in a good deal of correspondence and visiting.

By December 1914 the BEF had expanded to such an extent that it was formed into the First and Second Armies. Douglas Haig was promoted to command the First Army, Charles Monro was promoted to command I Corps and Henry Horne was given command of 2nd Division. Wilfrid had to work hard with this chain of command to make sure that his men received the recognition they deserved and to retrieve his nephew, Desmond ('Dubby'), a son of his brother Eustace, from the Scots Guards.

With the two sides opposing each other across freezing and waterlogged trenches January's combat was limited to raid-and-defend tactics. In mid-December the French had launched their first offensive against the German trenches in the Champagne region, the First Champagne Offensive. This went on for four months until mid-March and, coupled with other attacks against the German front, resulted in 90,000 casualties for very little gain:

DIARY

Jan. 1st

A very wet night, and constant sniping. 2 k.,4 w.

Jan. 1st

I want you to send me out my waders as soon as possible. I can't stand this wet, the trenches are over our knees in mud and water, and I have got a good cold from it. However, everybody else has to stand it, so I suppose I can. I am much annoyed at Desmond and three of my subalterns being sent to the 1st Battalion Coldstream in the 1st Division. It is really monstrous. They will be in John Ponsonby's Battalion.

I saw the New Year in last night in the most depressing way, wet, cold, slush, and bullets and rockets. The Germans sang carols, so our men shot at them to make them keep quiet. This life is misery for the men, bad enough for us. Anyhow it is as bad for the Germans. I don't see how we can get on while the country is in this state. It is difficult to move at all except at a slow walk, and never was warfare made more difficult.

DIARY

Jan. 2nd

Relieved at 7 p.m. by Staffords, and marched to billet at Locon. Slight shelling all day. The Brewery was shelled to-day several times. Rumbold w., 1 k., 7 w.

Jan. 3rd – Jan. 7th

In billets at Locon. Constant rain.

· BACKGROUND NARRATIVE ·

Unsurprisingly, Wilfrid had caught a bad cough. He felt guilty at delegating duties, under doctor's orders, to his second-in-command, Ma Jeffreys.

Hugo Rumbold was injured on 2 January. He had been a leading theatrical designer. After the war, he continued with this career and became a theatrical impresario. He was a member of the Noël Coward set and died in 1932 in Pasadena, California, from injuries sustained in the war:

Jan. 3rd

I have enjoyed your letters from Madresfield. I can picture it all so well with your descriptions of the scenery we know so well. Nature is a great help. At least I always thought so till I came here, where nature has the devil in it. Dead flat, a few poplars, and mud, mud, mud, and water. Never was nature so horrible, and it was a relief to read your description of the sky at Madresfield, and think how beautiful it can be. The nights have been glorious, when it has not been raining, but the mud below is a nightmare. My wounded men have had to have all their clothes cut off them, as the mud is caked right through to their skins, through great coats and all.

We came out of the trenches last night, and go in again on Thursday, unless anything turns up before. It has certainly been a trying time. The wet and the cold dreadful. I have a bad cough and have been shirking in consequence, which I did not like, but the Doctor insisted, and old Ma did all the wet work for me.

I have no more time to-night, and much correspondence to get through.

Jan. 5th

I want some Boracic ointment or something of that sort to put on my feet. Somebody sent me some, and I put it on to help to keep the wet and cold out, and I find it makes a great difference, although it makes one's feet in a hideous mess. Anything though to try and keep less cold. The Doctor tells me any sort of oil or grease tends to make one's feet waterproof like a pair of boots, or at any rate helps to keep the wet out. We are trying to get it for the men, but I cannot persuade them to give me enough. I am glad to think of you in London to-night, and the boys will enjoy the jaunt.

We are having a quiet time these few days, and I sleep like a top after a heavy and sleepless week. It will be comparatively easy if we are allowed as they hope, twelve days on and six days off. It just makes the difference getting away from bullets for a few days. Of course, if the Germans bring their guns back, no billet will be safe, but we must hope they won't.

I rode into Bethune to-day, rather nice to see civilisation again, shops etc., but how dirty and squalid all foreign towns appear to be.

It still rains most days, and the inhabitants say the water must rise another foot before it stops, so I suppose we shall have to drown a bit more yet. My cough is better, but still bothers me a bit, but if I have nothing worse, I have nothing to complain of.

Poor Desmond's letters and parcels come here, and I forward them as soon as I can. I am still fighting for him. I hear Churchill is better, and going to live, poor chap, I thought he was gone when I saw him; a nasty wound in the head.

Jan. 6th

Writing late last night, and I suppose sleepy, I forgot to tell you about Sergeant Turner, so that you can tell his wife. He was missing on September 1st at Villers-Cotteret. I heard about ten days ago that his body had been found in a large grave at Rond de la Reine, near Villers Cotteret, so it is definitely established that he is dead. They opened the grave to find George Morris, etc., and incidentally found about twenty-five of our men.

Later. The Prince appeared again to-day, and brought us a gramophone. It seems to cheer everybody up here. Personally music is the only thing I cannot stand here. I should like to sit down and cry, and I remember the same feeling in South Africa on the few occasions on which I heard music, but I suppose I shall have to put up with the beastly thing. It is raining hard again, and this wet is sickening. We go back to the trenches on Friday, nominally for twelve days, but of course one can never tell what twelve days will bring forth.

I hear to-night that Dubby has gone to the Kiddies, so now we have found Officers for the whole Brigade of Guards. I am still trying to get them back, and have been trying to ginger up the Prince to get the King to stop it. I have squared the Corps General, and still have hopes.

Poor Gough was killed, as you have seen. You may remember that we saw him one day when I was home, near Wellington Barracks, the black haired boy, and Reggie Stracey, the last Officer of the original Kiddie Battalion, was killed last week. It really does sometimes seem as if everybody's time must come. One gets very weary of War. The opinion now seems to be that it may last for months. Well one never knows. It may end in a hurry some fine day. The most important thing, after all, is that it should end right, isn't it?

Jan. 7th

It has been a shocking wet day, and has poured all day; the wind has been very high too, so altogether it has been beastly. We go into the trenches to-morrow. I am told they are not so bad as the old ones. Anyhow we know they cannot be worse! It is all very well to say we can do no fighting. I assure you it goes on all day and night, nothing like what it was, but still we all try to shoot each other all day, and the Germans snipe all night. The guns let fly at intervals, and though it is nothing to what it has been, I know many people who wouldn't like it a bit. And of course, there are a few casualties every day.

I have at last got my application for Dubby as far as the G.O.C. 1st Corps, so I have hopes that I shall get the boy soon. If I do, it will be a triumph.

I have no news, except mud and wet. Some of the men are very rheumatic, I am sorry to say.

<u>DIARY</u>

<u>Jan. 8th</u>

Very wet day. I rode over in the morning to see the line we were to take over near Richebourg St. Vaast. Marched at 2 p.m. to take over from the Worcesters. Had 1 Company in the centre of the line with Coldstream on the right, and Irish on the left. Three Companies in support to the whole line.

<u>Jan. 9th</u>

Trenches were very wet, well up to the waist in places, and the Germans very close. After consultation with Brigadier we decided to leave advanced posts in the dry parts of the trenches, and hold the back line of the Rue de Bois with machine guns. We entrenched, made 'dug-outs', and put some of the houses in a state of defence.

Jan. 9th

I have never got a fur coat, and don't want one yet. As a matter of fact it has been quite warm except for the wet, which makes one chilly, but it is not cold doing anything. If it turns to frost, which I almost hope it will, it will be a different matter. So far nobody has seen one of these coats, although they were asked for six weeks ago. The waders arrived to-day, the first thing I must do is to cut off the feet, as I cannot get my boots over them. They will, however, make a great difference to keeping my legs dry. We are holding a horrid wet line again. The water was well over my knees to-day, and beastly cold. However, I am lucky, as I can change and keep more or less dry, but the boys have to last 24 hours. This awful rain prevents one ever being really dry, but luckily at present the Germans are not shelling much, and so we can get into houses, and have fires more or less. I believe they are as badly, or worse off, than we are. I write in haste to-night, but I cannot send the letter till to-morrow, when I will write again if I can.

<u>DIARY</u>

<u>Jan. 10th</u>

The village of the Rue de Bois was smashed to pieces. It was not a nice line to hold, as the line bent back on our left towards the 8th and 7th Divisions, and we got bullets from the front, left and left rear, a continual stream coming down the main road all night. Still very wet. 3 <u>k</u>., 1 <u>w</u>.

<u>Jan. 11th</u>

Very showery, but it did not rain <u>all</u> day!

· BACKGROUND NARRATIVE ·

Wilfrid's efforts to get his nephew back were finally rewarded. Desmond was fortunate to have done a short machine gun course during his training in autumn 1914 so was able to fill the Machine Gun Officer vacancy in his uncle's battalion:

Jan. 11th

My cough is much the same. We all have them and laugh at the noise we make. I got Dubby back to-night. He seems well and cheery. I must now try to get the others, but unless the Kiddies can be persuaded to send some Officers, of whom they appear to have plenty, I cannot see how I shall ever get them. I had to send a substitute for Dubby, and only got him on the plea that he was a Machine Gunner, so that course at Hythe did him some good.

The weather is still appalling. The water rose 18 inches in the trenches last night, and has been rising all day, and I am at my wit's end to know how to cope with it. We have tried everything – dug new trenches, which fill at once – pump all day, and it all comes back, and so on. It is a desperate business fighting the elements. The Germans are just as badly off, and we shell the poor devils all day, and feel we are getting some of our own back for that terrible month of November.

I am delighted to hear poor Goschen is alive, but I'm afraid he must be in a bad way. It is greatly to the credit of the Germans to have saved him. I know the labour I had to get my wounded out of those horrible trenches, and it is creditable that they should have taken so much trouble for an enemy.

The village we hold (Rue de Bois) is in an awful state and reminds me of Zillebeke. A charming village with an avenue, which must look quite nice in summer, even in this beastly flat country, all smashed to pieces and done for ever. The inside of the houses look as if an earthquake had taken place. I fell over something in the dark last night, and found it to be a child's bicycle. Rather pathetic! I have no time for more to-night. I have had a busy day and a good deal of writing to get through.

DIARY

Jan. 12th
A fine day! Continued making the line stronger, and erected bridges at night over the dykes and trenches, to enable a counter-attack to be made if necessary.

· BACKGROUND NARRATIVE ·

Wilfrid was in a reflective mood, providing as positive a slant as the circumstances allowed. His mood was clearly improved by the arrival of two pheasants and some butter sent from Goldings by his sister-in-law, Margaret ('Meta') Smith:

Jan. 12th

The water at last has stopped rising, and we have not had much rain to-day. We are trying to drain, but the country being like a billiard table, there is nowhere to drain to. It is very depressing weather, but we are all really very cheery. They tell us that the only place people out here are cheerful, is in the trenches. Everybody behind sit in their houses, in front of a good fire and listen to the rain, and pity the poor devils in the trenches! It is a miserable type of warfare. We lose a few men every week in a rotten sort of way, and have little to show for it. I think we get more of the Germans, as we are continually shelling them, and also are sniping a lot. I don't see much chance of getting forward till the weather improves, at least not in these parts. The French are getting on very well, particularly in Alsace, and I think generally the tide is definitely against the Germans. If only we could get at the Fleet it would be a great thing, but, till we can, we shall never give them a really hard knock.

I am stupid to-night, and cannot write sense, so I will stop.

I like your description of your fine day at home. I can picture every detail so well, knowing every inch of it, as I do. Please ask Ralph to thank Meta for two pheasants and some butter just arrived. I am going to enjoy one for dinner and one for breakfast. The first cold pheasant I have had except when I was home for a week.

DIARY

Jan. 13th
Rained hard. 1 <u>w</u>.

Jan. 13th

I hope you will get this to-morrow night, as I am sending it by a sick Officer who is going straight home, by motor to Boulogne. He has never recovered from 48 hours in the water on Christmas Eve, and is suffering from neuritis (Buchanan by name) and I have managed to get him a bit of leave. I daren't let any of them go sick, or they will be turned into a Kiddy or Coldstream before they can get back.

Yes! I should like a cake. They are always acceptable. Sometimes we have them every day for a week, and then a month goes without one. It is still wet, and the water rose 4 inches to-day. We move to another line the day after to-morrow, which is worse, so I suppose we shall have to rack our brains still more to cope with it. Dear me!, how tired one gets of the eternal crack, crack of bullets. It is not as bad as shells, but it is trying, and in this place they seem to come from every direction. How one longs for the day, if it ever comes, when one can walk about in moderate safety again!

I have no news for you, and just write this as it will get home so quick.

DIARY

Jan. 14th
Rained hard. 1 <u>w</u>.

Jan. 15th
Relieved by the Indian Division 4 p.m., and marched to billets in Le Touret. Very cold. 1 <u>k</u>.

Jan. 15th

You ask why I have so much writing to do. I have had endless presents to the Battalion, and they all have to be acknowledged. I have had constant correspondence with Stretty. Endless things crop up which must be referred home, or the Battalion will suffer whenever we get back again. I have been trying for weeks to write up my diary, but have never succeeded in even beginning. Twelve days in the trenches sounds terrible to you, and I ought to have explained. We always at Head Quarters manage to sleep under cover, though often the house is somewhat dilapidated, and always draughty, and most windows are broken. We shall continue to do this as long as the Germans do not begin to shell us, which they may do any day, then we shall have to go and bury ourselves again in the wet ground.

The weather is really wonderfully warm, but it is very damp.

We get a good deal of charcoal and coke, which we can burn without making much smoke, which is all important.

Tell Sylvia my chilblains are all right. I put on Iodine and have had no more trouble. Our trouble is more that our feet swell from being constantly wet. I generally manage to keep pretty dry, but the boys in the trenches, and the men suffer terribly from swollen feet, and cannot get their boots on after taking them off. This is the greatest trouble at present.

How odd that Mrs. Woodbridge should know young Craigie! He is a capital boy, keen as mustard, and doing very well. We hope he will remain a Grenadier after the war.

I have been anxious all day with Dubby in the trenches. I am expecting them back at any moment.

I hear the poor boy slipped crossing a wooden bridge this morning in the dark, and fell headlong into a dyke, which was a bad start for a day in the trenches. I am going to stuff him with quinine to-night. They all want something to keep off trouble, when they come in wet.

Later. They have just come in. Dubby wet, but very jolly, and seems happy here. We have been taking over a new line to-night, always a long and tedious business, and I am glad when the first night is over. One can never see what the place is like in the dark. The Germans are very busy at night, sending up rockets, and they send up any quantity. It goes on all night, every few minutes, and they light up the place like day. Some of the rockets seem to have parachutes which keep the light going for quite a minute. And now I must go and lie down for a bit. If all is well, we hope to get back a bit behind the line for a week, in a few days' time, but in war one can never look 24 hours ahead.

DIARY

Jan. 16th and Jan. 17th
In billets at Le Touret. Hard frost and snow showers.

Jan. 17th

What about my glasses! They have never come yet, and meanwhile reading by two dips is trying to the eyes these long winter evenings.

We had a Communion Service this morning in a Public House! We had it in the same place on Boxing Day, as we were in the trenches on Christmas Day. We have had these services in many weird places, the attendance varies considerably, and I think largely depends on the parson.

We have actually had a dry day, with a cold wind, which will dry things, if it doesn't rain again at night, which it generally does. The days are beginning to get longer, which for the first time for many years, I do not look on altogether with pleasure. Longer days will mean shelling, and that means trouble. However, it is all in the day's work, and we have to accept each day as it comes. It is difficult out here to imagine what it is like to be able to walk about without bullets flying about, and to be able to say for certain what you will do this afternoon or to-morrow. You never know what the next hour will bring, and that is wearing.

· BACKGROUND NARRATIVE ·

A letter to his brother-in-law FitzRoy, Lord Raglan, thanking him for the gift of a periscope, made clear Wilfrid's disapproval of the Christmas truces that had been made on some sections of the line. His letter is dated 17 January 1914, although it was clearly written in 1915.

Trench warfare required soldiers to be able to look out from their trenches without getting exposed to enemy fire. In response to this challenge, early trench periscopes were made by installing two mirrors at 45-degree angles at either end of a long box or tube. Commercial manufacture of box-type trench periscopes began in Britain in early 1915, but demand exceeded supply until 1916. Wilfrid was therefore grateful for FitzRoy's present. In his letter he refers to the R.O.R. (Regimental Orderly Room), which was a colloquial expression for Regimental Headquarters.

Henry Fludyer, mentioned below, was temporary OC of the Scots Guards from 1914 to 1916, then aged 67, having originally been their commanding officer at the turn of the century:

Jan 17 14

Dear FitzRoy

A few minutes to spare, so I can answer your letter for which many thanks. The Indians have not done too well, but it is largely due to bad staff work. They kept them in the trenches (where I am now) for 60 days. The whole place is mud and water and they were stone cold, and the natural result followed that they were pushed back a ¼ of a mile. In consequence we are now in the middle of a bog. The line they originally held was not quite so bad.

Many thanks for the periscope, which will no doubt appear in due course; I have been trying to get them for some time, but the R.O.R. had to get them made. They are invaluable. We have these infernal German gamekeepers opposite us, with telescopic sights, and they get everybody plum through the head. Almost all my wounds lately have been from the waist upwards, and so largely fatal. They are the most persistent snipers we have met. They go on all day and all night, and the bullets fly all over the country for miles. The house, my HQ is in, must be 1000 yards from the Germans but bullets keep cracking all round us continually. They are unpleasant, but we thank God the shelling has largely ceased, so we can get inside houses whenever available. There were several disgraceful truces about Xmas time and I am sorry to say that the Kiddies forgot themselves in the same way. The Germans tried it on with us, but I got the gunners to plant a few shells into the trenches, with the result that we shot at each other all day. That sort of fraternisation is rot. War is war, and you cannot make it anything else. We are having a much easier time than we had. 12 days in the trenches and 6 out. Also when in the trenches, we have 1 and sometimes 2 Battalions in reserve. Last November we never had a man in reserve.

We are being very badly treated about officers. The officers sent out to me, are shunted off to the Kiddies and Coldstream. The Kiddie Battalion in the 1st Brigade consists of four Kiddy officers and six Grenadiers. They have plenty of officers at home, but Taddy Fludyer and … will not send them out. It is very hard on our boys and will ruin the esprit de corps of the Brigade. The gunners are doing v. well, but we are still short of ammunition particularly for the heavy guns. On Xmas Eve when we had a bad day, the Indian gunners were with me, and they were quite splendid. They planted their shells again and again just right, within 200 yards of my line, and never touched one of my men. It was the finest bit of gunning we have seen, and we got some of our own back. We got cleared out of one of our trenches and the moment I told the gunner our men were clear, they let fly, and plastered the trench with shells. The Germans tried to get back and we got them to rights, not a man getting any more than a few yards.

> Yr Affect
> Wilfrid

DIARY

Jan. 18th

Took over line near Rue de Bois from the Herts Battalion 5 p.m. Very heavy snow all day and very cold. Trenches very wet.

Jan. 19th

A thaw set in, making everything even worse than before. The whole country was under water, and being dead flat, there was nowhere for the water to run to. The road I walked down about 8 a.m. was up to one's waist in water by mid-day. An unlucky shot killed two good N.C.O's [sic]. 2 k., 4 w.

· BACKGROUND NARRATIVE ·

La Bassée, a town about 8 miles east of Béthune, had been heavily fought over during the autumn of 1914. Wartime reporting of the Allied successes tended to be one-sided.

Henry Lygon, a cousin of Violet's, had just been attached as an observer to the Royal Flying Corps, whose primary role at this stage in the war was observing artillery fire behind the enemy front line at targets that could not be seen by ground observers. Wilfrid was somewhat optimistic about the safety of the role as the attrition rate for flyers was very low. Henry survived five months before transferring to the ballooning branch, which he left because it made him seasick.[4] He rejoined the Suffolk Yeomanry in 1916 and survived the war.

The froust that Wilfrid refers to was a contemporary expression for stifling warmth in a room.

Sergeant Littler was to be awarded the DCM with the citation, 'For conspicuous gallantry throughout the campaign. He has rendered invaluable service on all occasions, and has never failed in any duty allotted to him, however dangerous.'[5]

Jan. 19th

The waders were rather <u>de trop</u>, but they may come in for somebody. The difficulty is that all these extras add on to one's kit, and I am always kicking up a row about Officers' kits being too big, and do not like mine too large. Also it is impossible to send anything home, as there is an order that no clothing will be accepted at the P.O. This is done to prevent men sending home their clothes, and getting new ones, but it is hard on Officers. My poor Burberry has been wet through so often from wading through water, that it is somewhat battered. I thought it would be wiser to have another mackintosh in case this weather goes on.

The [story of our] success at La Bassée was true, but what they did not tell you was that we were kicked out again two days afterwards! There is an important point there that is a bone of contention, and it has been taken and retaken more than once. Flying is looked on here as the only really safe occupation, so Henry will be all right, and have a most interesting job. The cold, I am told, is frightful, and they cannot stay up long [in] this weather.

We are back in trenches. It snowed all yesterday, and the result is slush even worse than ever. The snow also shows us up, and you have to be very careful moving about, even by night. The worst trouble is that this weather makes the parapets fall down, and so they are no longer bullet proof, in spite of constant work. I lost a good Sergeant this morning, shot clean through the parapet. The snow has increased the trouble and adds to our difficulties. To-morrow we hope to go back some miles to peace for a few days, when I hope to have a bath, badly needed.

I have lost another Officer to the Kiddies. They start for me, and disappear en route, which is very annoying. I have had a few Officers sick, and I have to be careful not to let them go too far back, or they will get caught and made Kiddies. I always get them into hospital for a few days just behind, before they get too bad, and then they return in a few days. I won't let these boys go and get wet in the trenches when they are shaky. There is no necessity for it, and they will be much more wanted when we move forward. They rebel as a rule, but they are told to obey orders, and there's an end of it. I really am very lucky in my Officers, for they are a capital lot of boys, do their best and are keen, but they want looking after.

I manage to write often by making use of odd moments. Some days are full of messages and orders, and I never get a minute. Then we get a quiet day, and it passes except for routine. Here I am at a small farmhouse, which stinks awfully, (they all do) but I have a nice coke fire, and we get up a bit of a froust. The ceiling leaks, as the roof has mostly gone, and the snow has come through, but my excellent Drill Sergeant, (Littler) has managed to stop the worst of it. He is a topper – one of those men who makes it his business to see to my comfort, as far as it is possible, without being told to, and does or gets done all sorts of little odd things, and duly reports them finished before I know he is doing it.

I want a small flask – somebody has broken mine – to hold say – ¼ pint. I always carry a little brandy, and mine has been rather heavy.

DIARY

Jan. 20th

Relieved by S. Staffords at 5 p.m., and marched to Les Choqueaux in Corps Reserve. 1 w.

Jan. 21st to Jan. 24th

At Les Choqueaux. Very wet.

Jan. 21st

We are back at peace for a few days, and it is odd to walk about without bullets, and only distant guns. I've had a busy day and want some sleep, so I will not write more to-night, but hope to have more time to-morrow.

Jan. 23rd

I lost a good Sergeant the other day, Croft by name. I am told he was a Yorkshire policeman, and leaves five children. You might see they don't want. He was one of my old King's Company Sergeants. He was killed dead, and the same bullet mortally wounded the man next to him.

We have had a hard frost the last two nights, and I have been so thankful that the men have not been in the trenches. Some of my frost-bite men [*sic*]

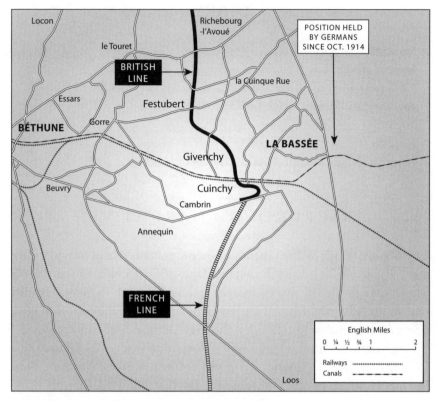

The British line near Béthune in early January 1915.

are beginning to come back. I think it is more neuritis and rheumatism than frost-bite, but I'm afraid some of them have suffered a good deal. I do so hate losing life when there is nothing to show for it, it is bad enough when we have something to show, but lately we have been losing two or three, sometimes more, men a day from stray bullets, which is always such bad luck. History tells us that 'the Army swore terribly in Flanders'! I can quite understand this. The language is really shocking at times, but there is every excuse. I never heard a Battalion who cursed so much, but it is trying to wade through mud up to your knees and then suddenly plunge in the dark into water up to your waist, with no chance of getting dry for 24 hours, if then.

DIARY

Jan. 25th

Marched at 10.30 a.m. to position of readiness in a wood near Gorre, in support of 1st Division, who had been attacked at Givenchy and Cuinchy. Remained there all day. Very cold. Returned to billets at 9.45 p.m.

Jan. 26th

At Les Choqueaux. Ready to move at 20 minutes [*sic*] notice.

· BACKGROUND NARRATIVE ·

The *Blücher*, which Wilfrid mentions below, was a German heavy cruiser that was sunk on 24 January during the Battle of Dogger Bank in the North Sea. Despite the British success in sinking this cruiser, which buoyed British morale, the Admiralty felt that the navy had failed to use the opportunity to inflict an overwhelming victory on the large German fleet which escaped.

The battalion's machine gun officer had gone sick on 22 January and Wilfrid's nephew, Desmond, was given command of the Machine Gun Section, as a result of which he moved to the Battalion Headquarters.

The Kaiser's birthday was 27 January:

Jan. 26th

A few lines, in somewhat of a hurry, so that you may get it possibly to-night, if you happen to be in London. We had a long, tiring, and very cold day yesterday. We were hurried off to help others in temporary trouble, early in the morning, and did not get back to our billets till 10 p.m.

It is grand news about the 'Blücher', etc. I hope the Kaiser's birthday will be further celebrated in the same way.

It is terribly raw here now, the mud sticks to your boots like glue, and it is just like having them in a bucket of ice – most unpleasant – really it almost makes one cry with cold.

Ma is off home for a week and Paddy Nesbitt. They both want a change. I'm afraid it is one of the penalties of my position to send others off and remain myself. Still one can never tell, and if things are fairly peaceful in a few weeks' time, I might get a few days. One can only hope. I can see that some of the boys will break down if they don't get a change, and I am glad to say that the authorities realise this, and I hope to be able to send somebody every week. I am told that the French don't like it, so we have to keep it pretty quiet. Ma just off, so I must stop.

Later. Tell Eustace that Desmond is much better. He is living with me now as he is Machine Gun Officer.

I have been disturbed about 50 times while writing, and my hands are so cold I can hardly hold the pencil.

DIARY

Jan. 27th
Marched at 6.15 a.m. to position of readiness at Essars in support of the 1st Division. Returned to billets about 3 p.m.

Jan. 28th
Ready to move at 20 minutes [*sic*] notice. Hard frost and snow.

· BACKGROUND NARRATIVE ·

Harold Bury, Gareth Hamilton-Fletcher, Arthur Lang and Jack Denny had been temporarily attached to the Scots Guards. Bury was the subaltern who Wilfrid had swapped for his nephew, Desmond. On 25 January all four were hit by a shell that exploded in their trench. The first three were killed and Jack was severely wounded. On hearing the news that her son had been wounded, Jack's mother was driven to the front by her chauffeur in the family Rolls-Royce. She took him from his field hospital to a hospital for officers in Park Lane. After he recovered, he spent the rest of the war as ADC to the Viceroy of India, Viscount Chelmsford, and returned to join the family bacon-curing business.

Gareth Hamilton-Fletcher's brother-in-law was Laurence Fisher-Rowe. He was to die on 13 March 1915 commanding 1st Battalion Grenadiers at the Battle of Neuve-Chapelle:

Jan. 28th

We ought to do in England, what the Belgians do for water. They have a large wooden broad wheel, about 10 or 12 feet in diameter. The dogs get inside and begin to run, and so of course turn the wheel, which pumps the water. Very cheap and very effective, but the dogs have to run a long way. They seem to like it, and I have often had them chased out, as it makes such a noise.

We have had no rain now for 4 days, for the first time since the end of November. There was a hard frost last night, and there is a bitter wind to-day, so the country is drying up, which will help us to get on, I hope.

I am sorry to say that four of my boys with the Kiddies were knocked out two days ago, one killed, two missing, and one wounded. I am so sorry. Poor Boys, had they died with the Battalion, they would have done what they joined for, but I'm afraid they will be forgotten in the future, as so few people knew them. Mrs. Rowe's brother, Hamilton Fletcher, is one missing. The Germans were supposed to be trying to give the German Emperor a birthday present of Givenchy, but they took a heavy knock, though of course we suffered too. That place has been a bone of contention for some time.

We expect to be back in the trenches in a day or two. I must say I am getting tired of being shot at, but after all it is what we came out for, and must put up with it. From many things I think there are signs of weakening, both on this side and the Russian, and economically. Although half the stories in the papers are lies, written with some ulterior objects, there is a lot one can read between the lines. Letters that prisoners are found to have on them are very different reading to what they were three months ago. There can be no question about the end, and it may come quicker than we think, though without doubt there must be much hard fighting before the end can come. It will be very interesting, for those who read the history of the War, to see what has been going on really on the German side all this time, and I expect it will be a surprise to most people. I hear the German Fleet was really coming out last Sunday to settle the business once for all, but they funked and turned back, so that we only got their advanced guard. What a pity we did not let them come out a bit further. Anyhow it will have hit them hard. There is no doubt the Germans know they are beat, and are only fighting now for terms, but that will take a long time.

· BACKGROUND NARRATIVE ·

Wilfrid's diary entry of 30 January records the need to leave some of his men behind at Les Choqueaux. A case of cerebral meningitis (spotted fever) had been discovered at the Guards Depot at Caterham in Surrey, and orders had been given for all drafts from England to be isolated:

Robert Smith, Wilfrid's father. (Private collection)

Isabel Smith, Wilfrid's mother. (Private collection)

Goldings in 1885. (Author's collection)

Cricket at Goldings, 27 July 1890. (Author's collection)

Learning how to dig trenches at Sandhurst. (Author's collection)

Wilfrid as a young subaltern. (Author's collection)

Shooting expedition up the Guadalquivir River, 23 November 1897. (Author's collection)

Wilfrid at Government House, Sydney, in 1899, standing behind his future mother-in-law Lady Raglan, seated in the centre, with Lord Beauchamp standing to the left. (Author's collection)

Engagement portrait of Wilfrid painted in Sydney in 1900. (Private collection)

Wilfrid and other officers in January 1902 before setting sail for South Africa. From left to right: Mr Sartorius, Major Fox Pitt, Lord Mahon, Wilfrid. (Author's collection)

Lord Mahon

Mr Sartorius

W.R.A.S

MAJOR FOX PITT AND OFFICERS OF THE GRENADIERS, WHO HAVE JUST SAILED FOR SOUTH AFRICA

Jan. 14th 1902
Wellington Bks

Ralph aged 7 months.
December 1903 - Normanton

Violet Smith in December 1903 with Ralph, aged 7 months. (Author's collection)

Wilfrid's home, Upton Lea, near Slough, in 1907. (Author's collection)

Wilfrid with Ralph and Lyulph in July 1907. (Author's collection)

Ralph 4 years & 2 months
Lyulph 2 years & 6 months
July 1907

Upton Lea

Below: The Earl of Cavan, Wilfrid's brigade commander, photographed as a lieutenant general. (Ponsonby, Vol. II, p. 48)

Wilfrid photographed in 1914. (Author's collection)

Lieutenant-General The Earl of Cavan. K.P. K.C.B.

Major-General G.D.Jeffreys, C.M.G.

George Darell 'Ma' Jeffreys, Wilfrid's second-in-command. (Ponsonby, Vol. II, p. 80)

Right: Sylvia, Wilfrid's daughter, with Jack the Airedale terrier and another dog. (Private collection)

German soldiers fighting on the Aisne. (Grenadier Guards)

Top left: Norman Somerset, Wilfrid's nephew, killed in action 23 October 1914. (Grenadier Guards)

Top right: Sydney Walter, Wilfrid's nephew, killed in action 24 October 1914. (Grenadier Guards)

Left: Lord Richard Wellesley, Violet Smith's cousin, killed in action 29 October 1914. (Grenadier Guards)

Top left: Humphrey Stucley, killed in action 29 October 1914. (Grenadier Guards)

Top right: Carleton Tufnell, killed in action 6 November 1914. (Grenadier Guards)

Left: Harry Parnell, 5th Baron Congleton, killed in action 10 November 1914. (Grenadier Guards)

Lord Bernard Gordon Lennox, killed in action 10 November 1914. (Grenadier Guards)

Cholmeley Symes-Thompson, killed in action 17 November 1914. (Grenadier Guards)

Officers of the 2nd Battalion Grenadier Guards at Méteren, December 1914, in lighter mood. Wilfrid is second from left and 'Ma' Jeffreys sixth from right. (Author's collection)

NCOs of the 2nd Battalion Grenadier Guards at Méteren, December 1914. (Author's collection)

Sergeant G.H. Thomas, 2nd Battalion Grenadier Guards, later Welsh Guards, presented with the DCM by Lieutenant General Sir Francis Lloyd. (Grenadier Guards)

Sir Montague Cholmeley, killed in action
24 December 1914. (Grenadier Guards)

Charles Monro,
GOC 2nd Division,
promoted to GOC
I Corps in December
1914. (Grenadier
Guards)

Harold Bury, killed by an exploding shell on
25 January 1915 while attached to the Scots
Guards. (Grenadier Guards)

Desmond Abel Smith, Wilfrid's nephew and
machine gun officer, photographed after he
was awarded an MC in January 1917. (Private
collection)

Arthur Lang, killed by an exploding shell on 25 January 1915 while attached to the Scots Guards. (Grenadier Guards)

Gareth Hamilton Fletcher, killed by an exploding shell on 25 January 1915 while attached to the Scots Guards. (Grenadier Guards)

Jack Denny, injured by an exploding shell on 25 January 1915 while attached to the Scots Guards. (Private collection)

Left: Wilfrid with Captain Brabazon, Coldstream Guards, at 2nd Battalion Grenadier Guards' HQ, Cuinchy. (Author's collection)

Below: Freddy Marshall, killed in action on 22 March 1915. (Grenadier Guards)

Above: Alwyn Gosselin, killed in action on 7 February 1915. (Grenadier Guards)

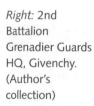

Right: 2nd Battalion Grenadier Guards HQ, Givenchy. (Author's collection)

Violet Smith in 1922.
(Author's collection)

HERE
LIES

Lt.Col.W.R.A.Smith C.M.G.
GRENADIER GUARDS
Died of Wounds
received in action near this spot

MAY 19th
1915

BORN September 13th.,1870.
DIED May 19th.,1916.

"But the souls of the righteous are in the HAND
of GOD, and there shall no torment touch them."

WISDOM.

Nothing is here for tears, nothing to wail,
  Or knock the breast; no weakness, no contempt,
Dispraise or blame, nothing but well and fair,
  And what may quiet us in a death so noble.

MILTON.

Wilfrid's grave in 1915.
(Author's collection)

Wilfrid's grave on the 100th anniversary of his death. (Author's collection)

Eton Volunteers marching out of Paddington Station to watch the Triumphal March of the Household Cavalry and the Guards Division on 22 March 1919. (Private collection)

DIARY

Jan. 29th

Marched at 10.30 a.m. to position of readiness near Gorre in support of 1st Division. Fine day but cold wind. A few shells. Returned to billets at 8 p.m.

Jan. 30th

Marched at 6.30 a.m. to position of readiness at Essars in support of 1st Division. Hard frost and very slippery, and we could hardly get transport along, many horses falling in the first few miles. Later cleared up and thawed. Returned to billets at 10.30 a.m. Parade 2 p.m., and marched to billets at the Orphanage, Bethune, leaving 200 men isolated at Les Choqueaux on account of 'spotted fever' at Chelsea.

Jan. 31st

Snowed hard and very cold, rode over to see the isolated draft, who were giving trouble.

· BACKGROUND NARRATIVE ·

Johnny Campbell was the eldest son of Lord Strathden and Campbell. He had rejoined the Coldstream in 1914, aged 48, as a reserve and had won a DSO 'for gallantry in the operation at Givenchy 21 to 23 December 1914, when he handled his company with great efficiency'. Campbell's eldest son Donald was to be killed, aged 20, on 19 July 1916.

Clive 'Closh' Bell had been a contemporary of Wilfrid at Eton and joined the Scots Guards. He retired from the army in 1908 and was elected MP for Honiton in 1910. He rejoined the Scots Guards in 1914. In January 1915 he was taken prisoner by the Germans and returned to England in 1918. He remained MP for Honiton until 1931. His surname had changed to Morrison–Bell in 1905 and he was created a baronet in 1923:

Jan. 31st

I'm afraid you must not expect me home as long as I keep well. I am the last to go, unless we get taken right back to the rear, of which I see no prospect whatever. We are holding a very important line, where there was a good deal of fighting last week. The 1st Division had a good many casualties, but nothing to the Germans, who were severely dealt with. It is a ticklish place to look after, but I think we shall manage it all right, though there is more shelling than we have known since the Zillebeke days, and so it is rather unpleasant. We were out three times last week to help the 1st Division, but were never needed, and so had long days standing about in the cold. It is snowing hard to-day, and is bitterly cold, but the frost has dried up everything considerably, and we are dryer than we have been for weeks. I had a bath this morning, and did not half like taking off my clothes! It was so beastly cold. Certainly, not washing helps to keep you a little less cold.

I got some excellent pheasants and butter from Meta again yesterday, and Colston sent me some last week, so we have been living like fighting cocks.

I am awfully sorry about Johnny Campbell and Closh Bell. They both went last week, and nothing is known of them, though the worst is feared. J. Campbell got the D.S.O. only a few days ago, which was splendid for him at his age. I should think he must be 48, and has a son in the Coldstream.

Writing in a cramped position, so it will be hard to read.

Desmond is quite himself again, looks thin, but healthy, and takes an interest in his guns.

· BACKGROUND NARRATIVE ·

Wilfrid's papers include a copy of a letter sent by the Duke of Connaught (Colonel of the Regiment) to Colonel Streatfeild:

> Government House
> Ottawa
> January 12th, 1915

My dear Streatfeild,

Most grateful thanks for three letters of the 23rd, 29th, and 30th.

I have been deeply interested with all the Regimental news you have so kindly sent me, and especially with the letters of Colonel Wilfrid Smith and Captain Morrison, and for the very gratifying order of General Capper. It is really splendid to hear how well both Battalions have done under most serious and trying circumstances which must have tried the nerves and endurance of all ranks to the very utmost.

As I expected, our Officers have set a splendid example of capacity and bravery.

It is hard to think what terrible losses all this splendid work has entailed on the Regiment, and how many first-rate Officers we have had to mourn. May they not have given their precious lives for nothing, but may their names and examples be ever preserved in the Regiment in whose honour they have fallen.

I hope that never again will Companies have to occupy so large a front as ours have done; with less good Troops the risk would appear to me to have been too great to run.

I am glad to hear such good accounts of our 4th Reserve Battalion. I thank you for so kindly sending on my message to the 1st and 2nd Battalions. I was anxious that they should know that although so far away they were in my thoughts.

I have not time to write more.

Believe me.

Yours very sincerely.

(Signed) ARTHUR.

7

February 1915 – Strengthening the Line at Cuinchy

Wilfrid's battalion spent February occupying the trenches at Cuinchy. The area known as 'The Brickstacks' was like no other on the front line. It sat on a plateau between the towns of Béthune and La Bassée, with the La Bassée Canal on its northern edge and the Keep on its southern edge. The trenches were often filled with water.

Ponsonby describes the activity during this month:

The usual routine was forty-eight hours in the trenches, and forty-eight hours' rest in billets at Beuvry. The weather, which at home is only noticed by people with weak conversational powers, becomes a matter of enormous importance when you have to stand in a ditch for two days and two nights. The wet and cold made the life in the trenches at first very trying, but later, when the spring began, the nights in the trenches became bearable.

Sniping and bombing with intermittent shelling were of constant occurrence. The sad news that some officer, sergeant, or private had been killed was passed down the trenches with wonderful rapidity, and was known at once by the whole Battalion. The line of trenches now occupied by the Battalion was much drier than those it had been accustomed to, and far more intricate. When the trenches were known the relief became easy, although it was always carried out in the dark, but at first, when the officers and NCOs took over the trenches for the first time, it was long before every one settled down.

The forty-eight hours' rest was spent in comparative comfort in billets at Beuvry, where the inhabitants still lived in spite of the proximity to the trenches. When the moment came to leave the billets and return to the trenches, the

Battalion moved up in small parties at a time, in case the road should be shelled. Through endless transport of all kinds the men slowly wound their way. They usually met food going up, empties coming back, ammunition and supplies of all sorts, and as it became darker the road was more difficult. They often passed French troops on the way, with the secondary French transport, a motley collection of every conceivable sort of vehicle. Yet with all these different streams of men and wagons there was never any confusion or accident. As the platoons neared the trenches, stray bullets usually began to fly, and occasionally shells. Then each company, on reaching its allotted communication trench, disappeared, and so reached the firing line.

The Battalion Headquarters were in the cellar of the ruins of a house, and here the business part of the work was carried on by clerks and orderlies. Sometimes shells fell on the remains of the house, but the cellar was never reached. A motor canteen presented by Lord Derby to his old Battalion now arrived, and proved a great boon. It could provide hot drinks for 300 men at a time …

The shelling varied: on some days it was mild, and on others for no apparent reason it became very violent. The difference, however, between the shelling here and that which the Battalion had been accustomed to near Ypres was, that while the German gunners at first had it all their own way, they were now not only answered but received back as many shells as they sent over. A great deal of work was done by the Battalion during the month, and the digging was constant night and day. The Keep was strengthened, many new communication trenches were dug, all very deep, eight to nine feet, and the right of the line, near the French, was made very strong. Supporting trenches were dug, and eventually the whole line was straightened out and wired. The majority of the men thoroughly understood how to dig, and the newcomers very quickly learnt from the old hands.[1]

Back in England, German airships, known as Zeppelins after the company that produced most of them, were becoming a threat. They had been used since the beginning of the war to bomb locations in Belgium and France but the first confirmed raid on England occurred on 21 December off the pier at Dover. The Kaiser approved a bombing campaign on 7 January 1915 but at first forbade attacks on London, fearing for the safety of his cousins in the British Royal Family. The first successful raid took place on the night of 12–13 January when two Zeppelins aiming for Humberside were blown off course and dropped their bombs on Great Yarmouth, Sheringham and King's Lynn.

German U-boats were becoming an increasing threat to British naval and merchant shipping. They had sunk their first British cruiser in August 1914 and had started to attack merchant shipping in October. In response, the Dover Barrage was begun in February. It consisted of a 15-mile series of light steel indicator nets anchored to the seabed at various depths. The nets were accompanied by layers of mines.

On the Eastern Front, the armies of Germany and Austria–Hungary were engaged in a bloody battle with the Russian Army in the Carpathian Mountains that ultimately involved more than 1 million troops on both sides fighting in the most difficult of winter conditions. Over 1 million lives were lost in a campaign that lasted through the winter and spring of 1915 and resulted in the defeat of the Austro-Hungarian Army. The Germans launched a supporting offensive in East Prussia on 7 February, known at the Second Battle of the Masurian Lakes. The Russians suffered significant losses that month as they stopped the Germans from advancing far into Russia.

DIARY

Feb. 1st

Ordered at 4.30 a.m. to move at once towards Cuinchy, which the Germans had attacked at 2 a.m. Marched to Beuvry, where I received a message to halt till further orders. Had breakfast and returned to billets at 9.30 a.m. Marched at 4.30 p.m. to Annequin and billetted. No. 1. Company went to support the Coldstream at Cuinchy, on account of their heavy casualties during the day.

Feb. 2nd

Took over trenches from Irish Guards at Cuinchy 6 p.m. from La Bassée Road (where we joined the French) to the Keep, where we joined the Coldstream. 1 k., 1 w.

Feb. 3rd

In trenches at Cuinchy. Hopley w., 2 k., 7 w.

Feb. 4th

A good deal of sniping and bombing, 2 k., 15 w. Relieved by Irish Guards about 8 p.m., and marched to billets at Beuvry.

Feb. 4th

<u>Cuinchy.</u> We are very busy at present, and I have just had a very heavy 48 hours, Jeffreys being away has put a lot on me, and my Adjutant has been seedy, so it has been difficult, and we have been almost continually at it for the last 48 hours. However, the weather has been fine, for which one is thankful, though it brings more activity to the Germans, but at the same time it bucks us all up. Once more I live in a deserted village, smashed to atoms. The Church has practically gone, and some of our communicating trenches run through the churchyard, perilously near graves, which is most unpleasant. We have had some anxious days here, but the Germans must have suffered very heavily here; the number of their dead tell that, and I think we have established our ascendancy at last in a place which has been lost and won three times. We think it takes us to keep it. I live in a cellar – a jolly good one, but it is a gloomy life living with the light of a candle day and night. The beggars put a shell into our house two days ago, and brought some of it down. However, nothing but a real whacker will smash my cellar, at least I hope not. They shoot hard all night, which shows great nervousness on their part. The Brigade have had a good many casualties, one way or another, but considering the number of bullets about, it is wonderful we don't have more. I lost a good Sergeant yesterday, Buttle, I don't know whether he is married or not.

I can't write much as I cannot see much, this pencil writing is so hard in a bad light.

I hear you are all at home in dread of a raid still. I am sure the Germans are much too busy to have any men for such a job, and they seem to have lost heavily in Russia. Prisoners lately, have been much dispirited, and say they simply long for the end of the war. All that is good, and that their Officers are also sick of it. They will have to fight all the same, but it is a different matter fighting men who don't want to.

The Brigade is in great form, and we hope to repeat our success at Ypres.

I hope to get 48 hours off to-night in billets, and then we come back for another 48 hours. It is such a comfort to be on a dry line again. No time for more to-day.

Feb. 5th
In billets at Beuvry.

Feb. 5th

I cannot see that there is much danger from Zeppelins. They ought to be seen long before they reach the coast, and it is only fair to believe that we have made all preparations to down them wherever they are. Aeroplanes are a different question, and may come, but they can only be dealt with by our Aeroplanes, of which I am told we have plenty and shall have more every week. I hear that when the Zeppelins were reported to be approaching Sandringham, His Majesty was urged by the courtiers to retire to a cellar, already arranged for his comfort, and his reply was 'D … the cellar, bring me my rifle', and a sporting rifle was at once brought to him.

Such a lovely day to-day, the first day of Spring, which usually is the first day of hope that the Winter is passed. What a Winter it has been! May we never have such another.

I had a glorious sleep last night, undisturbed by a lot of heavy gunning, which I am told took place. What a curious life this is. A few miles back we live in houses and rest; the inhabitants are all here, and we have every comfort as far as it can be got. After 48 hours' rest, we march back to the trenches, in small parties in case of shelling en route, past our guns, making night hideous at intervals, and as it gets darker, among transport of all sorts. Food going up, empties coming back. Ammunition and supplies of all sorts – all in pitch darkness. Why there are not more accidents is a mystery. Gunners bringing back empty wagons, others bringing up ammunition for the guns. French troops jabbering like a lot of monkeys. French transport, which is a motley collection of every sort of vehicle under the sun. All on a pavé road, which is diabolically hard and uneven. As you get nearer, say a mile or more from the trenches, stray bullets begin to fly, and in time the various Companies get to the various places where they get into the communicating trenches. They take all they want for 24 or 48 hours. Food, braziers, charcoal, fur coats, sandbags, spades: some have gum boots round their necks, and they look very different to the King's Guard of six months ago! And so they enter the long communicating trenches to the fire trenches, take their places, and the old lot file back. If you know your way and have been there before, it is all pretty easy, but if you haven't, each Captain has to spend a long night getting to know his section and making it safe.

I go to my Head Quarters, now in the cellar of a once good house, and arrange telephone communication with everybody, and reserve supplies of all sorts, and there I sit, with messages coming and going continually, and various people to see, sappers, gunners, etc. I go round the line once or twice a day or night, and see what work should be done, and whether it has been done, and many other things. In my gloomy cellar we have our food and sleep, if circumstances permit, while night bullets whack the house and drop about the garden, which was once very nice, and is now a ruin. And so for two days, when the relief arrives after dark, and gradually the men withdraw from the trenches and form up in a comparatively safe place. Each Company then marches off down the same old road, very tired, and very slowly, and by 10 p.m. with luck we are all back in the old billets, where the men find soup waiting for them, and sleep for 12 hours if they like. It may be a lovely night, or it may be black and wet. Heavy shooting may begin and delay the relief, but these are the only variations in our existence – an extremely fatiguing one.

We get more shelling now than we did, but our guns help us as they never could in November, and so we submit to bombardment with hope that our guns will make them stop soon, and all this goes on for miles and miles, night after night, and has gone on now since December.

I find many of my Officers very shaky, and wish I could get more. I have only five subalterns with Companies, but I am well off for Captains. I am pleased with Desmond, he shapes [up] very well, seems to know what he is about and knows something of his job.

Feb 5 15

My dear Ralph

So you are back at school after your long holidays. I hear from Mummy that you have both been such good boys while you have been at home, and I am very glad that you have been so good, as I could not be at home to lick you if you were naughty. I hope you will get on well at school this term and manage to get higher up in your class. It will never do for the cheeky little brother to be higher up in his class than you are!

I wonder whether you have any new boys this term. It is drier again and we are dryer now than we have been for 2 months.

Give my love to Luff. I will write to him the next time I write.

Yr Affect
Father

DIARY

Feb. 6th

Marched at 2 p.m. with two Companies to Brigade Head Quarters at Cambrin, in reserve while an attack on the Brickstacks was being made. Attack successful.

Relieved the Irish Guards at 6 p.m., and dug a new line, which was completed and safe by 2 a.m.

Feb. 7th

A heavy bombardment in the afternoon for 40 minutes, but no attack followed, apparently because the Germans would not come on. Much worried all the morning by the small 'Fiz-Bang' gun, which killed Gosselin. Graham w., 2k., 11w.

Feb. 8th

Quiet day. The French took the Mill on our right, which made us much safer. Relieved by Irish Guards at 7 p.m., and marched to Beuvry. Battye w., 1 k., 4 w.

· BACKGROUND NARRATIVE ·

On 7 February, Archie Graham had been badly wounded. Alwyn Gosselin was killed instantly by a piece of shrapnel that struck him while he was bending down trying to dress his wound. Archie's mother had a dream that he had been injured and went to France, where she found him in a field hospital and brought him back to England. He returned to service and became a stockbroker after the war.

Wilfrid's battalion headquarters were close to those of 'Pinto' Pereira, who was commanding 1st Battalion Coldstream:

Feb. 8th

I had a great loss yesterday in poor Gosselin. He was undoubtedly the best Captain I have at the moment, and I shall miss him enormously. I was talking to him about a quarter of an hour before he was killed, and he was dead before I got back to my Head Quarters. A great blow to us all, and we are very sad. A boy, Graham, only out a week, was badly wounded too, and has lost his right arm. So I am very short of Officers again, particularly now that I have nearly 1,150 men. It really is cruel luck the way our Officers are killed. One expects them to be hit sometimes, but the number killed is out of all proportion, and is sheer bad luck. Yesterday I had 850 men in the line, and in the morning I had three casualties, two Officers, and one good sergeant.

In the afternoon we had a regular bombardment, which reminded us of the old days at Zillebeke. Mercifully very few casualties, but my house was horribly knocked about.

Pinto who lives 100 yards off me says that they shoot at his house and hit mine! At least eight hit mine, and made an awful mess and noise, and two hit the house in the middle of the night. Luckily my cellar is pretty solid, but it is a sin to live in a cellar with a tallow dip [in] this lovely weather. It was once such a nice house, I should think belonging to well-to-do people. I hope that now most of it is knocked down the Gunners will shoot at something else!

I have had a shocking throat for the last few days. To-day it has practically gone. The warmer air and the sunshine is a great help.

More to-morrow, I hope, if we get out safely to-night, and have 48 hours' rest.

DIARY

Feb. 9th

In billets at Beuvry.

Feb. 9th

Please thank Meta for two pheasants, which Alas! had to have a decent burial! They had been longer on the way than usual, I suppose because I cannot get all parcels up to the trenches, and they have to wait till we come out.

I have had bad luck with Officers: 1 killed, and 3 hit in two days is shocking luck. I suppose that we ought to think of the many that miss us.

I find the mackintosh too heavy, and have gone back to my Burberry, only using the mackintosh in billets. It gets so clogged with mud that I can hardly move in the trenches, and tires me so. Also the weather is so much better, and our present line so much dryer, that my Burberry is better, and really wonderful with ordinary rain. The rain now is more showery – it was incessant – now we can cope with it, formerly we could not. I had such a good sleep last night, eight hours without a move. To-morrow we go back for our 48 hours as usual. No more to-day. This is written in rather a hurry to go by an Officer who is going on sick leave, so you will get it soon.

DIARY

Feb. 10th
Marched at 5 p.m. to relieve Irish Guards. 2 <u>w</u>.

Feb. 11th
In trenches. 6 <u>w</u>.

Feb. 12th
Relieved by Irish Guards at 7 p.m., and marched to Beuvry. Very cold.

Feb 10 15

My dear Silvia [*sic*]

Thank you for your nice letter. I am glad you like the Pram Rug. I wish, like you, that I was with you, but I am afraid that cannot be for a while. I cannot come home until we have finished off these Germans. You must miss the boys very much, but you still have Jack who [*sic*] you love so much.

I wonder how your poor teeth are getting on. I hear that you are a good girl with your plate. Give my love to Mummy.

Yr affect

Father

· BACKGROUND NARRATIVE ·

Bertram, Wilfrid's younger brother, aged 35, was to go out to Egypt in May 1915 with the South Nottinghamshire Hussars, a mounted Territorial regiment. He volunteered for special duties and served as a military landing officer at Suvla Bay, Gallipoli, for which he was awarded the MC. By the end of the war he had been promoted to lieutenant colonel commanding 23rd (2nd Football) Battalion Middlesex Regiment with whom he won a DSO in 1918:

Feb. 12th

Thanks, for your long letter of the 9th, just received in my cellar.

I am so sorry to hear about Bertram's typhoid. It is bad luck for him, and will knock him out for coming out here for a good many months, by which time I hope the war will be over, though opinions vary very much how long that will be. I'm afraid I have not much time to write to the boys, but I try to write to one of them every week. The bother is that I never know when one week ends and the next begins.

We are going out in a few minutes for our 48 hours' peace, I hope – but it is always a busy 48 hours as I have so much to do that I cannot do in my cellar. The cellar has been very stuffy and frousty the last two days. The only window had to be blocked up with sandbags, as the beggars pay so much attention to my poor house. However, they smashed the balcony the other day, and have taken away most of the front wall, since when they seem more satisfied, though they come uncommonly close to it sometimes.

A great blow I had yesterday when I got a letter from Atholl telling me that Paddy was not coming back. Of course, if he is ill it is no good his coming, but he is the only subaltern left who was serving before the war; the only other two have been taken from me for the Staff, and I am glad they shall go, for they are good boys, (Gerard and Marshall) but still it is a loss. The bullets have been very unkind to my poor Officers and good sergeants lately. It is a curious thing, but if I have to send a man back to duty, or try him for a serious offence, he gets hit shortly afterwards. I had to get rid of my groom a week or two ago, and I feared he'd get hit, and of course he has been hit badly, to-day. [Atholl Forbes was the Regimental Adjutant in London who informed him that Paddy Nesbitt would not be returning to his battalion.]

DIARY

Feb. 13th
In billets at Beuvry. Snow and very cold.

Feb. 14th
Marched at 5 p.m. to relieve Irish Guards.

· BACKGROUND NARRATIVE ·

BEF officers had gone to France with swords but quickly realised they were redundant:

Feb. 14th

A Sunday of comparative peace before going back to our 48 hours' labour in front. I went to Holy Communion this morning in a school-house, which is a temporary hospital, the parson, Fleming, officiating. He is a good fellow, and has been with us on and off all through. He gets me news of my wounded in hospital, and is not too much of a parson.

I have got my fur coat at last – after waiting months – I don't know that I really want it, and have got on very well so far with my old one, but Fatty tells me it is the fashionable coat now, so I got one – lined with goat, and £3 odd in cost. The great advantage over the old one is that it comes down to my knees.

I am trying to send home some handkerchiefs which you can have properly washed, and sent out again later on. I don't know whether you will get them, as they will not send clothing by post, but we will try. There are many things I should like to send home, which I have accumulated and don't want, but at present I don't see how to do it. I am also sending my sword (by a Sergeant who is going home on leave) to the Regimental Orderly Room, and no doubt Atholl will send it on to you. We don't carry them now, and I am afraid of getting it lost.

It is raining hard again, and very cold wind and unpleasant, but luckily we can hope for some fine days at intervals now.

Just got your letter of 11th. You need not be afraid of this line, it is no more dangerous than any other. In a way it is safer, as being dry we can hold it properly, whereas the wet lines were very difficult to manage. The first week was rather anxious work till we got definitely established, but we are all quite happy about it now, and if the Germans like to come they will get a warm reception. It is a much more interesting line than any we have had since Christmas.

I see bad news about the Russians in East Prussia, but we can never tell whether the papers lie or not. The German news some days ago, said heavy fighting was in progress to re-capture what we took from them here. It was an absolute lie. We kicked them out, and for the first time they could not get their men to come on and try to get it back. It was the first time we have seen them hang back.

DIARY

Feb. 15th

In trenches. 1 <u>w</u>.

Feb. 16th

Relieved by Irish Guards at 7 p.m., marched to Beuvry.

Feb 15th 1915
West Downs
Winchester

My dear Father

Lyulph and I came to school yesterday, and arrived at Winchester at 7.15 from London. All the way up to the house Lyulph made jokes; and we laughed so much that we nearly cried; we came up from Slough in the morning with Mummie by the 11.00 train. We enjoyed the holidays very much, and Mummie was so kind and nice; always thinking of us first. We went for a walk this afternoon to see a common which is being made into a camp, outside the mud was so thick (made by the steam engine), that it came over your ankles; after that we had a Scout kit inspection, then we had tea, and then learnt nots [*sic*].

This morning, we went for a short run before breakfast, then we had breakfast, then we did work, till 1 oclock [*sic*], then we went on the field, then we played football, (I was in the Senior game) after that we did work; then had tea. I hope that you are quite well again after your cold; and I hope that you will get leave soon. It seems very funny not seeing you for such a long time, it is so horrible without you in the holidays.

A chum of mine has a toy anti-aircraft pom pom gun it gets hot after ten shots the shots are corks, he is firing over my head now, so I have to keep on stooping to avoid the shots. I have just had tea. I hope you will get this letter soon; I am just going to do work, and after that we are going to do first aid. I have not got much more to say. I am in the bear patrol, and have gone into a different dormitory, I do not sleep with Lyulph yet. I had a letter from Grannie this morning and she said that Cousin Sisle had strained her ankle. Lyulph sends his best love.

Your loving son
Ralph

· BACKGROUND NARRATIVE ·

The body of Mrs Rowe's brother, Gareth Hamilton-Fletcher, was never found. He is commemorated on the memorial at Le Touret Military Cemetery along with the other officers who died in January 1915, including Harold Bury, Arthur Lang and Montague Cholmeley:

Feb. 16th

Your letter of 13th from home, reached me yesterday, which is very quick. I'm afraid Mrs. Rowe's brother stands a very poor chance, he was thought to be badly hit, and I'm afraid Johnny Campbell has a poor chance too. I think they are all lying a few hundred yards in front of us, very sad, for it all ought not to have happened.

My throat is all right at the moment, but comes on at times. It depends on the weather, I think the ground being so foul, it gets down one's throat. Alas! Life can never be the same again, too many old friends have gone, and the change has been too great for anything to be the same again, and as for the future, one has too much to do to keep alive in the present, to think much about it.

No time for more to-day, I will write again soon if I can.

DIARY

Feb. 17th

Beuvry.

Feb. 18th

Marched at 5 p.m. to relieve Irish Guards.

Feb. 18th

Just got your letters of 15th and 16th. I generally get one every day, though I hear that the mail boat has been stopped to-day on account of the German threats. We have shorter times in and out of the trenches now, as we have five Battalions in the Brigade, as you know, and so we have a good Reserve which we never had in November. I am sadly short of Officers, and cannot raise quite two per Company. I have four sick, and of course the more go sick, the more are likely to follow, as the work is much harder. I think it is about time the 1st Division came back and relieved us.

Feb. 19th

In trenches. Visited by General Horne, and took him round the trenches. 1 k., 1 w.

Feb. 20th

Hail storm in the afternoon which flooded trenches. Relieved by Irish Guards at 7.30, and were very late getting to Beuvry on account of the wet trenches, the last lot not arriving till 1.15 a.m.

Feb. 21st

In billets at Beuvry.

Feb. 21st

The mails have all gone wrong lately, as the boats have been running irregularly, so I have had no letters for some days. I expect a large batch will come in to-day. I am sure you will be as miserable as I am at the wretched way they have treated the Battalion, in the Mentions in Despatches. It would seem that to be mentioned you must be killed first. Not a single Officer in the Battalion, except myself, has been mentioned yet, who is still alive, and it is a poor compliment to be mentioned when all whose names I have brought forward have been ruthlessly cut out by somebody high up who knows nothing about it. The two N.C.O.'s. [*sic*] mentioned are Grenadiers, but are employed with the Division, and I have never seen them, nor have they done a day's duty with the Battalion. All the privates mentioned, are, I believe, dead. This is the second time they have cut out the Officers I mentioned, who are alive, and this Battalion has had more casualties in Officers and men than any Battalion in the Brigade except the Irish Guards, whose casualties are somewhat open to criticism. It is over three months since I sent in any list, and this is the result. What is so annoying is that I know my list was forwarded by Fatty and Monro without alteration, and it was a very moderate list, so it must have been cut about by the War Office, or somebody high up, very sickening.

Later. Just got your two letters delayed <u>en route</u>. I hear everybody is quite happy about the Russians, and that they are only doing what they always said they would do, if they were attacked. No doubt the Germans make the best of it and their account is not pleasant reading.

We had an awful storm yesterday, hail and snow, which makes an awful mess of the trenches. Fatty has just been to see me, and I hope the 'Mentions' will be in after all. There has been a mistake, which General Monro is doing all he can to get put right, so I am happier than I was last night.

153

DIARY

Feb. 22nd

Marched at 5 p.m. to relieve Irish Guards.

Feb. 23rd

In trenches.

Feb. 23rd

If all goes well, I hope to leave to-morrow night, and arrive in London Thursday morning at dawn. Have everything ready for me, if you can.

· BACKGROUND NARRATIVE ·

Wilfrid went on five days' leave on 24 February, his last visit home.

DIARY

Feb. 24th

I left at 1 p.m. for London. Battalion relieved by Irish Guards at 7 p.m.

Feb. 25th

In billets at Beuvry.

Feb. 26th

Marched at 5 p.m. to relieve Irish Guards. The main road was shelled for the first time for weeks, and 1k.

Feb. 27th

In trenches.

Feb. 28th

Relieved at 7 p.m. by Inniskilling Fusiliers, and marched to billets at Bethune. Half Battalion at the Orphanage, and half Battalion at the Girls' School.

During the whole of this month a great deal of work was done by the Battalion. The digging was constant day and night when in the trenches. The Keep was strengthened, many new communication trenches were dug, all very deep (about 8' to 9'), and the right of the line, near the French, made very strong. Supporting trenches were dug, and eventually the whole line was straightened out and wired. The first fortnight was anxious work. After that we had obviously got the better of the Germans, and had a quiet time. We buried a great many Germans on this part of the line.

8

March 1915 – Rest in Béthune and Transfer to Givenchy

Wilfrid returned from leave to join his battalion resting in Béthune. It remained there for the first ten days of March and held concerts and boxing competitions. The battalion was then held in reserve for a few days, in support of what proved to be a disastrous offensive at Neuve-Chappelle. Once back on the line, it would be relieved every forty-eight hours by the Irish Guards to go into billets in Le Preol. Ponsonby describes the scene:

> … the trenches, which were comparatively new, were shallow and the parapet not bullet proof. The village was a complete ruin, the farms were burnt, and remains of wagons and farm implements were scattered on each side of the road. This part of the country had been taken and re-taken several times, and many hundreds of British, Indian, French, and German troops were buried here. The roads were full of shell-holes, bricks, tiles, cart-wheels, and debris of every description. The shelling and sniping went on intermittently, but the habits of the enemy were known, and when the shelling began it was generally easy to estimate how long it would last, and when it would begin again.[1]

The Germans' strategic plan for 1915 was to maintain the defence line on the Western Front whilst launching an offensive attack to crush the Russians on the Eastern Front. The German commander, General von Falkenhayn, ordered the transfer of 100,000 troops from the Western Front, which he believed would leave the German Army strong enough to prevent the French and British from breaking through the line.

The French had suffered significant losses throughout the winter of 1914–15 for little gain but their commanders believed that they still had the necessary forces at their disposal to break through the German defence line, particularly with the transfer of German forces to the Eastern Front. In early 1915 they planned to direct the full weight of French forces through the German defences guarding the Douai Plain and cut the Valenciennes–Douai railway line that supplied the German armies active on the Western Front. Sir John French upset the French by refusing to participate in a joint attack on La Bassée. General Joffre, the French commander, postponed his offensive and suggested that the British carry out an offensive on their own. Sir John French decided to launch an attack on the line at Neuve-Chapelle. This was the first major attack launched by the British against a well-developed German trench system with cleverly sited Maxim machine guns. The aim was to capture the Aubers Ridge, a piece of higher ground in mostly flat country that gave advantage to the side that held it. The route to the ridge passed through the small village of Neuve-Chapelle.

On 10 March, 40,000 British and Indian troops gathered on a 2-mile-wide section of the line. The attack was preceded by a thirty-five-minute bombardment from 350 Allied guns, guided for the first time by the reconnaissance planes of the Royal Flying Corps. This consumed more shells than had been used in the whole of the Boer War fifteen years earlier. A subsequent barrage lasting thirty minutes pounded the second lines.

The attack initially achieved success by breaking through the lightly defended village, but soon became paralysed by poor communications and lack of munitions. The advance ground to a halt. The Germans brought in reinforcements from Lille and launched a counter-attack on 12 March. British troops attempting to take the Aubers Ridge were entangled in undamaged barbed wire and their losses were enormous. Fighting ceased on 13 March. The British suffered 12,900 casualties for no meaningful gain. The 1st Battalion Grenadiers lost 341 killed or wounded, including their commanding officer, Lieutenant Colonel Laurence Fisher-Rowe.

A breakthrough had been made but could not be exploited, a scenario that was to be repeated along the front until spring 1918. The British Army high command drew comfort from their ability to penetrate the German defences, blaming the failure of the offensive on a lack of artillery, shortage of ammunition and insufficient reserves.

The government was slow to respond to the chronic shortage of guns and ammunition, which was exacerbated by deteriorating industrial relations. This became the so-called 'Shells Scandal', a major factor in the fall of Asquith's government in May 1915.

A new front was opening up in the Dardenelles, following a request from Russia on 1 January for an attack against the Turks to ease the pressure caused by the Turkish offensive driving through the Caucasus Mountains. Winston Churchill, as First Lord of the Admiralty, had used this as an opportunity to push for one of his favoured schemes, to force the Dardenelles, the narrow straits leading from the Aegean to the Black Sea, with the older British battleships in the East Mediterranean Fleet and then to take Constantinople. The Royal Navy commenced bombardment of Turkish forts at the entrance of the Dardanelles in February. This offensive failed to silence the coastal batteries however. On 18 March a British and French fleet was sent in to complete the task. The Turks secured a significant victory, sinking three battleships and severely damaging a further three, primarily with mines. As a result of this, the British naval commander, Vice Admiral Sir John de Robeck, informed Churchill that he could not capture the Gallipoli Peninsula without the help of the army.

DIARY

March 1st to March 6th

In billets at Bethune. Had boxing entertainment in the Theatre with Irish Guards on the 6th.

Feb 28th 1915

West Downs

Winchester

My dear Mummie and Father

I so enjoyed seeing you both last Friday. We all went for a walk this afternoon, it is quite a nice day today; it started to rain just as we came in. We are going to chapel in a few minutes. I have not got much to say as I saw you last Friday. The lecture last night was quite nice, he could speak a bit of broken English so that we could understand most of it. After lunchtime today we had a book read to us, and we had oranges, and while reading was going on myself and some other boys had fights with the orange pips. I have not got much more time to write. I wonder if you have had nice weather at home since you have been back. I expect that you enjoyed a nice quiet Sunday at home, after always moving about. I wish you could get longer leave, and in the holidays. I hope that you will have nice weather when you get back to France. After you left on Friday Lyulph and myself went and scouted with our patrols; on Saturday Mr Helbert and all the other masters, went and inspected another troop about two miles off. It gets dark very late now, and I am writing in the classrooms without a light, and it is a quarter to six, there are about eight boys in the sick room here with colds. We saw an aeroplane the other day, coming from London and going towards Germany. I have got hardly any envelopes left. Give my best love to Sylvia and Jack. We are both quite well.

Your loving son
Ralph

March 3rd

<u>Bethune.</u> I had a horrible journey – a smooth crossing, getting to Boulogne by 10, where we had a good meal. The train did not start till past 1 a.m., and we were eight in a carriage: changed at St. Omer about 4, and arrived here about 7.30 after as tedious a journey as you could wish for, very little sleep, and raining hard on arrival here, and only 60 miles from Boulogne!

· BACKGROUND NARRATIVE ·

After a difficult journey back to the front, Wilfrid found himself in the comparative comfort of the home of a wounded lawyer in Béthune. The Prince of Wales came to dinner:

March 5th

I got your letter dated the 3rd at luncheon to-day, so it has come very quickly. I sent a Postcard to Sylvia with a picture of our house on it, given to us by the 'lady of the house', as the waiter said, the lady being the <u>domestique</u> left by the family. It is the best house we have been in, with really nice pictures and furniture, the owner is said to be a lawyer, and is <u>'blessé'</u>. We live in the housekeeper's room, and were permitted to have all the house lighted up when H.R.H. came to dinner two nights ago.

I have been busy writing up my diary, which I am sending you. I do not think there is much of interest in it.

It is rather dull in this town, but one is thankful for a quiet time which I do not expect to last beyond Tuesday, when we probably go just N of where we were before.

· BACKGROUND NARRATIVE ·

Wilfrid rode over to look at the trenches that he was due to take over. He paid a visit to his fellow Grenadiers in the 1st Battalion: the commanding officer, 'The Old Friend' Lieutenant Colonel Fisher-Rowe, his second-in-command Major 'G' Trotter, the adjutant Lieutenant 'Conny' Fisher-Rowe, Captain 'Bobby' Lygon and Lieutenant Darby. The 1st Battalion was part of 20th Brigade 7th Division, which included battalions of the Scots Guards, Gordon Highlanders and Border Regiment. They clearly did not think very highly of their commander, Brigadier General Heyworth.

DIARY

March 7th

Rode to Givenchy at 6.30 a.m., and looked round the trenches – all in a dirty state, and the whole line appeared very unsafe, the parapets not bullet-proof, and the communication trenches up to your waist. Interested to see a place that has been such a cockpit for months. In the afternoon went to see the 1st Battalion at Estaires. Saw Old Friend, Conny, G. and Darby, all seemed very well, and talked a lot about the coming attack.

March 8th

Concert in the Theatre in the evening. H.R.H. to dinner.

March 8th

It is very cold to-day – a bitter wind and snow showers. In between the most brilliant sun, which is odd. I went to see the 1st Battalion yesterday, they are only about 15 miles off. I saw the Old Friend, G. Trotter, and Bobby. I don't think they are very happy in that Brigade. They have a rotten Brigadier, and the line Regiments they are with are not too good. I am very lucky to be in a proper Guards' Brigade. It makes a great difference to one's happiness and everything else too. I shall be very glad to get my Adjutant back to-morrow.

I keep very busy every day, and the mass of papers the Officials send me daily seem to increase week by week.

· BACKGROUND NARRATIVE ·

The trapping of the German submarine *U-8* on 4 March was the first success of the newly completed Dover Barrage. In 2014 its propeller was found by police in Kent after being removed illegally from the sunken wreckage by divers. It was returned to the German Navy in June 2015 at a ceremony in Portsmouth:[2]

March 8 15

My dear Ralph

I got a nice letter from you just before I left London. It has been v wet since I got back here and today it is snowing and a very cold wind. I hear that Sylvia is staying at Malshanger and that she was going to see you one day. When we crossed over the Channel last week, we came with all the lights out for fear of submarines, but nothing exciting happened. I hear they have caught a submarine at Dover. [Malshanger House, near Winchester, was the home of Wilfrid's sister Edith Walter who had lost her only son Sydney at Ypres in October. It was close to his sons' school, West Downs.]

Write and tell them all your news, and give my best love to Lyulph – I have no more time to write today.

Yr Affect
Father

DIARY

March 9th
Bethune.

March 9th

It has been very cold and frosty the last two nights, which has dried up things considerably, but it is snowing hard again now, and so I suppose we shall go back to mud and slush.

On Sunday we had service in the local Theatre! Very different surroundings to the previous Sunday. This Theatre has done duty for many different things, concerts, boxing, etc. Really it was one of the best services I have seen. The Theatre was packed, and it was quite a good size, and a voluntary service, which I so infinitely prefer to a compulsory one.

We had a concert last night, with a great deal of talent. It is much better to employ the men than to let them loaf about the town and get into trouble.

I have no news to tell you, or rather no news I can tell you.

DIARY

March 10th

Marched at 7 a.m. to position of readiness in wood near Gorre in reserve to 2nd Division. Attack made by 6th Brigade at Givenchy, a most gallant, but disastrous business, and as far as I could judge afterwards, it never had a chance of success. The guns were not given time to break the wire, and there was want of co-operation between the Artillery and the Infantry. Two, if not three, attacks were made, and all appear to have behaved most gallantly, but no good was done, and the casualties were about 800 in the Brigade. At 3 p.m. I was ordered to move up to support the 6th Brigade in their last attempt, which, however, never came off, and we returned to Bethune, which we reached at 8 p.m. Very cold day.

March 11th

Moved at 5 a.m. to same place as yesterday. Another attempt was to be made at Givenchy, but orders from the Corps stopped it. At 5 p.m. we went into billets at Le Preol, and the Brigade took over the trenches at Givenchy, the 6th Brigade being pulled out. Their losses had knocked them about badly. I gather 28 Officers were killed, and the worst of the business was there was nothing to show for it.

March 12th

Relieved Irish Guards in trenches at 5 p.m. Worked hard to get trenches in good order. The number of dead a dreadful sight, and many have been lying about for months.

March 12th

Yes, we did some good digging on the last line, but it was fairly easy work, and the men were glad to have something to show for their work. They have worked just as hard on other lines, but everything was washed away again and again. We have had some long days lately, from 4 in the morning till late at night, very raw and cold, and the noise of the guns is terrific again. Thank goodness this time it is more ours than theirs, and we all hope the Germans feel as uncomfortable as we used to in November. We are just N. of where we were before (Givenchy), but our billets (when we get them) are in a swamp.

I never saw a more beastly unhealthy place, but not worse than many we have been in since Christmas.

DIARY

March 13th

A good deal of shelling and sniping all day, and indiscriminate shelling at night, which destroyed all sleep. We completed a new trench and buried many dead. Any number lie between us and the Germans. They won't let us bury them and won't do it themselves. 3 k., 1 w.

March 13th

I lost another good Sergeant to-day, Wiggins, a reservist. I am told he leaves a wife and children, and worked as [a] chauffeur in London. He was shot dead through the head. An excellent and valuable N.C.O., who has done first-rate work since he came out in December; he is a great loss. I attended his funeral with the parson this evening in a small cemetery we have arranged here, and a cross will be put up to-morrow.

I think we have given the Germans a knock this week, though we have taken but a small part in it. It is only beginning, but it may lead to greater things. I am in a peculiarly desolate place, once a charming village, the only high ground for some miles, but very important to whichever side holds it. It has been battered to bits, like many places we have seen before. The church is flat, except for a small strip of the tower, which stands like a poplar above everything else, and looks as if a touch would bring it down, and sooner or later it will fall as they shell all round it every day. The tombstones are all over the place, and you have to look twice before you realise that it <u>was</u> a church. I have only found two houses with more than the ground floor left, and those are mere skeletons, and shaky at that. One cannot conceive that the village will ever re-appear again, for the work of clearing will be too great. The farms are all gone, and the remains of wagons and farm implements block the roads and are scattered far and wide. The civilians fled months ago, for it has been a bone of contention since the early days of November, and many hundreds of English, Indian, and German troops rest all over the ground, and many more have been lying between our lines for months, neither side being able to get at them. One never conceived such a thing to be possible in civilised warfare in this century, but the Germans appear to be utterly indifferent as to whether their dead and wounded are collected or not. Hit or killed, seems to be all the same to them. They really are devils of the middle ages. They will turn a machine gun on any man who appears to be alive after he has fallen, and they sometimes throw bombs, with some burning liquid in, at wounded men to finish them off. War must always be a dreadful business, but it is inconceivable that Christians should carry it on with all the brutality of the pagan.

I write this in a cellar, as usual the house above has completely gone, and I have no idea what class of house it used to be. I should think mine was a coal cellar from its darkness, the only hole being one we have made in the wall, to a communicating trench through what may have been once [*sic*] the dining-room. It is a pitch black night, and I have just come in from stumbling round the village, the roads full of shell holes, bricks, tiles, cartwheels, and debris of every description, and the usual accompaniment of nightly bullets.

It is just six months since I took over the Battalion. What years it seems, and in what a number of odd places I have laid my weary head. I hope I shall be allowed to see the game out.

I have had a bad cold, but have got the better of it, thanks to quinine, etc. taken in time.

I like writing to you in the dead of night, when everybody has gone to sleep, and I sit up for messages.

DIARY

March 14th
A good deal of shelling and bombing, which makes work difficult. 1 k., 7 w. Relieved by Irish Guards and returned to billets.

March 15th
In billets at Le Preol. Conference with Brigadier at 10.

March 16th
Took over trenches from Irish Guards at 5 p.m. Shelling during relief, and heavy shooting all night. Shelling again at 11 p.m., and lasted all night at intervals.

March 16th

It is very sad that the 1st Battalion should have caught it again. All I have heard is that they were caught on a road by shells, a thing I have often had great anxiety about, and have always, when I have been allowed, prevented, but high authorities will not always allow you time to shake out. It is 'Push on', – 'Don't waste any time', etc., and unless you are adamant amounting to insubordination, you are bound to have to run unnecessary risks. You cannot move about a Battalion at war-strength quickly under shell fire. I do not know whether this happened on this occasion, but I hear there were 200 casualties, of which 34 were killed, so the proportion of Officers is enormous and difficult to understand. Eleven killed and wounded. I was hoping to get out a few more Officers, but now the 1st Battalion will want all that can be spared.

Our attack last week is reported to be successful. We heard it going on, but did not do much ourselves.

I got a good sleep of 10 hours the night before last; having had very little all the week, I was badly in want of it, and a bath next morning put me right again.

A few birds are appearing again, which is so jolly. I saw a lot of rooks flying across the lines the other day, with an aeroplane among them – such a mixture of nature and war. All the winter we have hardly seen a bird, and it is a great loss. Rooks cannot live here, there are so few trees, but I suppose they are migrating, for they were flying very high, and I had to look through my glasses to see what they were.

The first signs of spring are just beginning, which tells us that the worst of the winter is over. When I see all these villages in ruins, and farms burnt, and all the animals dead, I sometimes wonder if even the coming generation will ever see it all straight again after all this desolation and ruin, but the signs of spring show that it will all come right again, though it may take 20 years. I do not think the villages will be rebuilt in the same spots for the cost of clearing away the bricks and mess would be so great, but they will be gradually rebuilt, a few hundred yards away, and called by the same names, and the old ruins will be left as a lasting memorial of the victory (let us hope) of right over wrong. In the same way as we in England sometimes find relics of the old Roman battles, so these poor villages will, hundreds of years hence, mark the places where we have lived through many troublous days.

March 16. 15

My dear Lyulph

I do not think I have heard from either of you two boys for a fortnight, so I suppose you are having a jolly good time and forgetting how quick it is going. Our time does not go so quickly. Each day sometimes seems like a week. Luckily it has been drier lately, so we have been warmer. The first signs of spring are just beginning, which tells us that the worst of the winter is over. Is it not comforting to know that nothing can stop the spring and summer coming back? When I see all these villages in ruins and farms burnt and all the animals dead, I sometimes wonder whether you boys will ever see it straight again. For it looks more than impossible for anybody to ever get the country straight again.

But the signs of spring show that it will all come right again, though it may take 20 years. I do not think the villages will be rebuilt in the same spots, for the cost of clearing all the bricks and mess would be so great, but they will be gradually rebuilt a few hundred yards away and called by the same names, which you are reading daily in the papers, and the old ruins will be left as a lasting memorial of the victory (let us hope) or right over wrong. In the same way as we in England sometimes find relics of old Roman battles, so these poor villages will, hundreds of years hence, mark the places where we have lived through many troublous days.

I suppose the time is coming for you to go back home for Easter, though I have no idea when Easter is this year. Mind you are good boys, as good as you were at Xmas, and look after Mummy well. My love to Ralph.

Yr Affect

Father

DIARY

March 17th

Conference with Brigadier at 9. Shelling heavy for 40 minutes at 10 a.m. Some big shells falling all round my Head Quarters, and much too close to be pleasant. New trench proceeding well – buried many more dead. 3k., 8 w. Casualties mercifully very small.

March 18th

A good deal of shelling – the line is improving every day, and we have begun several communication trenches, which ought to have been done weeks ago. Relieved by Irish Guards at 5 p.m. 4 w.

March 18th

I'm afraid I have missed the post to-night, but I will try and get this back by one of the boys who go home to-morrow, for a few days. We have had a bit of a shelling, the last two days – very unpleasant. They are giving us a few of their old big ones, which I suppose seem bigger for our not being used to them, as we used to be. The beggars have taken to shelling us at night. I must say that we have provoked them, I trust successfully. Two nights ago they began to shell at 11 p.m., and kept on promiscuously till 10 next morning, when they gave us an hour of the best. The poor village, previously pretty well battered, was further knocked about. I saw one house absolutely disappear into the air, and the bricks went flying far and wide. Of course, any wires went at once, as they always do in heavy shelling, and after long anxiety I found I had only 3 <u>k</u>., and 1 <u>w</u>., and it was all done by one shell. One has a certain amount of comfort in the thought that it had cost them many hundreds of thousands of pounds.

I did a record [sic] last night. About 2 a.m. I am told eight shells fell near my buildings, at least three of which hit it, and I am charged with having slept through the lot! Well, I had only four hours in which to sleep, and had none the previous night, so I had no time to spare, but it shows what weariness of the flesh will do.

I'm afraid you must all have had a shock at the list of casualties after Neuve Chapelle. They are heavy! I don't suppose you will be told the total for some time, but you can't attack without them, and it gives us some idea of what the Germans must have suffered in the Autumn, for our casualties never equalled their dead, which we know as a fact, and yet in this attack their casualties were undoubtedly much heavier than ours, and the moral effect of that terrible bombardment must be great. It was awful to listen to, and absolutely the first time we have been able to do to them what they so often used to do to us, and we gave it to them with interest. If only the people at home would work instead of striking, we should be able to get on. It is rather sickening to feel that we cannot get the support in Artillery we want, because our own people will not work at home, and then they are offered a 'medal' to induce them to work, and we laugh at the Iron Crosses! At least the men who get Iron Crosses are the bravest of the brave, while our shirkers at home will get much the same reward. I suppose that is democracy! It was borne in on one yesterday when we suffered under German shells. A month ago ours would have instantly replied, and they would have shut up. Yesterday I could get no help. Why? Because men will not work at home, for the sake of farthings an hour! I wish they could see their pals in the state I often see them after shelling. They would have a shock, after which they would put their farthing an hour at the proper value.

I had to send two Officers (Seymour and Hughes) to the 1st Battalion – both great losses. I heard from Copper [Seymour] yesterday that he found what was left of the 1st Battalion very cheery. Apparently they got under maxim gun fire, which did the damage, but that is all he told me.

I will try and write more to-morrow, if I have time. I must go to bed now, and get some sleep.

DIARY

March 19th

In billets at Le Preol.

· BACKGROUND NARRATIVE ·

Sergeant Horace Holness was awarded a DCM, 'For conspicuous ability and gallantry from 6 to 10 November, near Zillebeke, when he defended his trench under very heavy shell fire, and again on 18 November when the enemy attacked in force and both Officers were killed, he commanded the company most creditably for two hours until relieved.'[3] He was commissioned with the 1st Manchester Regiment, survived his injuries at Neuve-Chapelle and went on to become a warder at the Borstal juvenile prison:

March 19th

I saw the Prince to-day, who told me a certain amount about the 1st Battalion, but the story is rather confused, and I must wait till I hear something more definite before I pass it on. Anyhow the shell fire story was wrong. I am rather low tonight at the thought of the way the strikes go on at home. The Germans have certainly scored one in getting the Turks to go for us. It has necessitated a second Expeditionary Force with all the paraphernalia that that entails, and so far weakens us here, and Constantinople is by no means a small job. If it comes off, it will be a great coup and be worth the trouble, but if things go wrong, it will hamper us here very much, and to think that people at home will not supply us with ammunition is really sickening, and the one person to blame is Lloyd George. He has stirred up all the ill-feeling for years which he is doing his best to keep down now, but we are paying for it day by day.

I lost another good Sergeant yesterday. He is not dead yet, but has never regained consciousness, and I hear he cannot get right. He was one of poor Bernard's standbys, and has done first-rate all the time. Luckily not married. Another of Bernard's standbyes [*sic*] was wounded the other day – Holness. I got him a D.C.M. and a commission, and he was wounded with the Manchesters at Neuve Chapelle. Dear me! What a number I have seen come and go.

Such a long, good sleep last night, and now I must go and try to get another before, I suppose, a sleepless night to-morrow.

DIARY

March 20th
Relieved Irish Guards at 5 p.m. 1 <u>k</u>.

March 20th

Such a lovely summer day, but cold with snow last night. I have been enjoying the sun by an open window all the morning, and getting some air before retiring to my cellar very shortly.

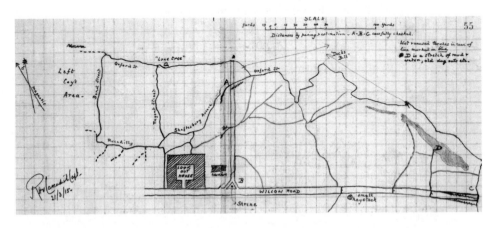

Plan of the British line at Givenchy, drawn by Captain Cavendish, 21 March 1915. (Author's collection)

DIARY

March 21st

A good deal of shelling and bombing in the morning. Completed our trench up to White House, which we demolished. The line is at last much safer. We have used thousands of sandbags, and the men have worked well under very unpleasant conditions. We get happier every day about the line, but why the Germans have left this part in peace I cannot understand. It seems to me they might have walked in at any time they liked. They won't now. 7 w.

March 22nd

Quiet day in the trenches, but some shelling behind the line. As we get the place stronger, the Germans appear to be less aggressive. Moved to a new 'dug-out' as Head Quarters, and left my much shelled cellar, which stank horribly. Relieved by Irish Guards at 8 p.m. Freddy Marshall k., and 6 w.

March 22nd

I saw a letter from G. Trotter yesterday. They lost 10 Officers, and 247 men the first day in the attack, and the Old Friend was killed going down a trench the second day.

The German aeroplanes are getting active again with the longer days. We had three over yesterday, and I hear Zeppelins have been to Paris. I suppose there will be some way of dealing with them if they get too annoying.

How the days lengthen! I get up at 4.30, and it is just getting light, and not dark till after 7. A hard frost this morning, and very cold.

I see we have lost some ships in the Dardanelles, but that was only to be expected with all the floating mines and a strong current running.

We hope to get out for two days to-night.

DIARY

March 23rd

In billets at Le Preol. A lovely day, like Spring.

March 24th

Relieved Irish Guards at 7 p.m.

March 24th

Alack and alas! Poor dear, young Freddy [Marshall] got a bullet through his heart on the afternoon of the 22nd. The most shocking piece of bad luck. He was having tea with the doctor at his dressing-station and left to go back to his Company, when just as he reached the road, a stray bullet came and killed him dead. That bullet must have had its mission – over houses and round corners – till it reached its billet. I had had a long talk with him only an hour before. His happy, rosy, jolly face always did one good. He always looked the picture of health and happiness, with his cap which always assumed a jaunty position on his head – full of fun and spirits and jokes about the Germans. Three hours afterwards, as the sun was setting, we laid him to rest for ever. I haven't got over it yet. He is such a loss, and I shall miss his rosy face for many a long day. I am always expecting to see him come into the room, and I can't get his happy face out of my mind.

Do you remember the five subalterns who all joined at the same time, about three or four years ago? Congleton, Marshall, Nesbitt, Sydney [Walter], Tufnell. They were the best batch we had had for years, and now only Paddy [Nesbitt] remains, and it has been my sad lot to bury three of them. It really is enough to break one's heart.

Such lovely Spring weather, and a warm rain last night. I begin to feel I shall be able soon to cast [off] some of my very thick clothing, which makes one too hot by day. It is still very cold at night sometimes though.

DIARY

March 25th
Very wet, and rained nearly all day. Very quiet. I think the main work on this line is nearly finished.

March 26th
Cold but sunny. The quietest day in the trenches for a long time. We seem to have got some new troops in front of us, who are much less aggressive. 1 <u>w</u>. Relieved by Irish Guards at 7 p.m.

March 27th
In billets at Le Preol.

· BACKGROUND NARRATIVE ·

Violet's cousin Frank Farquhar died on 21 March of wounds sustained the previous day at St Eloi while he was superintending some trench work. A Coldstream officer, he had been serving as military secretary to the Duke of Connaught, Governor of Canada, when war broke out. He raised and commanded a battalion of the Princess Patricia's Canadian Light Infantry comprised mainly of British-born Canadians with previous military service. This was the first Canadian battalion to see action:

March 27th

A few lines by Desmond, who I am delighted to be able to send home for a week. I had no time to write the last few days. It rained nearly all day on Thursday, and the filth was once again awful. Yesterday was a glorious day, following a frost and a N.E. wind, and everything is drying up again quickly. This morning is a glorious Spring day, but cold wind. I always get breakfast alone quietly these off days, as I am up long before anybody else. It gives one a peaceful time – the only time I get quite to myself, except sometimes in the dead of night. The glorious morning was ushered in with a great deal of gunning, I suppose at aeroplanes. What a sin it seems to be fighting in this weather! And yet it is better than all the mud and slush. The trees are just beginning to come out, which looks so jolly.

I am very sad about poor Frank's death. Alas! Most of our friends have already gone, and week by week more go. Still we are getting on, and if only we can get plenty of ammunition, we shall get on sooner or later. I wish the Dardanelles would get on. I am always rather afraid it is only a Winston Churchill show, and will end like Antwerp. If so, it will be a loss to us here, as we could do with all the troops that can be sent, and I suppose, being committed to it, we must see it through.

I will write more to-morrow if I have time. The number of people who come to see me is appalling sometimes. I have been interrupted a dozen times during this!

DIARY

March 28th
Relieved Irish Guards at 6 p.m. 2 w.

March 28th

Such a lovely day, but very cold. We had an open air service to-day, as there is no room anywhere else. I remember well those lovely evenings in the early Spring at Normanton [one of the houses in which Wilfrid and Violet had spent their honeymoon]. It seems, as you say, a long, long time ago, and quite like another life. Fancy our having got to Holy Week. Out here, of course, it seems impossible. People at home seem horrified at the losses at Neuve Chapelle, but so far as I can make out, you have never been told what they were, and they will probably be published in driblets, like our Ypres casualties, which were still being published at the end of January. Of course, the 1st Battalion casualties sound, and are, dreadful, but they have had practically none for months, while we have had about 220 since Christmas, but it is not realised by anybody who does not send in the returns.

I have really no news for you. We have rumours of trouble in the Dardanelles. I trust they are not true.

March 28th 15

My dear Ralph

I was v. glad to get your nice letter. I had not heard from either of you for so long. Mummy sent me your marks. I was pleased to see that you have been getting on better. You do not get many marks in classics, but you seem to get on better in mathematics, and so you must try to become first in it, to make up for your not being very good in classics. Tell Lyulph I am very glad he has done so well. He has got more marks in classics and so he gets up higher in his class than you do.

I see you are not going home for Easter. I wonder when you will go home. Perhaps it is a good thing, as it will make the Summer term shorter. We are having better weather again now, but very cold and frosty at night. The sun is warmer now and the days are longer. The hedges are beginning to come out and the flowers are showing. In some of the gardens where all the houses are lying in ruins, the daffodils and primroses are just showing their heads. You cannot stop nature can you — war or no war.

When digging a trench the other day, through what was the parson's garden, we found a quantity of precious papers, (stocks and shares, which represent money) buried. I suppose he had buried them to hide them from the Germans. Now they are safely with the French authorities. I wonder if he (the parson) will ever get them back.

My best love to you both.

> Yr Affect
> Father

DIARY

March 29th

Shelled during afternoon – very cold. 1 <u>w</u>.

March 30th

Bombed and shelled during afternoon, tried to rouse the Germans all last night and early morning with no success. They seem very tame, but snipe much too well. I think we are top dog on this line now. Relieved by Irish Guards at 6 p.m. 2 <u>w</u>.

March 31st

In billets at Le Preol

· BACKGROUND NARRATIVE ·

Three heavily armoured trains were built in Antwerp during September and October 1914 using six 4.7in and two 6in guns, from scrapped cruisers which had been brought by the Royal Naval force sent to help defend the city. Each train had two or three artillery guns and a crew of seventy Belgian volunteers and two British gunners. They fought around Antwerp until 7 October, when they withdrew to Ghent and were then used in the First Battle of Ypres. They saw service along the Western Front down to La Bassée until they were withdrawn in late March 1915:

March 31st

It has been bitterly cold lately. A great deal of frost at night and a bitter wind. The days bright and sunny. It has played the devil with all our parapets which crumble away like sand, and entail a lot of work.

The papers have been very interesting lately. By sending a cyclist a few miles to Bethune, I get 'The Times' of yesterday by 2 o'clock to-day; so we feel quite civilised and up-to-date, so very different to what it used to be. I think you might send me out a picture paper, of which we are very short. Either the 'Sphere' or 'Illustrated'. It would go on to the men who appreciate them.

I went to bed at 9.20 last night, and never moved till 7.30, when I was woken up by the guns shooting at an aeroplane. I had had two very sleepless nights, as there has been a lot of shooting lately at night. Some of the boys sleep till 10 and 11 o'clock in the morning, after coming out of the trenches. So many of the men who have been out a long time are cracking up and want a rest. I have got rid of several lately, with the doctor's help. It is not surprising: except for December, when we had nearly three weeks' rest, this Battalion has been shot at for seven months and more. Even when we are resting here, we hear the shooting all night, and the shells by day, while our armoured train fires from the line a few hundred yards from us, and makes an infernal noise, and an occasional shell falls with a great thud in a field or two off us [sic] – so we are never really at peace. Such is war!

9

April 1915 to 17 May 1915 – Strengthening the Line at Givenchy and the Emergence of New Hazards

Wilfrid's battalion remained in the trenches at Givenchy until 12 May, enjoying a four-day break in Béthune halfway through this period. Ponsonby recounts that:

All throughout April the battalion remained in the same trenches, and was relieved every forty-eight hours by the Irish Guards, when it went into billets at Preol. A new trench howitzer was produced by the artillery with a range of 520 yards, which put us more on an equality with the enemy, and gave the men confidence. The mining had now become a regular practice, and every one was always listening for any sound that might denote mining operations. The shelling continued regularly, and at times a battalion coming up to take its turn in the trenches would be subjected to an unpleasant shelling.

The Commanding Officer, Lieut.-Colonel W. Smith, was accustomed to what he called 'stumble round the trenches' every day, and many visits were paid by Lord Cavan and his staff, who became quite proficient in evading the various missiles which the enemy daily aimed at the trenches. On one of these occasions the Prince of Wales, who was a constant visitor, tried his hand at sniping, and as there was an immediate retaliation, his bullets very probably found their mark. The men were delighted to see His Royal Highness shooting away at the enemy, and when, as sometimes happened, the evening shelling of the Germans – 'the evening hate,' as it was termed by the men – began while the Prince was in the trenches, the men were always anxious to hear that His Royal Highness had finished his tour in safety.[1]

On 17 April the British launched an attack on Hill 60, an area of high ground south-east of Ypres that had been captured by the Germans on 10 December 1914. This was the first time the British used offensive mining operations to blow out the German defences. The British succeeded in capturing the hill, but it was to be lost again to the Germans on 5 May.

The Second Battle of Ypres began on 22 April and continued until 25 May. The Germans commenced the battle with a new weapon, poisonous chlorine gas, which blew slowly across the two French divisions who were defending the line just north of Ypres. The Germans broke through the line and gained a significant amount of ground in the northern part of the Ypres Salient. Two days later, on 24 April, the Germans extended their territorial gain with the help of a gas attack and captured the village of Saint-Julien.

After the first German chlorine gas attacks, Allied troops were supplied with masks of cotton pads that had been soaked in urine. It was found that the ammonia in the pad neutralised the chlorine. These pads were held over the face until the gas dispersed. Other soldiers preferred to use handkerchiefs, a sock or a flannel body-belt, dampened with a solution of bicarbonate of soda, tied across the mouth and nose until the gas passed over. Soldiers found it difficult to fight like this and attempts were made to develop a better means of protecting against gas attacks.

In early May, the British committed the First Army to a renewed offensive against the German line in the Neuve-Chapelle area in support of a major planned assault by the French against the Vimy Ridge to the south. The Battle of Aubers Ridge took place on 9 May with the objective of taking the higher ground near Neuve-Chapelle that had been attacked two months earlier. The British had then nearly broken through the German line but the German defences were subsequently strengthened. While the British captured some first-line trenches, the German defences proved to be much stronger than expected. The attack was an unmitigated disaster, winning no ground or tactical advantage and resulting in 11,000 casualties, one of the highest casualty rates in the war, particularly for officers. The 4th (Guards) Brigade was assigned to hold the Givenchy–Cuinchy line while the 1st, 8th and Indian Divisions were to carry out the attack.

Continuing the pledge to assist the French by discouraging the Germans from redeploying forces to the Vimy battle, the British ordered another attack to the south of Neuve-Chapelle which became known as the Battle of Festubert. This was to involve Wilfrid's battalion. The action began on the night of 15 May, following sixty hours of artillery bombardment which had failed to inflict significant damage on the Germans' front-line defences.

Despite the need for reinforcements on the Western Front, Lord Kitchener had despatched a division to the Eastern Mediterranean on 10 March. By mid-April a Mediterranean Expeditionary Force (MEF) of 75,000 men had been assembled on the Greek island of Lemnos for the invasion of Gallipoli following the ill-fated naval encounter in March. The landings started on 25 April. Early news received in England was good but quickly turned bad as the Allies met fierce Turkish resistance on the difficult terrain of the Gallipoli Peninsula. By the end of May, the Allies had suffered 20,000 casualties.

On the Western Front there was increasing frustration with the lack of reinforcements. Kitchener's New Army of volunteers had yet to arrive and significant resources were being diverted to the MEF. In the meantime, older retired soldiers and reservists were arriving on the Western Front.

At sea, U-boats had become a threat to passenger ships. On 28 March RMS *Falaba*, a British passenger-cargo ship was torpedoed and sunk off the Irish coast by a U-boat, killing 104 people, including one American passenger. This nearly brought the United States into the war. Five weeks later, RMS *Lusitania* was sunk with the loss of 1,191 lives including 128 Americans. She had briefly been the world's largest passenger liner, and had won the Blue Riband for the fastest transatlantic crossing in 1912. This provided the British with a propaganda opportunity that helped to shift US public opinion against Germany and bring about the United States' eventual declaration of war in 1917.

On the Eastern Front, Germany and Austria-Hungary inflicted a heavy defeat on the Russians at the Battle of Gorlice-Tarnow in southern Poland when they took the city of Gorlice on 3 May and forced a Russian retreat. The Russians suffered a further defeat in the Battle of Sanok on 9–10 May. Russian losses were very high: 412,000 were killed in May alone.

DIARY

April 1st
Relieved Irish Guards at 6 p.m.

April 1st

I've just got your two letters of Sunday and Monday. Something went wrong with the post yesterday. A glorious day to-day and a bit warmer. I am told it is Bismarck's birthday, and we expected there might be a <u>hourroush</u> in consequence, but so far nothing has happened except the usual shelling, to which we make a most inadequate reply. I suppose some day the British workman will wake up and understand that we cannot get on without the workshop being kept going.

The account of the sinking of the passenger ship is shocking, and shows, I hope, what brutes these Germans are. We out here knew that by now, and it is time people at home knew it. The barbarous way they treat their dead, and ours too, is only too well known. Of course, it doesn't matter what you do to a dead man, but it is shocking to think that a White race should not think it right to bury them, and collect wounded, who can fight no more. [Wilfrid's reference 'White race' means 'civilised'.]

After all a hundred years ago there was always a truce for getting in dead and wounded, and nobody but Germans would think of not allowing it.

I have no news for you, and am just off to the trenches. It is so lovely I should like to sit out in a garden, if there was one!

DIARY

April 2nd
Quiet day. Tried to rout the Germans at night, but they were very quiet and would not be drawn.

April 3rd
Relieved by Irish Guards at 6 p.m. Very wet.

April 4th
In billets at Le Preol.

· BACKGROUND NARRATIVE ·

Lord Esher was a Liberal politician and courtier who had influenced many pre-war military reforms. He was the de facto head of British Intelligence in France:

April 4th

I woke up this morning after 9 hours' sleep to an extraordinary quietness, and for a brief moment I thought I was in a land of peace and quietness, and then I remembered where I was. Oddly enough there was no sound of bullet or shell till nearly 10, when a distant 'whoff' disturbed the stillness of what, for once, seemed to be a Sunday morning, and I had a quiet breakfast all to myself. Perhaps the Germans were keeping Easter Day. What years it seems since Christmas. Thank goodness we are not so wet as we were then, nor have we had such a precarious day as that never to be forgotten day was.

We came out of the trenches last night, and after dinner I sat in an armchair and listened to the gramophone. Now that I have barred songs sung by raucous women, and Ma has done the same about raucous men, I rather like the orchestral tunes. They are marvellously good and make a change to the continual noise of rifle and gun, to which we have been continually subjected since we came here on the 10th of March. We always try to get a decent dinner the night we come out of the trenches, and sometimes we get fish from Bethune, which is a pleasant change. A glass of old brandy, which is a good finish up to dinner, and to which I have taken a great liking since I have been out here. It is a capital pick-me-up and we try to keep a bottle going.

I have had three letters from you to-day. Your ordinary one, one Desmond brought, and one which ought to have come yesterday, but went to the Coldstream instead. It caused much merriment when my only letter consisted of a packet of envelopes!

It is quite true that the Cavalry were all ready at Neuve Chapelle, and if they had been able to be let go, one cannot tell what might have happened, but it is an exaggeration to say too much about what <u>might</u> have been. They thought the line was well broken, and the Cavalry were to have been let go, but some machine guns in some houses prevented a proper breaking of the line, and it never was broken sufficiently to let them go. It was only pushed back.

We had a Communion Service this morning at 10 in a pub! Waggett came again as Fleming could not come. We have no place large enough to hold a service in [sic] for even 100 men, and so we have to have open air services, which is a bore, as it is very wet underfoot after a wet night.

What is holding up the New Army as much as anything is, I am told, saddlery. They can't get enough for love or money.

I wish this Dardanelles business was over. It will only be justified by success, and is a Winston and K. show. It is a great pity. If anything goes wrong with them or us, it will lead to recriminations on both sides. Neither side is strong enough for the business in hand, and we ought to concentrate our forces, and beat the Germans here. However, we can only hope it will be a great success. I hear the Navy are quite satisfied up to now, and had expected the loss of six ships by now. Still it is a bigger job than most people at home realise, and the weather seems to have been constantly against us. How jolly it must have been for you to get home again last week, and you must have enjoyed your time in the garden. I know so well what it must look like at this time of year; all sorts of jolly things showing life again, which brings hope that the future will all come right somehow and somewhere.

I have been writing this at odd times all day, so I am afraid it is somewhat disconnected.

I have just seen Monro who told me that Esher had had luncheon with him to-day, and said that they anticipated more trouble with labour as time goes on. It is no question of drink, etc., but merely the fact that they earn such good wages that they won't work. Aren't our people rotters? It is all very well saying they are patriotic, but they are not, and they think of nothing but their own beastly pockets. What a rotten nation our politicians have made of us. And now I must stop, as I have been busy all day and have not looked at the paper.

I have not got Seymour back, and see no chance of it.

Perhaps these photographs will interest you. One marked 'G' is my Head Quarters where we are now. I have left it, and moved farther off to a 'dug-out' as the beggars have got the house 'plum', and put so many shells near that I couldn't stand it. Since I left it they don't seem to have shelled it so much. It has turned out a lovely evening.

DIARY

April 5th

Relieved Irish Guards at 6 p.m.

April 5th

You wish I could sleep till 10! I could sleep for a week if I dared let myself, but it is no use thinking of that till the show is over. A very nasty, drizzly day. The trenches will be awful I expect.

I have spent my two days' rest in ceaseless business, except when I have been asleep! I must sit down and have a bit of a rest before I go into the trenches, so Good-night.

DIARY

April 6th

Very wet. Trenches filthy. 1 <u>k</u>.

April 7th

Quiet day but wet. Took H.R.H. round the trenches and he had a shot. Relieved by Irish Guards at 6 p.m.

April 8th

Le Preol.

April 8th

I missed writing to you yesterday. I had a very busy 48 hours in the trenches, and was just going to sit down to write yesterday afternoon, when H.R.H. turned up with orders to take him round the trenches. I was jolly glad when I got him safely back to my Head Quarters, as the afternoon is sometimes a nasty time, as the Germans are very disagreeable towards tea-time on occasions. However, he enjoyed himself immensely. I took him to the safest part of the line and let him have a good look through a periscope, but I had to keep on insisting he should get his head down, as his curiosity was liable to get the better of his judgment. He had a shot at the Germans with Ted Colston's patent, which enables you to fire without exposing anything except your hand. There was an immediate return, so I suppose he got somewhere near a Hun, and he was much pleased! I heard afterwards that there was a scramble in the trench among the men for the cartridge case, and considerable ill-feeling, because the owner of the rifle failed to secure the trophy! We began to shell about this time, and I thought there would be a reply, and so I moved him on and took him back, pleased as Punch with himself. He had tea, and got, as he sometimes does when he gets over his shyness, quite talkative, and expressed himself strongly on the subject of Oxford and his career. He never knew what they were going to try and make of him next! And so we got back about 7.30 and had a good dinner of fish and other things, and then the gramophone which plays very excellent valses, and carried me back to many happy times with you.

We have had a lot of rain the last few days, and I came back last night looking as if I had had a fall out hunting. However, it is a luxury compared to what it was at Christmas! It is fine growing weather, and even in this benighted country there are some signs of Spring. The plough is eradicating shell-bobs, etc., and I suppose soon we shall have leaf on the trees. I remember well the day we went to Kew – a charming spot, and I hope some day you will take the boys down there and show them all the beauties of nature. At this time of year it is charming and so restful after London.

What a fight must be going on in the Carpathians! I do trust the Russians will have a smashing victory, but I expect it will be a hard fight, as they say 7 German Corps have gone down there to help. I think the whole tone from the papers is very different as regards the feelings of the Germans to what it was a few months ago. Out here the official view is that the Germans are done. I think they are, but they will no doubt resist up to the end, and may be able to do us a good deal of harm before they chuck it. If we were in their position, we should try to do as much damage to them as possible first.

I have been thinking of you to-day with the boys at school. I hope you will have had a happy day. I shall like to think of them home again with you next week.

Jules Pereira came to see me yesterday; he is out with some Terriers. I cannot say what a pleasure it was to see somebody who was a subaltern with me. We were in the same Battalion for years. He looks very old now, but wants to come back to the Regiment. He is, however, over fifty, and so he is really too old. George Macdonald is even older! Do you remember I told you about the papers we found in the parson's gardens? Well, he wrote and thanked us for sending them back, and said that there were several other things in the garden, and sent a plan of where they were buried. So we dug away, and found a lot of silver spoons and forks, and watches, and a chalice. We did not find everything, because a box containing a lot of things had been smashed by a shell and the things had been scattered to the four winds. He was very lucky that the Germans did not find them, or he would not have got any of them back!

We have had constant rumours about going to the Dardanelles, etc., but I don't believe a word of it. What is, I believe, a fact is that K. won't let any of the New Army come out here till he sees what is going to happen at the Dardanelles. A great pity, that business. If we had more men and shells, I believe we could push on to the Meuse now, but all that must be left to high authorities who alone have the necessary information.

A nice idea yours, about the souls of the departed at Ypres. I'm quite certain the Germans never knew how thin we were. After the Prussian Guard attack, an Officer who was [a] prisoner asked where the second line was, and was told there was none, to which he replied, 'If we had only known that'. I hope we may never have to live through such days again. Bright sunshine followed by drenching hail storms, which are most unpleasant. Regular April weather, but rather too cold.

I have not much to tell you after my letter of yesterday, but just write these few lines.

April 8 15

My dear Lyulph

I hope you are having good fun today with your sports and that you will enjoy having Mummy down for the day.

Do you remember I told you about the papers we found in the Parson's garden[?] Well, he wrote and thanked us for sending them back and there were several other things in the garden and sent a plan of where they were buried. So we dug away, and found a lot of silver spoons and forks, and watches, and a chalice, which is used in church. We did not find everything, because a box containing a lot of things had been smashed by a shell, and the things had been scattered to the four winds. I think he was very lucky the Germans did not find them, or he would not have got any of them back again.

We have had a lot of rain lately, and today we had some heavy hail and storms – but the sun is nice in the intervals and it is nice to feel the horrible wet winter is over and that we shall not have to live in the water again, as we did this time.

Give my love to Ralph and Sylvia when you see her. I hope you will have happy holidays.

Yr Affect

Father

DIARY

April 9th

Relieved Irish Guards 6 p.m.

April 10th

Quiet day after a wet night. Bad accident with bombs, result of which 3 k̲., 2 w̲.

April 10th

Just going back to the trenches.

I see the poor little Snipe [Sartorius] has died.

He was shot in the stomach, poor fellow. That makes 10 Officers in the 1st Battalion. All very sad, but I am sorry people talk so much at home. They had much better set their teeth and realise the future of our children will be a poor one if we are not prepared to make these sacrifices, and they ought to rejoice that we were able to do as much as we did. It has taught many things which we cannot put down, and told us much that we wanted to know, and is certainly one step nearer the end. The show here, was, I admit, a failure and a bad one, but not so Neuve Chapelle: with the experience we gained there, the loss of life might be reduced if we had to do it again. You never appear to have been told at home what our losses were, and it will probably be a shock to learn they were over 11,000, but when you think what every attack cost the Germans last November, it is wonderful it was not more, and that they, the defenders, should have lost at least 18,000, makes it a great success, though none the less sad for those individuals who have lost all that makes life worth living. It is sad to think that so many of those boys who were dancing about London last summer in the flower of their lives, are now gone, and most depressing if one allows oneself to dwell on it, but it is a fine thing to find that they have still got the good stuff in them that made England what she is, and we ought to be thankful that it is so.

I am writing this in the dead of night in my 'dug-out', to the constant music of rifles and guns. We keep bombing the Germans, and they are as jumpy as they can be, and shoot like the devil, it is a lovely starlight [sic] night, and rather cold, and this shooting will go on at intervals till 4.30 to 5, when it gets light. I suppose some day it will all cease, but one gets weary of it at times, though I never say so to anybody. One has to be satisfied that things are going better than we could have expected some months ago, and live in the hope and faith that in God's good time the Germans will crumble like a pack of cards. They seem to be losing heavily in the Carpathians, and I hear to-night that the French have had a great success at Verdun. The Germans attacked there 15 times, and fairly got it. The only thing to do is to go on killing them, till they collapse for want of men.

Who should turn up to-night to go into the trenches, but Hugh Warrender! He is a Major in the Terriers, and has done no soldiering for seventeen years. I always used to say that if this war came on, everybody would have to fight, soldiers or not, and it is better to go with a good Regiment than a rotten one.

What a comfort it is to have lived one's life in a good Regiment, and to have been in it for a war like this, that is a fight for the life of one's Country, and not a little Colonial war. That makes such a difference, don't you think so?

And now I must stop and get some sleep. I get up at 4 a.m., and lie down about 12 at night, so the hours of sleep are not long, and often broken by heavy firing or shelling, but I am thankful to be strong enough to stand it. I hope you will get this quickly, as Acraman takes it to-morrow, and it ought to be in London by Monday afternoon.

DIARY

April 11th

Quiet day. Another accident with bombs most deplorable. 1 <u>k</u>. Relieved by Irish Guards 6 p.m.

April 12th

Le Preol.

April 13th

Relieved Irish Guards at 6 p.m.

April 12 15

My dear Silvia [*sic*]

Thank you for your nice letter. I wonder if you know what all the flags at the top of it mean. What did the little bird say when it came out of the Easter Egg? How pleased Jack must have been to see you again. I hope you have given him my love and that he is still a good dog. Fancy your Robert playing at soldiers in the trenches! I hope there they are more comfortable than mine are. You will be glad to get the boys home again. Give the rascals my love and a good kiss from me.

Yr. affect
Father

April 13th

It is a most curious thing, which I see is commented on in the paper to-day, how often when everything has been smashed to atoms, the local crucifix still remains. I know three cases of it within a mile of where we are. In one case the building has absolutely vanished, but the cross and the figure remain. In another the whole shrine remains, although the houses all round are flat. Every village has its shrine, and sometimes two or three. A common feature in, I suppose, every Roman Catholic country, but they very often get off being smashed. I have no doubt the French think it is an omen for good, and perhaps it is so. Some of these poor villages have been battered for months, and why anything is standing in them is a marvel. After all even a shell has to be directed by some power, of which we know nothing.

I am thinking of you all at home together to-day, and wish I was with you. Give the dear boys my love. I hope they will have happy holidays. I can imagine you all together on a nice Spring day – you so glad to be out of London, and the boys so glad to be at home and talking sixteen to the dozen. This is the third holiday I have missed.

DIARY

April 14th
Quiet day.

April 15th
Relieved by Irish Guards at 6 p.m.

April 15th

We do 'relieve' earlier now than we did, but that is for a good reason. It varies in different places. Such a lovely day to-day after a misty morning. How you must all be enjoying it at home! Just out of the trenches and very tired, so no more.

DIARY

April 16th
Le Preol.

April 17th
Relieved Irish Guards at 6 p.m. Good deal of firing and bombing all night. 1 w.

· BACKGROUND NARRATIVE ·

Sir John French's Seventh Despatch, covering the Battle of Neuve-Chapelle, was published in *The London Gazette* on 14 April. French criticised Sir Henry Rawlinson, commander of IV Corps, for being slow to bring his reserve brigades into action once Neuve-Chapelle had been taken on 10 March:

April 17th

It is nice to get news of the boys. I often hunger for them. It is sad to miss so much of their childhood. I have practically missed four holidays now, as I saw so little of them last Easter.

The weather is glorious, and it seems more summery every day. We shall soon have to think of shedding some clothes, but the wind is still cold at night. I think the long socks will go very soon now. They have been a God-send during the Winter, and have worn very well.

French's dispatch is interesting. He certainly gives it to Rawlinson, who we heard all along was to blame, although he tried to cart everybody else, and that was the origin of all the talk of Stellenbosching everybody. [The expression *stellenbosching* derived from the Boer War, where officers who had done badly were sent to a farm at Stellenbosch, without losing rank, to look after horses.] He is not at all a nice character, always thinks of No. 1., and lets everybody else go to the devil. I am afraid also he is a political soldier, of all horrors!

The French people here are civilised. We are not two miles from the German lines, and yet the sowing and tilling is well forward, the ploughs being pulled by oxen or cows where there are no horses. All the gardens are getting rapidly dug up and sown, and places, which have been under water for months and looked as if nothing ever had grown, or would grow there, are now sown and tidy. It has made such a difference to the look of the country. All the Winter it has looked too awful for words – nothing but desolation and misery: now it is beginning to smile again, and is a change one never realised was possible. Now that the Winter is over, to look back on it is a nightmare. While it was on, we took each day and night as it came, but now we can look back on it, we all say what misery it was. The daily gloom, the appalling mud, snow and continual rain was something one can only look back on with horror, and wonder that we got through it. The sickness was extraordinarily small, largely I think, due to the excellent food, but at times it nearly broke one's heart to see the awful state of the men and their clothing. Mud and misery week in and week out. Then the constant anxiety lest the Germans should make a push, and the knowledge that we were absolutely immobile on account of the mud, and the state of the men's feet, absolutely tied to roads which might be swept by machine guns – our parapets crumbling day by day on account of the wet, built up every night with the knowledge that a few hours of the old Ypres shelling would knock them flat. It was a daily battle with weather, and some day, I suppose, we shall know why the Germans missed their chance and let us alone. Shortage of ammunition probably, for their guns. I don't want to go through it again, and if we are alive and have to spend next Winter on the Rhine, I think it will be less depressing Country.

We're just going back to our 'dug-out'!

<u>DIARY</u>

<u>April 18th</u>
Quiet day.

April 18th

I got your letter of 16th to-day, which sounds so home-like and spring-like. I know exactly the sort of weather you are having, and the look of the place. How happy you must be with the children all at home again. It has been lovely here to-day, but very cold in the small hours of this morning, and again to-night. I am writing with my great coat, etc. all on in my 'dug-out'. I think it must be freezing. But during the day it has been glorious, and we have made a seat outside, where we have been sitting a great part of the day in the sun, whenever the Germans have allowed us to. We have a little pyrus japonica planted outside, which we got from what had once been a garden. It reminds me so of ours at home and is a beautiful colour. The country is so hideous that even the sun does not help it much. The trees are all tall poplars, and very few of them, and they show no signs of life and are mostly smashed about and look dead …

… Talking of crucifixes, I don't think I told you that there is one on the remains of the only wall left standing, of the church here. The wall has been smashed up to the Crucifix, but that is not touched, in spite of the thousands of shells which have been hurled at it. We look at it whenever we come back, and there it remains in silent protest to its surrounding desolation. It is rather remarkable.

We hope, if all goes well, to get out for four or five days to-morrow night to go to Bethune which will, I hope, be a change, if not a rest. The worst of it is that there is so little to do in these towns, one cannot go far, and it is hard to get exercise. Still it will be a rest, and we have had but little since the 9th of March.

Nothing to what it has been in the past, but still each month makes it seem more of a continual strain.

How the maxims do chatter to-night, that is ours. We keep on shooting when we see the Huns trying to work, and so annoy them. We have not a very truculent lot in front of us just at present. Did you hear the yarn of the Hun who shouted across (not to us), 'Do any of you come from Manchester? I've got a wife and three children there.' The answer came back 'You'll jolly soon have a widow and three orphans if you don't watch it!' There are several yarns of this sort, but one forgets them.

And now I must go and lie down, as I got no sleep to speak of last night. They kept on shooting all night and waking me. It is light now by four, and doesn't get dark till 7.30, so the days are anyhow long and the nights short. I hope to put in some long nights during our rest.

DIARY

April 19th

Mine sprung at 3.20, 50 yards in front of our line. No damage done, but it was a tremendous explosion. Relieved by 15th London Terriers at 7.30 p.m., and went to billets at Bethune.

April 19th

… Another glorious day to-day, after a bitter night. It has been quite hot all day, and the Germans having been fairly peaceful this afternoon, I have been basking in the sun. Oh! The change from the wet of a few months ago. The sun seems to go right through one, and do one all the good in the world, only it makes one sleepy when one is short of sleep. I hope to be relieved in a few hours. I have had my boots on for three days and nights out of four since March 10th. It will be a treat to get them off every night for a few nights.

DIARY

April 20th
Bethune.

April 21st
Bethune. Concert in evening.

April 22nd
Bethune.

April 22nd

Bethune. I haven't written a letter of any sort for two whole days! Think of it! We came in to rest on the evening of the 19th, the joy of seeing a white table cloth and a real bird. I sent Ma in early to see after some things, and incidentally suggested that we might have a good dinner, and I got it. Fish, Plover's Eggs, and Champagne!! And then a long sleep, and we have had three peaceful days, peaceful in a way, for there is always a lot to do and to arrange, with the never-ending interruptions, which sometimes nearly drives one off one's head, flying from one subject to another, each of which requires one's whole attention. I hoped to have got some exercise, but except for a ride yesterday afternoon (on the roads, because there is nowhere else to go), I have hardly done more than walk round the town. However, the weather has been fine, though cold, and I have a good night's sleep every night, and a pleasant dinner with a few other Officers. Our rest has been abruptly ended. We were to have stopped out till Sunday, but circumstances necessitate our going back to-morrow. However, I have collected more Officers, Derriman, Copper [Seymour] and Creed having joined this week, so I have more Officers than I have had since Christmas. Please God they will not be as speedily reduced as they were then.

We too thought of Hawthorne Hill, which was to have been last week. Ah me! What changes!

I sent off a parcel yesterday of some winter things, if one keeps more than one wants, it only becomes a nuisance.

The account of Neuve Chapelle was very good and as far as I know, is extremely accurate. Our casualties would have been nothing like so heavy but for two things – in one place the wire was not out, and our guns caused a lot of casualties. You at home cannot realise the extreme difficulty of both these things. The guns do marvels, but it is often very hard to see the results of fire, and in this case unfortunately some wire was not out. Then it is awfully hard to tell friend from foe at a distance. We have been trying for the last ten years to devise some means of doing this, and it is still as difficult as ever, and accidents will happen. Deplorable, but not to be shouted about. You must take risks, and remember the many times those risks which have come off have saved many lives. The Japs did it continually in their war, and the Germans have done it under my own observation. But we learned a lot at Neuve Chapelle, which we expect will help us in the future. Anyhow it is well to dwell on the glorious success, and not to think too much of the accidents, always remembering the extreme difficulties under which we fight. It is very easy to read about it afterwards; it is quite another matter to make proper arrangements beforehand, and do the right thing under modern terrific shell fire.

Hill 60, which you are reading about in the paper is, as far as we can make out, the hill (so-called, merely a rise in the ground) on which we spent the terrible day of October 31st, never to be forgotten.

I enclose a good account which I cut out of the 'Daily Mail' for you, of the Germans opposite our trenches.-

Extract From the *Daily Mail*.

… The Germans spoke with great respect of the khaki-clad enemies, describing them as tough customers, good fighters at close quarters, and excellent marksmen. Presently the Battalion Commander gave orders to shoot off a couple of mines from one of the mine throwers towards the British Lines. It fell five yards short. The English at once shot off one of their mine throwers. It landed 50 yards to the back of us and went off with an ugly detonation. If they fall in a trench they kill everything within 90 feet. The air pressure tears your lungs to pieces, the Captain explained.

I am glad our trench mortars are so effective. We have been giving them a bad time with them the last few weeks.

No more for to-day. I always seem to have to write to you at fever pace! I only hope you can read them. I so seldom get a really quiet time for writing, and just write at odd times when I have ten minutes to spare, so there is naturally a want of consecutive thought.

My love to the boys, I am glad they are enjoying themselves. For goodness sake don't let them put the place on fire!

DIARY

April 23rd
Moved at 4 p.m. to take over B.3 line at Givenchy. Two Companies in line and two in billets.

April 24th

Ditto.

April 25th

Mine exploded at 8, and a certain amount of firing and shelling.

April 25th

<u>Givenchy.</u> I have had no time to write to you the last few days. Taking over a new line, (which is next to my old one) although I knew it a bit before, has been busy work. I seem not to have had a minute for anything for the last three days, and the number of questions per hour I have had put to me, must be colossal! As soon as I get half way through one conundrum, somebody else comes in with an urgent question on some totally different subject, and I sometimes feel as if my brain would go. However, the weather has been mostly fine, which is something.

The Germans have been very annoying lately, and being on a new line, I have not been able to annoy them as much as I should wish, but I have hopes of getting level with them soon.

We had a Communion Service this morning, but I had to hurry off immediately afterwards, so I missed the other service. Fleming is back again, having been ill.

I was much annoyed with 'The Times' for saying that Hill 60 was lost on the 31st October. On that day we held a place three-quarters of a mile in front of Hill 60, and the French got kicked out of it on November 6th. Hill 60 was still ours on November 17th, and I don't know when it was lost.

I'm afraid they will have a big job taking the hill I held on to on the 31st, and I cannot understand why they should have lost so much, but of course it is very easy to say this.

The wind has been bitter the last few days, but to-day it has dropped a bit, and is warmer.

I'm afraid I have not time for more to-day as I have a good deal still to do, but I had to write a few lines to catch the post.

I was glad to get out of Bethune. I had a great longing while there for home and peace. Once back again here, I'm all right again. Sometimes the weariness gets the better of human nature.

DIARY

April 26th
Good deal of anxiety about mines. Heavy shelling at the time of relief.

· BACKGROUND NARRATIVE ·

Asquith had set up a 'Munitions of War' Cabinet committee to investigate and instigate measures to solve the munitions supply problem. Kitchener, the committee chairman, had frustrated efforts to increase the rate of shell production and in a letter to Asquith dated 14 April stated, 'I have had a talk with French. He told me to let you know that with the present supply of ammunition he will have as much as his troops will be able to use on the next forward movement.'[2] On the basis of this, Asquith denied press reports of inadequate munitions supplies:

April 26th

Thanks so much for the cigars. I smoked one last night over the luxury of a fire – which has been very rare all the Winter, as they have nothing but stoves out here, and the taste carried me back to my arm-chair and home. Thanks so much for such a pleasure.

We have a comfortable room to sit in on this line, and as I said, a fireplace, which is very pleasant and cheery in the evening. But the bed! Very little mattress on an old iron bedstead, and my poor bones do so ache, after lying on it for a few hours. However, it might be worse.

Yes! Asquith was a liar about the ammunition, but probably was not told the truth. I wish he had to sit and be shelled without reply for weeks, and then he would know whether operations had been hindered or not. This house was once so nice, with a garden out of the back with a high wall round. I walked round in the early hours of this morning, and wondered what it looked like this time last year! To-day the wall has partly gone, and the field just our side is covered with holes made by good big shells, 25 yards in circumference and 10 to 12 feet deep, (measure it and you will realise) which will not fill up for years. The garden has been dug up in places to make covered walks, the rest of it, of course, left to nature; but the fruit trees that remain are in blossom, and the strawberries green – the rest weeds of all sorts, but here and there a piece of rhubarb, a peony, and artichoke.

My Drill Sergeant has made me a magnificent 'dug-out' in case of trouble, but it will destroy three or four beautiful pear trees, whose roots, I see, are cut, and the top of the 'dug-out' he has decorated with 'flowers', which include two artichokes, one good plant of dandelions!, and various other weeds, which no doubt he thinks beautiful! And two or three gooseberry bushes. The house has not a window whole, and the staircase is tottery, and the roof has few tiles left, but the piano is left, and our temporary doctor (while the other is home for a week) plays on it extremely well to my joy. The whole place looks as if it had enjoyed prosperity in happier days – now, alas, it is surrounded by graves, French, English, and Indian. Such are my present surroundings, and yet nature is doing her best, hiding us daily more and more with leafy hedges, and the trees just beginning to show leaves, at least those which will ever bear leaves again, of which there are few. To-day it was quite hot in the middle of the day, and I sat out for a short time in the sun, on a garden seat that had three legs out of four smashed, but was propped up with bricks and boxes!

The Germans have scored near Ypres and made a good advance, but I hope and believe all will be well there, and we are prepared for their beastly gases if they play those tricks here. I have been busy all day getting muzzles for the men, making them out of wire covered with lint which will be soaked in bi-carbonate of soda, which is ready in the trenches, the moment they turn on the gas. Hang them! I have been very weary the last few days, the days are so long and the nights so short, and there has been a good deal of anxiety lately owing to mines, at which we have not been wholly successful, but we are not going to let them be top dog here if we can help it.

I thought the cake excellent, and if we still remain in trenches, another would be a treat, and it travelled well. I'm afraid I have no time for more to-day.

April 26 15

My dear Sylvia

Thank you so much for the excellent cake you and the boys have sent me. We had it for tea today and everybody said it was so good and asked if the children had made it. I said I thought you had probably put in the cherries! And perhaps eaten some at the same time. We shall enjoy it for a day or two while it lasts. So thank the boys from me and give them a kiss.

Has the medicine been good lately? With my love

Yr affect

Father

DIARY

April 27th

Heavy shelling at the time of relief. Most lovely weather.

April 28th

A good deal of shelling.

April 28th

I made a mistake about Hill 60. It is a large hill, but the summit is a small mound, which I was thinking of. I have reason to remember it, as I had one of my marvellous escapes there on November 1st. I went to see the Brigadier when the Germans broke through the line, and on my way back past this mound or knoll, I cantered across instead of trotting down the road. I had only just got past, when four whackers landed just where I had passed. Had I walked or trotted I must have been caught. At that time we were resting for a few hours, after our terrific day of 31st October, and behind this hill, and were pulled out to begin another strenuous eighteen days of continual fighting.

I am sorry they have lost St. Julien. We attacked it on about October 18th, and got across the Langemarch Road, and some way further on, and it has been held ever since. Now they are back where we attacked when we first came to this horrible country from the delightful Aisne. I believe they are quite happy about it, but the Hun is a clever fighter. He always attacks, and knows our weak spot, and as you see, he has attacked the junction of the English, French, and Belgian, which weakness is entirely caused for political reasons, and would never be allowed for military reasons. By political I don't mean party politics, but higher politics. No nation wants it to be said that they did not help to get back Belgium, as if it mattered a hang who does it as long as it is done!

It has been very hot to-day – glorious, but winter clothes for the first time have been a burden, and very tiring, and yet one is afraid to chuck them at once. Also I have not had my clothes off for a week, and only my boots on alternate nights, and the warm weather makes that very fatiguing at first. However, I shall leave off things by degrees, and post them home.

I'm afraid you will find this hard to read, as I am writing it in an armchair to rest myself. I am sitting up waiting for one of our mines to be blown up – 10 p.m. – and must make sure of the result before I lie down. It is curious sitting here near the open window, which is nice and cool after the hot day, listening to the constant sniping which goes on all night, and occasional shells which the Huns send over at odd hours. All the blossom has come out tremendously the last few days, and looks so glorious; the swallows have come and one wonders what they think of the changed conditions. They don't seem to notice it, though many of their nesting places must have been destroyed.

My doctor has returned from home to-day. He tells me that everything goes on the same as usual at home, and that people do not realise what we are going through. Thank Heaven they don't!

We have got our room decorated with blackthorn blossom and a few tulips which we found in the garden here. So odd to have these lovely things within a hundred yards of the German lines. Such a mixture of luxury and danger, which has been the case all through this campaign so far. So odd after what we are pleased to call our Colonial campaign. I wish some of the New Army would come out. We think we have done our share of the fighting for a bit, and want to see some of these others come along and relieve us. What the good of them at home is I can't think – eating their heads off and doing nothing. Even the authorities at home do not realise what this war is.

DIARY

April 29th

Shelling on and off during the day and night. Much anxiety about mines.

April 29th

Another lovely day like summer, with the same glorious nights like you say you have. It is not altogether an advantage to us, as it shows up so much now that the Huns are so close.

Just got two letters from you. I have had to begin my letters at night lately, as I am so busy all day that I cannot always find time to write.

I hope to have a bath this evening if the Huns permit. I have not had my clothes off for a week, and the heat is rather oppressive in winter clothes. What luck for you to have such weather for the holidays.

I hear the trouble at Ypres began in the same old way. The French Terriers ran, as they used to last Autumn, and that in turn opened the flank of the French and the Canadians. However, I think they will be stopped all right, though it has rather upset matters for the moment.

No time for more.

DIARY

April 30th
Quieter day. Mines turned out to be nothing. 1 <u>k</u>., 3 <u>w</u>.

May 1st
Quietest day we've had on this line.

May 1st

I was roused before 4 this morning by a furious cannonade, which I was certain meant a Hun attack. However, it turned out to be about 7 miles off, and I watched it from the top of my house and believe nothing happened except that it disturbed my sleep and a good many others too, I expect, so I am jolly sleepy to-day, having lost even more sleep than usual.

The wind is getting up, and I suppose it heralds a change, truly the weather has been glorious, but rather oppressive first off. I cannot get the men to leave off their cardigans and greatcoats. The moment my back is turned, on they all go, aren't they funny creatures of habit? They like to wear the same clothes they wore in the desperate weather of December and January.

A lot of stirring news in the papers to-day about the Dardanelles. I do hope all will go well there, but you will see that after the war there will be a great controversy about the wisdom of that expedition. I believe though, that you will find that Greece originally promised to come in, if our Fleet got to work, and then backed out of it, thanks to the Queen of Greece being a sister of the Kaiser, and that left us in the lurch. But if my supposition is correct, it will still be inexcusable not making certain first, considering what we have got on our hands here. Having got through a winter of mud, frost-bite, and various other things, I have now to begin to battle against summer troubles, flies, bad smells, etc., which I suppose will be even worse than the Winter. The whole country is such a manure heap, dead animals of all sorts, manure, refuse of all sorts from thousands of men and horses being collected together in a comparatively small stretch of country, that it will exert our utmost powers to keep the men's health good, and bad water will be one of the greatest [concerns].

I see the swallows closer in this country than I ever have before, and I believe it is because they don't see me when my head is on the level of the ground. I happened to see two the other day as I went down a trench and I kept quite still and saw them within a few feet; all their beautiful colours which one generally only knows from pictures or dead birds. It was quite a pleasure to see anything so lovely alive: we have had to see so many hideous sights among the dead the last seven months. And now I must stop for to-day.

DIARY

May 2nd, 3rd, 4th and 5th

All very quiet days. Most lovely weather bar anxiety about gas and mines.

· BACKGROUND NARRATIVE ·

William Rhodes-Moorhouse was the first airman to be awarded the VC. On 26 April he was instructed to bomb the strategically important railway junction at Courtrai. After a 35-mile flight he dropped down low, released his bomb and immediately faced a heavy barrage of small arms fire from rifles and a machine gun in the belfry of the church at Courtrai. He was severely wounded by a bullet in his thigh, and his plane was badly hit. Returning to the Allied lines, he again ran into heavy fire from the ground and was wounded twice more. He managed to get his aircraft back, and insisted on making his report before being taken to the casualty clearing station. He died the next day:

May 2nd

I seem to have several of your letters to answer. I don't mind this line, it is next door to the old one, and I knew a good deal about it before, but it is an extremely fatiguing one, as we are here continuously and do not get our two days out. We have been here eleven days now, and I have only had my clothes off once for a bath in the afternoon, and generally sleep in my boots. Early risings and generally late to bed, a constant mass of correspondence (official), and a good deal of work to superintend on the line, makes it hard and continuous work.

I heard the cuckoo yesterday, and two were seen in the trenches. Such a pleasure to hear it, it seemed so peaceful and odd, and then a beastly shell came over just as I was listening to it.

A lot of respirators have been sent out, but they are all wrong. They must have a wire cage or one can't breath[e] at all. I have made several out of telegraph wire, and covered them with anything I can get. The white ones sent are not calculated to be inconspicuous! I hear several hundreds are going to arrive to-morrow.

Fancy anybody thinking we are helped by withdrawing some 80,000 men from us here to the Mediterranean in order to entice 13,000 Germans away! That is not one Division, and we have to deal with many Corps of 40,000 each. I am delighted to hear they have done so well, but their losses must be heavy, and will have to be replaced, and all that will drain us here. Even if successful, I believe history will say that it caused the war to last many months longer – if not a year – than it would have had all the available troops been sent here.

I didn't go to Church to-day – I was too busy. Our parson, Fleming, had a brother killed with the Canadians the other day, poor fellow. I think the account in 'The Times' is fine reading. Gallant fellows, I know what they must have gone through. Nothing has ever been published of what any of us did before Christmas! And now I must go and get some sleep. One never knows what the early morning may bring, and it gets light very early now.

I hope they will publish about the gallant flying man, Rhodes Moorhouse, at Ypres, who bombed successfully and brought his machine back safely to her shed in spite of being hit in the legs and stomach. He died shortly afterwards, but it was a fine piece of gallantry.

May 3rd

Much colder to-day, and I am back to my woolly, but minus my thick vest which I am glad to get rid of after all the clothes one has had to live and sleep in all these months.

Those brutes have been at their dirty games of gas again last night. Thank goodness they seem to have got it back with interest. We heard the bombardment they got in reply, and it was terrific and seems to have utterly defeated the gas. We are all ready for them here, but it makes me anxious when the wind is in the East, for fear the men will not take the precautions they are told to, but I am at it day and night rubbing in the importance of it, and one can only trust they will play the game when the time comes, as they always do, but it is always difficult to make a man do anything that gives him trouble, till he has had a lesson, and we can't afford to waste men learning lessons. No time for more to-day.

· BACKGROUND NARRATIVE ·

Wilfrid was heartened by the return of 'Crawley' de Crespigny to his battalion. A colourful commander of great energy and ability who ended the war as brigadier general commanding 1st Guards Brigade, he was reputed never to have read a book in his life:[3]

May 5th

It has turned so thundery and hot, and a thunder storm yesterday has made everything very wet again, and has hindered work; but it is good for the country, which is getting very summerish, spoilt only by this war.

The Russian business (if true) is a bad one, and I don't like the position at Ypres. Not that it really matters a hang whether Ypres goes or not, except from the sentimental point of view. You will see that some day that business will be severely criticised … The lists in the daily papers are very terrible, and I am afraid they will continue through the summer. You will have to make up your minds to this. I only wish we had more men getting ready at home.

De Crespigny came back yesterday, to my joy. He tells me that the crowds at the Race Meetings in the cheap stands are as large as ever, while the others are empty. Oh! For compulsory service. He is a wonderful fellow, he went home really very ill, but recovers very quickly, and actually won a steeplechase while he was home, on a horse that was only broken in last Christmas! He is a very hard nut, and I am lucky to get him. I only hope I shall not lose any of my Captains. I keep losing good Sergeants, at present, mostly from sickness. I have had too much here, but it is a terribly unhealthy place, and we have been here a long time. We are really on the same line as before, but another section of it. I was one side of the village, and am now on the other.

I have not much to say to-day, and it is so stuffy that I am woolly in the head, and must get on to some other things which have to be seen to.

DIARY

May 6th
Very hot – a good deal of shelling at times – alarm of a mine in evening, which proved nothing.

May 7th
Very hot – quiet day.

May 7th

My brain has been overworked lately, there is more than one man can do with all the details of the line, and correspondence and food and ammunition, and a hundred other things.

I have been very anxious lately about mines, most difficult to deal with, and liable, not unnaturally to alarm the men; so it has to be dealt with tact and confidence, which I often do not feel. But that is nothing to the gas, which I admit is most alarming, not only in itself, but how to deal with it, and it causes one daily and nightly anxiety, particularly when the wind will stay in the East. However, one can only take all the precautions one can think of, and leave the rest to Providence. A horrible form of warfare, and I do hope we shall do the same, and that people at home will realise that it may come to our breaking the Convention of Geneva <u>or</u> being beat. That is the point and must not be allowed for the sake of any false pride. Don't think I'm seedy, I'm very well, but want a rest, which I shan't get – so there! We have been on this Section of the line a fortnight now, and do not go out at all, and I see no immediate prospect of a change, but who knows, we shall shove on some day if you keep sending us men and ammunition.

Your mention of Finder recalls many games of golf. [Finder was the dog of Lord Richard Wellesley, a cousin of Violet, who had been killed with 1st Battalion Grenadiers in October during the First Battle of Ypres.] How sad to think of it all, and yet what happy times we have enjoyed for some years, and how nice our little home has been. I often wish I was working in the garden again, but I always felt that was rather waste of time, and that some day I should have a busy time, and by Jove! I have. I often can hardly believe I am myself responsible for a whole Battalion and an important line! It seems so absurd. It doesn't worry me a bit and seems to come quite natural, but the Battalion has grown since the war; it is no longer only a Battalion, there are Machine Guns, Bombers, Miners, Trench Mortars, all to be looked after, and anybody who does not play his part, puts me and the Battalion in the cart.

I have sent off my coat to-day with some regret. It has been a good friend and I have lived in it day and night for months, but it will be too heavy if we move, so it must go, and I suppose soon I must part with my thick woolly, which has been a good friend also. And now I must stop. Send me out a few acid drops, they help when one is thirsty, and the water is all so bad.

May 7 15

My dear Ralph

I am v. glad to hear that you have been distinguished in Geography and Mathematics. It is most creditable to you and I am much pleased. I hope you will do the same next term. And that Luff will also when he has been there a year. It has given me so much pleasure.

So you are back at school and I hope you have had happy holidays and now you must both work hard during the term. It is very hot and I am v. busy, so I cannot write more today.

My love to you both dear boys.

    Yr Affect

    Father

<u>DIARY</u>

<u>May 8th</u>

Quiet day.

<u>May 9th</u>

Attack by 1st Army on the right, which proved a failure after a tremendous bombardment. The French got on well on the right.

May 9th

A busy time has prevented my writing much the last few days, and now I am writing at odd moments in the midst of a furious battle. I say 'midst' but really so far I have been little more than a spectator, as I have had a wonderful view from the top of my house of the battle all round me. I have been at it since 3 a.m. and it was not till about 6 I made up my mind that at any rate for the moment I was not going to catch it, we were really bluffing, and do not seem to have taken the Huns in one bit, though I rather hope the reason for our peace is that our guns may have succeeded in knocking out some of theirs at the start. But on each side of me the battle has raged since dawn, and is still raging – on the left a perfect inferno has been going on, at times terrific, and then a lull, only to break out again in its fury. Through my telescope I could see everything going up in the air, houses, trees, sandbags and dirt, those devils have been getting it hot, and must have had an awful time. How the attack has got on I do not know at present. The one thing that always hangs us up is those infernal machine guns.

They have got so many and are so good with them – we have got so few and dare not risk them as we can't get them replaced. On the right the French are at it hard for miles, and I hear successfully. Dull thunder goes on continually, when it does not develop into a roar. Through my telescope I can see houses or something burning furiously in many places. Aeroplanes presumably dropping bombs and parapets being knocked all to pieces. I have never had such a good view of a battle, nor had time to give it so much attention. Meanwhile we have had more peace than we have had for days and days, though I have no doubt we shall have to bear our part in due course. I only pray it will relieve the pressure at Ypres, and that we may really at last smash their lines.

I'm afraid this is hard to read but my hands are cold in my 'dug-out', where I have been most of the day, as all my telephones have been arranged here in view of the probability of our getting shelled. We have worked hard for days at preparation for this: but I can't give you any details. It is an odd thing to see all this going on from the top of the house, and then to look down just behind the line and see a service going on, which was the first thing that reminded me it was Sunday. (Why does one always fight on Sunday?) However, it has often been successful in the past, let's hope it will again.

The country has come on very much the last few days – and all the trees and hedges are out, and the sun is glorious, though the wind [is] very cold. The whole view is totally different to what it was when we first came here on March 11th nearly two months ago. The next two months ought to alter the whole aspect of affairs, if we can get enough men and ammunition, and if the Dardanelles goes on as well as it has begun. That is a fine feat of arms, and something for any nation to be proud of, the landing must have been magnificent, and is a feat we have never performed since, I think, 1802 when Abercrombie landed in Egypt.

How odd to think of you spending a peaceful Sunday at home! And now I must end – don't be surprised if my letters are not so frequent as they have been.

I don't want a muzzle, I have three – one your mother sent me, and two patterns specially recommended, one by the doctor, and the other by Haldane! A high east wind to-day has made one happier. The beastly gas won't work in a high wind. And so to bed, or sleep for a few hours. I got up at 3, and now it is 10, and I have no orders yet for to-morrow; they will probably come in at 1, and necessitate getting up at 3, but that is normal war.

DIARY

May 10th

Up at 3 a.m. for attack to continue, but nothing happened – meanwhile French getting on well.

May 10th

If I wrote too much in my letter yesterday you had better keep it to yourself for the present, perhaps nothing much will be said about it as it was, sad to say, not a great success. The French are having a furious battle to-day, and, I hope, are getting on.

No more as I am weary, up at 1 a.m., when orders arrived, and up for good at 3 a.m., since when I have been busy.

DIARY

May 11th

Very hot. Quiet day.

During the whole time at Givenchy, the Battalion did a tremendous amount of work, and altered the whole appearance of the place. We took it over with miserable trenches and no means of getting there without going overland and being shot at and shelled day and night. We leave it with the whole line very strong, and communication throughout underground from one end to the other, and generally more than one way of going round – a strong 2nd line, and endless strongly defended posts in case of accidents. We have been the only Brigade that has held Givenchy without a disaster. We had heavy casualties at first, but we leave it with the Huns under perfect control – and confident of holding it against anybody. May our successors do likewise.

May 11th

I had such a good bath to-night before dinner after a hot day. Also clean linen. Such a pleasure, and I feel fairly clean at last. The third bath in three weeks, which will be up in a day or two, during which time I have never had my clothes off and generally slept with my boots on. We leave to-morrow, to go to where I know not, though I have a suspicion. I have got to hate the Huns at last. I think the Lusitania put the lid on their iniquities. So shocking to think that a Christian people could by any way of reasoning think it anything but a crime against civilisation. I am told, but I don't know whether it is true, that she had a gun or guns on board for some months, but it was taken off, as the Yanks said they would feel obliged to intern her if she came into a neutral port armed. I have no pity much for the Yanks, they came out very badly on the whole during the war – their one idea is to make as much money as possible out of it. I do hope it will all end by the Huns being turned out of every country in Europe.

Great Joy to-night as we hear the devils attacked behind their gas in the north, but our respirators worked, and we killed hundreds of them. It will give the men back their confidence, which I was afraid they would lose. I am sure this war will end by the giving and taking [of] no quarter. The men are getting to look on the Hun as unfit to live on God's earth, and they don't want to be taken prisoners after all the yarns they have heard.

I had a grand sleep last night, seven hours without a move, and I am right as rain again, but two nights of three hours each had tired me, following much anxiety.

We've had such a dinner to-night, asparagus and gooseberries out of our garden! And on our table we have tulips, lilac, bluebells – all found in gardens round the ruined houses. It really does one's heart good and makes it seem civilised.

I have quite got to like this line, it is so interesting, and we have done so much to make it strong that we should rather like to put it to the test. Anybody who can't hold it now, can't hold anything. It is over three months since we first came to this part, and were told it was a dreadful place. Thousands of lives have been lost here, and everybody hated it. We lost a bit at first, but we hit back hard and got the mastery, since when the Huns have left us alone, and we have done most of the worrying. I really think it is a thing for the Brigade to be proud of. And now to bed.

May 12th

I have no time to write anything more to-day, so I send what I wrote last night.

· BACKGROUND NARRATIVE ·

Italy had been nominally allied to Germany and Austria-Hungary under the Triple Alliance but had refused to join them when war began in August 1914. Under the London Pact of 26 April 1915, it joined the Triple Entente of Russia, France and Britain, and officially revoked the Triple Alliance on 3 May 1915. It declared war on Austria-Hungary on 23 May and the other Triple Alliance powers later that summer.

Wilfrid's following reference to the Germans 'working like niggers' was a very common expression in those days:

May 13th

I am sending you to-day three letters containing maps and air photos for our future regimental records. They will interest you and others, but you must keep them under lock and key for some time yet. Eventually the R.O.R. will be glad of them, but I want to ensure they are kept safe till we have driven the Huns a long way off. The air photo is entirely German trenches, we left the line yesterday, and I really think the Brigade may be proud of it. We took over the Cuinchy Line, as you remember, on January 30th, at a time when the Huns were top dog, and had established a funk – from there we went to Givenchy, and now we have it in such a state that any troops who can't defend it, can't defend anything, and moreover, the Huns are quite tame now. The labour has been continual and incessant, and we have had anxious times, but, next to the Aisne, I think it is the finest piece of work that we have done, and the Battalion has done its share. The Prince marched with us again yesterday. He is mad with the Huns, and dying to be allowed to shoot some himself!

So Italy really comes in to-morrow, if rumour be true. I suppose that will mean another million men against the Huns. The French have killed thousands lately, but I have no doubt they have lost a good deal themselves.

If the Lusitania really rouses the idle beggars at home, it will not have been lost in vain. We want men, any number of them, to replace those who must fall in any advance. Some day it will be realised that if only we could have gone on after Neuve Chapelle we should have done great things, but we couldn't because they struck work at home at the critical time. Since then the Huns took a fright and have been working like niggers to prevent the same thing occurring again, and the task is so much more difficult and costly now. I have watched them working for weeks past and they are fine workers and fighters. From the top of my hill I have been able to see for miles, and watch their defences getting stronger and stronger.

A pouring wet day to-day. I am so sorry for the men who are in some orchards with no cover, and this is how they have to spend a day's rest. However, they are singing lugubrious songs, which shows they are happy! I am in a small farmhouse, and so I keep dry, though there is not much room.

Wilfrid with Ma Jeffreys, photographed by HRH the Prince of Wales after he had been taken to the trenches at Givenchy. (Grenadier Guards)

The ruined church at Givenchy photographed by HRH the Prince of Wales. (Grenadier Guards)

The enclosed photographs were taken by the Prince the day I took him round the trenches at Givenchy. It is not a beautiful one, is it? But I always wore a Burberry to keep my clothes clean in the trenches, and he snapped one before I knew where I was. The other is a photograph of the church and the surrounding desolation, though it does not show anything like what it is really.

May 14th

I am sorry for your anxiety, which is inevitable. We are up against a very tough job, and things did not go well the other day, which is most disappointing, and I can't help wondering what the Battalion will be like this day week, though it does not do to think too much about these things.

The French have done well, but must have lost heavily, and the thing cannot be done without heavy casualties, but they start off with large numbers. Each of these battles would have been thought a great thing before this war.

I have been among the guns to-day, and the noise was simply awful. My ears still sing with it, and it has been incessant day and night for the last two or three days, please God we shall be successful!

· BACKGROUND NARRATIVE ·

This letter was found in Wilfrid's pocket after he was mortally wounded on 18 May:

> May 5th 1915
> West Downs
> Winchester

My dear Father

We came to school yesterday, we had a very good journey down; but our train was very late. Lyulph sleeps next to me in the same dormitory; it is very nice. We are just going to bed. Beautiful weather. I have taken six wickets, since the beginning of the term. An aeroplane came over our heads, while we were playing cricket this afternoon. We are soon going to wear our flannels. And in about two days we are going to begin to swim, it will be great fun. Thank you very much for the letter I got from you yesterday; I am so glad that you thought we worked well last term. I was Vice Captain on my side in the second game, on my side, and Lyulph was Vice Captain on his side in the Junior game as well. I cannot believe that I shall be twelve in ten days. Two days ago we had a violent thunderstorm, all the cricket fields were flooded and no-one thought that we should be able to play cricket in the afternoon; but in half an hour the fields were quite dry; and so we were able to play cricket. Excuse me writing to you badly, because I am writing in a great hurry to catch the post, and as we are just going to bed. On Thursday we are going to a large park, five miles off, and we are going to play a scouting game against another school; I will tell you what happened in my next letter. No time for more.

Your loving son
Ralph

Envelope enclosing Ralph's last letter to his father. (Author's collection)

10

Wilfrid's Death at the Battle of Festubert

Wilfrid was mortally wounded in the head during the Battle of Festubert, on 18 May at about 5 p.m. He died in Béthune Hospital at 2 p.m. the following day, never having recovered consciousness. He was buried at 9 a.m. on 20 May in the British Military Cemetery at Le Touret.

The attack had begun early on 15 May but the 4th (Guards) Brigade did not assume battle positions around the Rue de Cailloux until after nightfall on 17 May. Undetected by British intelligence, the German forward units had withdrawn about 1,200 yards behind their original front line to a new defensive line. During 18 May, British units had limited success in gaining ground across terrain veined by flooded ditches but the new German line remained undetected and unharmed. The 4th (Guards) Brigade, with Wilfrid's battalion, advanced in the late afternoon towards Ferme Cour d'Avoue but was met by merciless machine gun fire in which Wilfrid was wounded. Unable to progress, the attack was called off.

The Battle of Festubert continued until 25 May. The British suffered nearly 17,000 casualties, mostly during the first four days. Eleven officers commanding battalions and a brigade commander were killed in action or died later of their wounds. The British advanced up to 1,300 yards, but in most cases this only took them to the new German lines.

The failure of the attack was due partly to a shortage of shells for the artillery, which was to become an issue of such importance that it led to the fall of the Liberal government and the rise of David Lloyd George as leader of a coalition government for the rest of the war.

Wilfrid's last letter to his wife covered the opening stages of the battle:

WILFRID'S DEATH AT THE BATTLE OF FESTUBERT

May 17th

I think I have just time to write you a few lines, though I don't know how
many. I had a jolly Sunday yesterday. We started off at 3 a.m., and spent the
whole blessed day in reserve in a jolly place between our guns and the German
shells. The noise was the worst I have heard for months, and it never ceased all
day, and when we left at 8 p.m. the Germans were letting off a bit of steam by
properly shelling a village. House after house went up in the air, and the whole
place was a maze of smoke, brick-dust, etc. I don't think anybody was there, so
it didn't matter, but no living creature could have got through while it lasted,
which I suppose was their object, to stop us reinforcing our own people. I
had a head fit to split long before evening. We were lucky, as though we were
shelled on and off all day, (and in the afternoon they brought up some heavy
guns) I only had ten casualties, and none bad. We got food and rest by 10.30,
and then up again at 3.30 a.m. this morning and breakfast at 4, ready to move
at a moment's notice, but so far – 2 p.m. – they have not wanted us, and I got
another hour or two's rest this morning. As far as I know we are getting on
pretty well. The gunning has been awful. It is the first time I have really heard
our guns <u>lavish</u> with ammunition. Day and night they have been letting off,
slowly but jolly accurately since last Wednesday or Thursday, and it must have
been mighty unpleasant for the Huns. Yesterday they fairly let fly, and the shells
were screaming and shrieking over our head all day long – very pleasant to feel
most of them were going the right way. They went on slowly all night, and
are still at it today but we are behind them, thank goodness. I only pray they
have enough ammunition to keep it up. I am afraid the 1st Battalion lost a few
Officers yesterday, but who, and whether killed or wounded, we don't know.
It was a glorious day yesterday, and it is odd how little the animals of nature
care about a fight. The birds were chirping and quarrelling as if nothing was
happening, the bumble bees were buzzing about, and the bugs and flies and
mosquitoes, something too awful. A glorious blue sky, with our aeroplanes
going backwards and forwards like huge eagles, and the trees all getting their
summer garb – while man was doing his very best to destroy everything,
and succeeding!

We are back where we were in some of the wettest part of January, and it is
odd to see that the sea of mud (which was) is really going to grow something,
where it is allowed to. It seemed impossible at that time. To-day it is wet, and
everything filthy, so I don't mind if they don't want us till it stops raining.

I am sorry to see that the Plungers [Bengal Lancers (Hodson's Horse)]
have caught it at Ypres. It seems rather [a] waste to use Cavalry in that way.

The Russians too have had a decided set-back, how bad remains to be seen, but they have probably killed a lot of Huns, which is the only way to end the war, the horror of which outdoes anything in History as it is so world-wide. The men are very bitter against the Hun now, all the worse for him. The prisoners I saw yesterday were not nearly such fine men as they used to be. I hope the best have gone.

I have been able to write for longer than expected, and have not much more to say. I'm afraid you will have an anxious week, but after all, all weeks are anxious, and have been for months, and as usual, we must hope for the best.

· BACKGROUND NARRATIVE ·

While waiting for the attack, Wilfrid had time to write a short letter to Lyulph:

May 17 15

My dear Luff

I think it is your turn for a letter, and I have to thank you both for your letters, particularly a nice one I got from Ralph a few days ago. I am glad you are getting on with your cricket. I hope you will both play well some day. Do you remember the jolly games we had at home when you were quite tiny and how you got cut over the fingers in twice in the same place? About the first time you ever batted. It is such a wet day. Yesterday was very fine and a great battle has been going on all the time. I am writing while we are waiting to go on and the guns are making a tremendous noise, as well as the German shells which come back in reply. I hope we shall give the Huns a good licking, don't you[?] I am sure Mummy must miss you both v. much, but you seem to have had happy holidays.

My best love to both of you dear boys.

Yr Affect

Father

PS Tell Ralph if I don't write for his birthday it won't be that I have forgotten him, but that I am too busy.

Ma Jeffreys' diary contains the following account of the Battle of Festubert between 16 and 19 May. Major Basil Barrington-Kennet ('B.K.') was killed on 18 May and was buried next to Wilfrid. He was a leading aviator

Map showing
the location of
2nd Battalion
Grenadier Guards
at the Battle
of Festubert.
(Ponsonby, Vol. I,
p. 248)

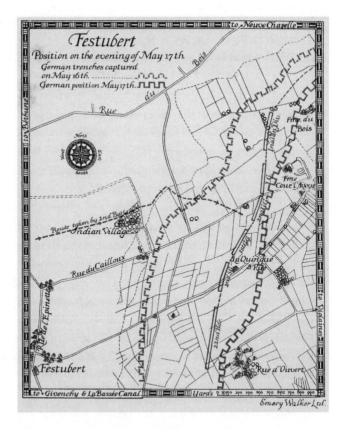

who briefly held the world record for long-distance flight in May 1912. Commissioned in the Grenadiers, he was attached to the Royal Flying Corps when it was formed in May 1912 and became its first adjutant. He returned to the Grenadiers in 1915 out of loyalty to the regiment:

> … when the 5th and 6th Brigades of our 2nd Division assaulted the Rue Du Bois lines. The 4th Brigade was in reserve to them, and 2nd Batt. (ours and Irish) were moved up to Rue Du Bois at day break in close support. The attack succeeded (as did that of the 7th Div. on the right) and we were not called on to do anything, but we had to sit all day behind breastworks at Rue Du Bois and got frightfully shelled. As a matter of fact we hardly suffered at all, as nearly all the shells were short or over, but the noise alone was terrific, added to that of our own artillery which was firing just over our heads.
>
> We had about 10 casualties and withdrew at 8pm and bivouacked near Le Conture. We were ordered to be under arms next morning at 4am and had

breakfast at 3.30am but were not called upon till 2pm when we got orders to march to Le Touret. We were then given orders to go forward through the 7th Division (who had got somewhat mixed up) and occupy the line of La Quinque Rue. The Germans were shelling all the roads, and it took a long time moving the Battalion up across country in artillery formation. When we reached the reserves of the 7th Division we found a good deal of confusion, many units mixed up, and no guide was given to us to point out the line we were to take up so we had great difficulty in finding where they really wanted us. However, an artillery observing officer eventually pointed out the various positions on the map and we went forward.

The ground after heavy rain was in an awful state of sticky mud and pitted with shell holes; so that we still only got along very slowly and it was getting dark when we got up to the firing line, composed of a mixed lot of Scots Fusiliers, Borderers and Yorkshires and was quite dark by the time we got through them and formed a firing line. That being so we did not attack, (as the country was strange and we had no chance of reconnaissance) but entrenched ourselves about 500 yards short of La Quinque Rue, which the Germans held. Grenadiers on the right and Irish Guards on left: two Coldstream Battalions in reserve. I took charge of our front line (2 and 3 Companies) and 1 and 4 were in support under the C.O..

Just at dark an officer of the 1st Batt. (Dudley Smith) came across to me with a patrol, and told me the left of the 1st Batt. was about 100 yards to our right rear, so that the 2nd Batt. were practically in line. We had to work very hard to put the place in any sort of defence, as having come so far across country our tool carts were miles behind and the men only had their little entrenching implements, which were not very good in sticky clay. The Germans fired a good deal when we first came up, causing both us and the Irish Guards several casualties. We had practically no sleep and by day break had some sort of line with communication of a precarious sort via various much smashed German works between firing line and supports. The whole ground was littered with German dead besides a good many of ours. About 6.00 am we got orders that we and the Irish Guards with 2nd Batt. of the 20th Brigade on the right were to attack La Quinque Rue at 9.30 after a preliminary bombardment. As, however, it was too thick for the Artillery to bombard, these orders were cancelled, and we heard to our great surprise that the 20th Brigade was to be withdrawn and not replaced by other troops so that there was a big gap of some hundreds of yards on our right. Charles Corkran came over to see us for a few minutes before the 1st Batt. withdrew. The weather cleared about 10 am and the Germans began to shell us intermittently, making things very unpleasant but not hurting us much. We received orders that the attack on La Quinque Rue would take place later and that the Canadians would come up and attack on our right. About 3.15 we got orders to attack at 4.30 following on 40 mins bombardment, whether the Canadians had arrived or not, from which we concluded (rightly as it turned out) that the Canadians were late. At 4.30 No 3 Coy advanced and the Irish Guards on the left.

Attack by No 3 Coy

Wilfrid and I watched the attack develop from a mound of earth behind which we lay. The shell fire had not hurt the German machine guns, which opened a tremendous fire from the vicinity of some ruined houses. Wilfrid was shot in the first 5 mins. Henry Seymour and I dragged him into cover and I then ran forward to a point nearer the firing line, whence I could see better and get a bit of cover.

The leading platoon of No 3 did not get a 100 yards, the next platoon got to it but not beyond it; the 3rd platoon the same. B.K. [Barrington-Kennett] was killed: Creed and Cary wounded and Corry was the only officer left in the Coy. He displayed great gallantry and did very well. The Irish Guards' attack which was on a wider front got about as far as ours, but was also held up by machine guns, they brought up reinforcements after reinforcements, but could not get on and lost very heavily. I ordered no 2 Coy to reinforce no 3 and to try to get forward, but P.A. Clive came back to me and represented that it was impossible to get across the fire zone, and I said that he need not try and gave orders to simply hold on till dark. About 5.30 pm the Canadians began to appear a long way out on our right and met with very little opposition and got on a good way. I think if they had come at the right time and place it might have made a lot of difference to us. When the attack was held up I reported to the Brigadier and said I intended to try and get in by night, which I think we could have done. Under instructions, however, from the Corps Commander we were ordered to consolidate where we were and join up with the Canadians by digging out to them (the latter a big job). We worked all night and next day and handed over last night to the Coldstream and are now in reserve. The whole 2nd Division is to be relieved and go into reserve tonight. The shell fire these last few days has been very heavy – it was terrific during the attack – but it really was very ineffectual and caused us very little loss. That is I think all I can tell you.

My private humble opinion is:

1. That on Monday we ought to have had our orders earlier and an officer should have been sent to guide us, in which case we should probably have been able to take the position that evening, or at any rate got up in time to see the ground and take it after dark. The Germans had not had much time to strengthen it.

2. That if we were to attack on Tuesday it was a mistake to withdraw the 1st Batt. and bring up the Canadians very late (probably without anyone to guide them either.)

3. That we ought to have been allowed to have a shot by night on Tuesday. As it is, we did nothing Wednesday, the Coldstream (strangers to the ground) relieved us Wednesday night and so could do nothing and are to be relieved themselves tonight by a fresh Brigade and all the time the Germans are strengthening the place, which except for the machine guns was not much at first. The Battalion all very well, chiefly suffering from lack of sleep.

PS The attack was ordered off the map and no General or Staff Officer ever came to look at the ground.

Wilfrid's nephew, Desmond, wrote to his father Eustace on 20 May. He refers to Emmeline, his sister:

Of course by the time you get this, you will have heard about Uncle Wilfrid.

I'll tell you exactly what happened as far as I know it personally. Soon after I wrote my last letter on the 17th and just as I was sitting down to write one to Emmeline to wish her many happy returns of the day, we were ordered to move – during the 36 hrs. fighting before the 2nd Division had broken the German line on the left, the 7th Division on the right, we were ordered to join the gap between the two – very little information could be given us and what was, proved to be wrong, the 7th Division being nearly ½ mile from what it said it was.

We marched up, at times heavily shelled until it got dark, pitch dark and rain. Somehow we got up to the left of the 7th Division with the Irish Guards on our left. The mud, enormous shell holes, old communications and pic trenches made going, especially with machine guns, very heavy indeed. The dead and wounded covered the ground in places and were ghastly.

We occupied a line some 600 yards from our objective (a road) and sent a few Scots Fusiliers who were holding a part of it back. We spent the night digging in with the 1st Battn. on our right and the Irish Guards on our left. During

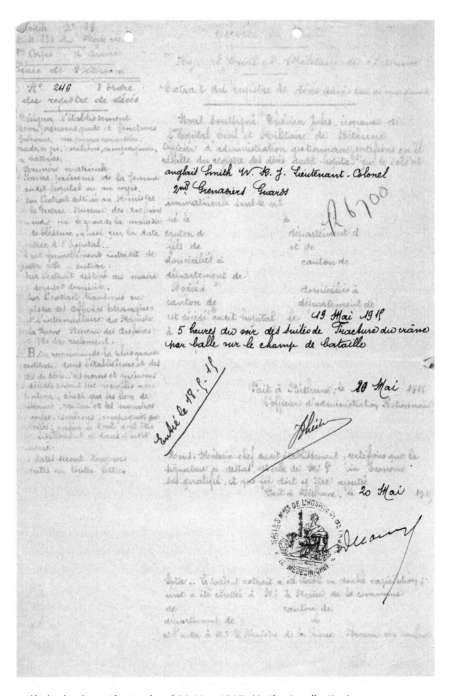

Wilfrid's death certificate, dated 20 May 1915. (Author's collection)

this time we had heavy casualties. Only Arthur Penn getting a bullet in his back and a few men getting knocked out and our sergeant. Next day, the 18th, we were ordered to attack the road (our objective) at 9 o'c. The Germans were in some houses on the road and had a line behind it. Communication was very difficult as our line was very sketchy and [it was] raining hard and [there was] water below the ground about 3ft down. No communication trenches except old German ones which were mostly blown in, so one was sniped whenever one tried to move. The 9 o'c attack was put off, but we were again ordered to attack at 4.30 p.m. in conjunction with the Canadians on our right (who were coming up in place of the 7th Division) and the Indians on our left. We and the 1st Grenadiers did go across open and flat ground with no cover, the Germans having machine guns in the houses on the road.

Before the attack, I with 2 guns crept down an old German communication trench to try and give covering fire to the attackers. We fired about 3,000 rounds but it was no good, none of the attackers got further than 150 yards. The fire was much too severe. It was at this time, while watching the operations from behind that Uncle Wilfrid was hit. He was, I believe, standing between Major Jeffreys and Seymour. He was hit in the head by one of the bullets fired at the 1st Grenadiers' attack on the left.

Everybody who saw him said that he felt nothing and was unconscious from the first. Yesterday we improved our line and the Canadians dug in on our right, so we handed over to the Coldstreams a fairly continuous line. I got back here at 1.30 am. We lost 5 officers, Barrington-Kennett commanding us, 3 killed and the C.O. died of wounds. Creed, Cary, Penn wounded and Craigie slightly wounded beside many top hole sergeants and men. Luckily we have many wounded in comparison to dead. The Germans could not have picked out to kill more important officers or men.

As far as Uncle Wilfrid, his loss to the Battalion cannot be fully realised. Of course, I feel it very much, but everybody does. He was one of the most popular C.O's [sic]. I have heard it said that he and Major Jeffreys were the ideal C.O. and Second in Command about here. I cannot say more than we cannot realise our loss yet. We buried him this morning. He was wounded on the afternoon of the 18th and died yesterday in Bethune. As I said I don't think he felt anything more than a smack in his head as the bullet hit him. I shall write at the first opportunity to Aunt Violet. We move to a place about 4 miles behind Bethune today with the whole of the 2nd division to refit, I believe. Uncle Wilfrid was up and doing all day on the 18th and I felt nervous about him as they were shelling constantly …

11

Wilfrid in Memoriam

Ponsonby describes Wilfrid's funeral and summarises his exceptional qualities:

> He was buried in the British Soldiers' Cemetery near Le Touret, and his funeral was attended by Lord Cavan and many officers and non-commissioned officers of his battalion. Never was a Commanding Officer more mourned by his men; he had endeared himself to them by his soldier-like qualities and constant care for their welfare. He was a gallant and distinguished soldier, imperturbable in action, never flurried or disconcerted in perilous situations, a strict disciplinarian, but the kindest and best of friends, and his loss was keenly felt by all ranks of the regiment.[1]

These qualities were echoed in the numerous condolence letters that Violet received from his brother officers:

Telegram to Violet notifying her of her husband's death. (Author's collection)

Major Jeffreys

I am so dreadfully sorry to have to tell you that Wilfrid died yesterday afternoon from a wound received on the previous afternoon.

I cannot tell you how much we shall miss him, and how grieved we all are at his loss, and I hope you will believe me when I tell you how the whole Battalion feels for you and sympathises with you and your children in your terrible loss.

No Commanding Officer ever gave more thought or devoted more trouble to the welfare of his Battalion than he did, and he was rewarded by the affection and respect of every man and Officer in it.

I think perhaps I shall feel his loss even more than the rest: for eight months we lived together, sharing the same lodgings, or 'dug-outs', and establishing such close relations with one another, as only many weeks of active service can produce, and I feel that I have lost not only a good and gallant Commanding Officer, but also an old and dear friend.

The Battalion was attacking a position, and he and I were lying on a mound of earth watching the attack develop, when a bullet from either a rifle or a machine gun (there was a very heavy fire from both at the time) hit him in the head. He never spoke a word, and became unconscious at once, and I feel sure never felt anything or suffered any pain. Henry Seymour and I dragged him back into shelter, and saw that he was just breathing, though unconscious, and he was at once carried back to the Dressing Station, where our Doctor did all that was possible for him, and sent him in an ambulance to the hospital at Bethune. I hear that he never recovered consciousness.

We buried him this morning in the little British Cemetery which has been established at Le Touret, where many other gallant Officers and men of the Regiment, and of the British Army lie. Major Barrington Kennett who was killed on the same day, is buried next to him.

Sir Henry Streatfeild, the Lieutenant Colonel of the Regiment

I cannot tell you how grieved I am to get the terrible news of dear Wilfrid's death and I want you to know how deeply the Regiment mourn his irreparable loss. Wilfrid was one of the best and straightest men I have ever met. His charming personality endeared him to Officers and men alike. His own Battalion would have followed him anywhere.

Personally I am very miserable at losing a true friend, and lately I have been in such close touch with him. Always, the Regiment he loved so well, was his first thought, and he was so loyal and considerate in these anxious times, when many difficulties and complications were so often arising.

Sir Frederic Ponsonby

Poor, dear Wilfrid, he is a terrible loss to the Regiment. He was such a splendid type of Guardsman, and such a good soldier. His death was a real tragedy for the Brigade.

Brigadier General the Earl of Cavan

It is with deepest sympathy that I write to tell you how Wilfrid died. We were ordered to attack some buildings, and the Grenadiers were in front on the right, and Irish Guards on the left. All started well under heavy fire, but as they got within 500 yards it became unreasonable, and I ordered them to stop – make good, and dig in. Wilfrid had issued excellent orders, and was watching the advance from a good observing breastwork well forward. The fire was terrific, and a bullet came through the opening, and hit him in the head. He lived from about 4.45 p.m. 18th, till about 3 p.m. 19th.

He has done great service for the Regiment all through these hard days, and his dogged stand at Ypres is historical. He is a terrible loss to us.

Major G.S. Clive

You know how much I have served with him since Gibraltar days, and how fond I was of him, so you will know what I am feeling for you and the boys.

'There is no greater glory than to
be crowned by the laurels of death
in the moment of victory'

This is very true; and it will be a priceless possession for his sons, for it was in the moment of victory that it happened.

Lieutenant Colonel Charles Corkran

You will know how brokenhearted all his pals are. I saw him that morning so fit and cheery; the 2nd Battalion had come up alongside of us in that fight, and practically relieved us. They pulled this Brigade back to refit, and the 4th Brigade continued our advance. The dear old man had been so cheery and with everybody's confidence in him, both as a pal and a soldier.

Captain Pike

I feel I don't know how to write and offer you every sympathy I've got in your terrible loss. The Regiment has suffered a loss which can never be repaired, and I have lost one of the best friends I have in the world, and the kindest and best of Commanding Officers. I shall mourn him till my last day, and can never forget his many kindnesses to me.

Captain Beaumont Nesbitt

My loss, and that of the Regiment too, is quite irreparable; how we shall miss him, and how can we ever hope to replace him?

I had to write and tell you how much I feel for you in your loss, and we in ours.

Major Gilbert Hamilton

Wilfrid was the kindest and best Commanding Officer I have ever served under. A wish from him was always considered as an order by us all, and the way he commanded the Second Battalion will go down as an example for all time.

Captain F. Thorne

I think you must know what admiration I had for Wilfrid. (I feel I can call the Commanding Officer by no other name, so please forgive me). He was always so splendid, and especially to young officers, like myself, to get them on as soldiers. As 2nd in Command of the 3rd Battalion, when I happened to be the Assistant Adjutant, we often met together in the Orderly Room as C.O. and Adjutant, and I shall never forget his goodness and help to me.

Colonel G.D. White

You may truly feel that your sorrow is shared by all the Regiment, and more especially by all those who, like myself, have had for many years the inestimable privilege of calling him their friend, in the fullest and truest sense of the word. His was indeed the 'knightly, stainless life, crowned with a soldier's death'. There are but few men I have ever known who had so gripped the hearts and the affections of all those with whom he was brought in contact.

Captain the Hon. W. Bailey

Will you please accept my deepest sympathy and that of all the junior Officers of this Battalion. I simply can't tell you how good he was to all of us; he was always kindness itself, and we can never replace the loss of the best and kindest Commanding Officer that we have ever had.

Lieutenant Desmond Abel Smith

We were ordered on the afternoon of the 17th to fill up the gap between the 2nd and 7th Divisions, which had both broken the German line in different places. We and the Irish Guards started off about 4 p.m., and went up in 'blob-formation' to avoid the shelling as much as possible. I with the Machine Guns, did not get up to the firing line till long after dark. I found two Companies up there (about 300 yards behind the 2nd line German trenches). We had established connection with the 1st Battalion on the right, and the Irish Gds on our left, and I imagine it must have been a creditable performance considering the darkness, state of the ground, (it was raining) and the mass of shell holes and trenches.

Next day, the 18th, we were first ordered to attack at 9 a.m. some houses on a road about 500 yards away, but it was put off at the last minute. All day we shelled the houses, and the Germans behind them, and we attacked about 4.30 with I. Gds on the left, and the Canadians on the right. All day he had been to and fro from the firing line to his Headquarters in an old German trench giving instructions etc., and he was watching the attack when he was hit.

Speaking as one of his Subalterns, I can say we all had the greatest confidence in him, and would have gone anywhere, feeling that he would always do the best for us, and never throw us away uselessly. I am sure that confidence in our leaders is half the battle out here, as there have been so many cases of lives being thrown away by bad leading and muddling, and I feel we do not yet realise what a loss the Battalion has had in losing him. We always heard that he and Major Jeffreys were the ideal Commanding Officer and Second in Command out here.

He was buried this morning at 9 a.m. in a graveyard not far from the fighting line, close to the 'Rue De Bois' between Le Touret and Richebourg, where he was brought from the hospital at Bethune. It was a very fine morning, and we could hear the shells bursting, and see the smoke left by some of them. The Brigadier was there, and Gort, Brigade Major, also Major Jeffreys, and many of the Officers from the Battalion – as many as could get away, as one had to be left with each Company. Fleming, the parson, whom we all like, buried him. The grave is, of course, carefully marked by a white cross with black lettering, made by our own pioneers, as are all the graves of the Officers and men of the Battalion. There are many Officers and men of the Brigade buried there, as it is close to the place where we had so many losses on Christmas Eve. I saw the graves there of Archie Trotter, Tritton, Gough, Guthrie, and several others you may know.

· BACKGROUND NARRATIVE ·

Desmond wrote later that year: 'Col Ma Jeffreys left 2nd Battalion Grenadiers for a Brigade and one could not help feeling that if Uncle Wilfrid was still alive he would have had one some months before.'

Desmond survived four years of war on the front with only two minor wounds, one in the hand, the other in the foot, enemy gas and a minor bout of jaundice. He was awarded the MC early in 1917 for his gallantry on the Somme and was acting brigade major by the end of the war. He went on to enjoy a successful business career that included becoming Chairman of the National Provincial Bank (later to become the National Westminster Bank after merging with the Westminster Bank), Anglo-Persian Oil Co. (later to become BP) and the Equitable Life Assurance Society. He always recognised the role that Wilfrid had played in his survival of the war by taking him from 1st Battalion Scots Guards as his machine gun officer in January 1915.

· BACKGROUND NARRATIVE ·

A memorial service was held for Wilfrid at Holy Trinity Church, Sloane Street, where he and Violet had been married fifteen years earlier, on 3 June 1915. Wilfrid's brother Bertram was in Egypt and therefore could not attend. A few days later he wrote to his sister, Marjorie 'Madge' Smith:

> June 6th 1915
> Summer Palace
> Ramleh

Dear Madge

... I have written so many letters to-day and in pencil as the pens are impossible. I received your long letter of 23rd today, your letter of 25th with a copy of Desmond's letter. So very many thanks for it and for letting me know as soon as possible. All the letters I have received this morning make me very sad and I am so glad to have got them here away from the Mess at Cairo. I am enjoying a quiet cool Sunday with Reggie [Abel Smith] and Myrtle [Reggie's wife]. It picks one up no end and I delight in a room to myself and a comfortable bed for the first time since I left England. Also a long lie [in] instead of the 4.30 rise.

I wish I had been with you all [at] the memorial service. I hope poor Violet got through it well. I hear she is so brave.

How I wish I could do something for her.

I would write more. I am glad Eustace cabled, thanks I gather to you and it was such a more satisfactory cable than Meta's with the bare facts.

I do so appreciate your letters.

Y

Bertram

Reggie Abel Smith, a nephew of Wilfrid's, also wrote to his aunt Madge at this time. He was serving with the Herts Yeomanry in Egypt. He won the MC for gallantry:

> Summer Palace
> Ramleh
> Herts Yeomanry
> Army of Occupation
> June 22nd 1915

My dearest Madge

What a dreadful blow this is, and the truth and the realisation of it is impossible to grasp at present! One grieves for poor Aunt Violet so terribly and the miss will be a great and awful blow to all of us. All the happy times we have spent with dear Uncle Wilfrid simply spring up in the mind and one cannot think that they will not be repeated. Thank God, he did not suffer after he was hit. That is one very great mercy. The other great comfort is to know how wonderfully well he had done, and how devoted all in his command were to him. Even so it does not balance the loss. My dear, I am sorry for you and the others, as it will be such a blow to you all, but you will know how I feel. My heart is very heavy with grief, as I was very devoted to him indeed ...

I feel thoroughly relieved really that dear Grandmother never lived to see this war. She would have minded about it so dreadfully. Every mail brings fresh casualty lists, and each time several more friends are killed – and one wonders what it will be like when it is all over. Goodbye, as I must let this go.

With much love
Your very loving
Reggie

In November 1915, Colonel St Leger Glyn wrote to Violet:

I felt I should like to go and see where my dear old friend and comrade was sleeping his last and now peaceful sleep, so the Adjutant, Bill Bailey, and I started off this afternoon. The Cemetery is on the south side of the Bethune–Neuve Chapelle Road. It is very nicely kept up: paths being made, but much cannot be done at present, it being only just behind the line. I left the Adjutant at the gate with the horses, and went by myself and stood for a few moments by his side. The dark clouds were hurrying along from the south-west, the rain was falling, or rather it was misting very heavily, troops, very dirty and mud bedraggled, were marching along the road from the trenches, and others, a trifle cleaner, were going up to the trenches for their turn of duty. Our guns occasionally roared but a hoarse defiance to the Huns, and every now and again a German shrapnel burst highish in the air to the north of the road, but for all that peace reigned in the little God's Acre, and I well knew that he was where perfect peace does always reign.

Before I left the Regiment I was just below him. He was, as you know, a dear old friend and comrade, and I could not leave the neighbourhood without going to see where he lay. We in the Second Battalion will never forget him. We will try to live up to the standard that he has set us. We are carrying on the system he laid down in the Battalion, and although many have changed since he laid down his life for his Country and Regiment, the spirit of those who remain, and of those who have come out to fill the gaps, is the same good, stirling [sic] spirit which made the 2nd Battalion Grenadier Guards the first fighting unit in the army.

The volume produced of Wilfrid's letters and diaries contains the poem 'For the Fallen' written by Laurence Binyon, published in *The Times* on 21 September 1914:

> With proud thanksgiving, a mother for her children,
> England mourns for her dead across the sea,
> Flesh of her flesh they were, spirit of her spirit.
> Fallen in the cause of the free.
> Solemn the drums thrill: death august and royal
> Sings sorrow up into immortal spheres –
> There is music in the midst of desolation,
> And a glory that shines upon our tears.
> They went with songs to the battle, they were young,
> Straight of limb, true of eye, steady and aglow –
> They were staunch to the end against odds uncounted,
> They fell with their faces to the foe.
> They shall grow not old, as we that are left grow old:
> Age shall not weary them, nor the years condemn –
> At the going down of the sun, and in the morning,
> We will remember them.
> They mingle not with their laughing comrades again,
> They sit no more at familiar tables of home;
> They have no lot in our labour of the day-time –
> They sleep beyond England's foam.

But where our desires are,and our hopes profound,
Felt as a well-spring that is hidden from sight,
To the innermost heart of their land they are known,
As the Stars are known to the Night.
As the stars that shall be bright when we are dust,
Moving in marches upon the heavenly plain,
As the stars that are starry in the time of our darkness,
To the end, to the end they remain.

Four years after his father's death, Ralph (aged 16) wrote to his mother about the Guards' triumphal march past Buckingham Palace on 22 March 1919. He went up with the Eton Volunteers to line the streets.

Ralph mentions the mascots that he saw marching in front of their respective battalions. The Irish Guards had their wolf dog and the Scots Guards were preceded by two cows, called Bella and Bertha. They had been caught in the autumn of 1914 by 2nd Battalion Scots Guards to provide milk for the officers. The two cows stayed with the battalion, survived the war and were shipped home as 'Officers' Chargers' in the spring of 1919. They enjoyed grazing in Windsor Great Park and Hyde Park before living out their retirement in Renfrewshire. Their memory is preserved by two silver statues that form part of the Scots Guards' regimental silver:

23/3/19
L. Todd's Esq
Eton College
Windsor

My dearest Mummie,

I hope you and Syl. got to Derby all right, we had such a nice time together. Lyulph is sending you the tickets for the concert, if you don't want them or don't know anyone to give them to, send them back to us, as their [sic] will be a great many people, who will want them. We went to London yesterday, and had awful fun. We marched up to Windsor Station and went up by the 10 o'clock special train. Then we got out at Paddington, and marched off with a brass band through crowds, we were quarter of a mile long! Then we marched right up to Green Park, w[h]ere we broke ranks, and had lunch. Then at 1.30 we marched down to the Mall. We were just in front of the crowd and had a lovely view and could see them just as they swept round the corner. I saw Lord Cavan, and the Prince of Wales was enormously cheered. I also saw General

Excerpt from Ralph's letter showing where he stood to watch the Triumphal March. (Author's collection)

Jeffreys. And Dubby, looking very smart, was riding in front of the machine guns, he was also wearing his 1914 medal. There were lovely chargers and in front of some battalions were the mascots i.e. a wolf dog and in front of one two cows! Then they all passed and the crowd had broken, when a policeman came galloping along, and it turned out that 6 battalions were left behind. So they passed too. The wounded in the lorries climbed up onto the roofs and made an awful noise. When they had all passed we went back to the park had tea and were dismissed for an hour, at 5.15 the Guards marched down Piccadilly so we rushed across and saw them go by again. Here they were cheered like anything, and baskets of flowers and confetti were hurled down from the Berkeley Hotel. When they had at length passed by, we fell in and marched back through terrific crowds, with the band playing Mississippi etc. and all the ladies crowded to the windows to see us go by. We marched back very fast, and when we arrived at Paddington the band halted … and played us in, and in the small space their noise was deafening. The train had to leave at 6.10, so as it was 6.12 we crowded in quickly, and cheered the band, and they played God save the King and we left. We arrived at Windsor at 6.50, and when we passed through Slough we all cheered etc. We marched back and were dismissed at 7.15. We came straight back and had a hot bath, and went straight to bed at 8 o'clock (most people went straight to bed but some fools stayed up) and we were in bed for 13 hours!! It was the end of a perfect day. It was very cold so I put on 2 prs of pants and 2 vests, 2 prs socks, 1 shirt and wooley [sic] waistcoat under my tunic, but I was none too warm even then. We had been 10 hrs on parade, and had had to stand still for 2 hrs, while they marched by, so it was very tiring. Some people fainted whilst standing, and the boy next to me almost did, if he had had, I would have taken him along 100 yds down the Mall to the Ambulance, before huge crowds, and while the Guards were marching past, but thank goodness he didn't faint! A huge Handly-Page [sic] [a bomber aircraft] hovered over most of the time. I could just see the King. Their bands were lovely and 2 played by us alternately the whole time. They were not cheered much in the Mall as their [sic] were no houses to cheer from or to throw flowers from. But they were cheered frightfully going down Piccadilly. Some Etonians in the Corps got leave to go just because they had cousins in the Guards! (I should think their [sic] were 3,000,000 people their [sic]). The day before Lord Cavan (who is an Old Etonian) came down and was presented. He made a speech and said he was very proud of the Etonians, who had served him during the War!! Isn't he a small man? But he looked awfully fine riding yesterday. I am afraid this letter is very boring. Only a week more Hurrah! No more news. Best love to all.

Your loving son

Ralph

Ralph went on to join the Grenadiers after he left Eton. His mother recorded in his baby book that he carried the colour in the Trooping of the Colour in June 1924. He had to leave the army on medical grounds in 1928 after suffering a serious accident, falling from his horse onto wet tarmac while riding at speed during an event in the barracks at Windsor. He eventually went on to farm in Herefordshire.

After leaving Eton, Lyulph worked for Shell in Malaysia. In the Second World War he fought with the Royal West African Frontier Force and the Royal Artillery in Burma, rising to lieutenant colonel. On his return to England he became a banker in London.

Sylvia married Arthur Hanning, also a Grenadier.

Appendix

Wilfrid is buried at Le Touret Military Cemetery, Richebourg-L'Avoué. He was awarded the following orders, medals and decorations:

The Order of St Michael and St George, Companion (CMG)
Queen's Sudan Medal
Queen's South Africa Medal and clasps
Order of Mejide, 4th class
Khedive's Sudan Medal and clasp
First World War 1914 Star and dated clasp
First World War War Medal
First World War Victory Medal and Mentioned in Despatches
1911 Coronation Medal

His CMG, First World War Star, War Medal and Victory Medal, together with his Mention in Despatches, signed by Winston Churchill, were sent to Violet. He is commemorated on the following war memorials:

Smith Family Memorial in the Cloister at Eton College
Grenadier memorial at Eton College
Colonnade memorial at Eton College
Parish Church of St Mary, Slough, Buckinghamshire
Smith Family Memorial at Royal Bank of Scotland Offices, 1 Princes Street, London EC2R 8BP
The Travellers Club, Pall Mall, London
The Church of St Michael and All Saints, Waterford, Hertfordshire
Cheam School

Notes

Chapter 1

1. Girouard, Mark, *The Victorian Country House* (London and New Haven, CT: Yale University Press, 1979), p. 407.
2. Abel Smith, Dorothy, *And Such a Name …:The Recollections of Mrs Robert Smith of Goldings* (Knebworth: Able Publishing, 2003), p. 89.
3. Ziegler, Philip, *Omdurman* (London: Collins, 1973), p. 162.

Chapter 2

1. Craster, Michael, *Fifteen Rounds a Minute:The Grenadiers at War 1914* (Barnsley: Pen & Sword Military, 2012), pp. 2–3.
2. Wright, Philip, *For Distinguished Conduct:Warrant Officers, Non Commissioned Officers and Men of the Grenadier Guards awarded the Distinguished Conduct Medal in the Great War 1914–1918* (London: Blurb Publishing, 2010), pp. 15–17.

Chapter 3

1. Hanning, Henry, *The British Grenadiers: Three Hundred and Fifty Years of the First Regiment of Foot Guards, 1656–2006* (Barnsley: Pen & Sword Military, 2006), p. 161.

2. Hanning, p. 141.
3. Craster, p. 95.
4. Craster, p. 96.

Chapter 4

1. Liddell Hart, Basil Henry, *History of the First World War* (London: Pan Books, 1972), p. 123.
2. Wyrall, Everard, *The History of the Second Division, 1914–1918, Vol. 1* (London:Thomas Nelson and Sons, 1921), p. 164.
3. Hamilton, Ernest, *The First Seven Divisions: Being a Detailed Account of the Fighting from Mons toYpres*, 15th ed. (London: Hurst and Blackett, 1916), pp. 299–300.
4. *The London Gazette*, 17 December 1914.
5. *The Times*, 5 November 1914.
6. Ponsonby, Sir Frederick, *The Grenadier Guards in the Great War 1914–1918, Vol. 1* (London: Macmillan, 1920), pp. 171–73.

Chapter 5

1. Ponsonby, p. 203.
2. Ponsonby, pp. 203–05.
3. *Household Brigade Magazine*, Winter 1960–61.

Chapter 6

1. Ponsonby, p. 207.
2. Ponsonby, pp. 208–09.
3. Ponsonby, pp. 211–12.
4. *Flight*, 13 July 1916, p. 587.
5. *The London Gazette*, 30 June 1915.

Chapter 7

1. Ponsonby, pp. 212–15.

Chapter 8

1. Ponsonby, p. 217.
2. BBC News, 16 June 2015.
3. *The London Gazette*, 15 January 1915.

Chapter 9

1. Ponsonby, pp. 219–20.
2. Cassar, George, *Asquith as War Leader* (London: Hambledon Press, 1994), p. 87.
3. Thorpe, D.R. (Richard), *Supermac: The Life of Harold Macmillan* (London: Chatto & Windus, 2010), p. 56.

Chapter 11

1. Ponsonby, p. 261.

Bibliography

Private Papers

Jeffreys, George Lord, Diaries
Smith, Bertram Abel, Letters
Smith, Desmond Abel, Letters and private autobiography
Smith, Ralph Abel, Letters
Smith, Reginald Abel, Letters
Smith, Violet, Diary 1901
Smith, Wilfrid Abel, Letters and Diaries 1914–1915, private albums, game
    book, accounts books and other correspondence

Published Sources

Abel Smith, Dorothy, *And Such a Name …: The Recollections of Mrs Robert
    Smith of Goldings* (Knebworth: Able Publishing, 2003).
Anon., *List of Etonians Who Fought in the Great War 1914–1919*. Eton
    College.
Cassar, George, *Asquith as War Leader* (London: Hambledon Press, 1994).
Cole, Christopher and E. Frank Cheesman, *The Air Defence of Great Britain
    1914–1918* (London: Putnam, 1984).
Craster, Michael, *Fifteen Rounds a Minute: The Grenadiers at War 1914*
    (Barnsley: Pen & Sword Military, 2012).
Edmonds, James, *Military Operations France and Belgium, 1915, Vol. 1: Winter
    1914–15: Battle of Neuve Chapelle: Battles of Ypres* (London: Macmillan,
    1927).

——, *Military Operations: France and Belgium, 1915: Vol. 2: Winter 1914–15: Battle of Aubers Ridge, Festubert, and Loos* (London: Macmillan, 1928).

French, Sir John, *The Fourth Despatch of Sir John French dated 20 November 1914.* Second Supplement to *The London Gazette* of 27 November 1914.

——, *The Fifth Despatch of Sir John French dated 5 December 1914.* Second Supplement to *The London Gazette* of 5 December 1914.

——, *The Sixth Despatch of Sir John French dated 2 February 1915.* Third Supplement to *The London Gazette* of 12 February 1915.

——, *The Seventh Despatch of Sir John French dated 5 April 1915.* Second Supplement to *The London Gazette* of 14 April 1915.

——, *The Eighth Despatch of Sir John French dated 15 June 1915.* Second Supplement to *The London Gazette* of 10 July 1915.

Girouard, Mark, *The Victorian Country House* (London and New Haven, CT: Yale University Press, 1979).

Hamilton, Ernest, *The First Seven Divisions: Being a Detailed Account of the Fighting from Mons to Ypres*, 15th ed. (London: Hurst and Blackett, 1916).

Hancock, Edward, *The Battle of Aubers Ridge* (Barnsley: Pen & Sword, 2005).

Hanning, Henry, *The British Grenadiers: Three Hundred and Fifty Years of the First Regiment of Foot Guards, 1656–2006* (Barnsley: Pen & Sword Military, 2006).

Hart, Peter, *Gallipoli* (London: Profile Books, 2011).

Hastings, Max, *Catastrophe: Europe Goes to War 1914* (London: Collins, 2013).

The Historical Section of the Committee of Imperial Defence, *History of the Great War: Principal Events 1914–1918* (London: His Majesty's Stationery Office, 1922).

Hoare, Philip, *Noel Coward* (London: Sinclair-Stevenson, 1995).

Jukes, Geoffrey, *The First World War: The Eastern Front 1914–1918* (Oxford: Osprey Publishing, 2002).

Lawson, Eric and Jane, *The First Air Campaign: August 1914–November 1918* (Conshohocken, PA: Combined Books, 1996).

Liddell Hart, Basil, *History of the First World War* (London: Pan Books, 1972).

Marder, Arthur, *From the Dreadnought to Scapa Flow, Vol II: The War Years to the Eve of Jutland* (London: Oxford University Press, 1970).

Massie, Robert, *Castles of Steel: Britain, Germany, and the Winning of the Great War at Sea* (London: Random House, 2003).

McCartney, Innes, *The Maritime Archaeology of a Modern Conflict: Comparing the Archaeology of German Submarine Wreck to the Historical Text* (Oxford: Routledge, 2014).

Neillands, Robin, *The Old Contemptibles: The British Expeditionary Force, 1914* (London: John Murray, 2004).

Nicol, Randall, 'The Tale of Bella and Bertha' (*The Guards Magazine*, Autumn 2014)

O'Connor, Mike, *Airfields and Airmen: Ypres* (Barnsley: Pen and Sword, 2001).

Ponsonby, Sir Frederick, *The Grenadier Guards in the Great War 1914–1918* (3 Volumes) (London: Macmillan, 1920).

Preston, Diana, *Lusitania: An Epic Tragedy* (New York, NY: Walker Publishing Company, 2002).

Reid, Walter, *Architect of Victory: Douglas Haig* (Edinburgh: Birlinn, 2006).

Rickard, J., *Battle of Neuve-Chapelle, 10–13 March 1915*, http://www. historyofwar.org/articles/battles_neuve_chapelle.html (19 August 2007).

Russell, Bertrand, *Prophecy and Dissent, 1914–1916* (London: Unwin Hyman, 1988).

Simpson, Colin, *The Lusitania* (London: Longman, 1972).

Slowe, Peter and Richard Woods, *Fields of Death: Battle Scenes of the First World War* (London: Robert Hale, 1986).

Thorpe, D.R. (Richard), *Supermac: The Life of Harold Macmillan* (London: Chatto & Windus, 2010).

Travers, Tim, *Gallipoli 1915* (Stroud: Tempus, 2001).

Tunstall, Graydon, *Blood on the Snow: The Carpathian Winter War of 1915* (Lawrence, KA: University Press of Kansas, 2010).

Wright, Philip, *For Distinguished Conduct: Warrant Officers, Non Commissioned Officers and Men of the Grenadier Guards Awarded the Distinguished Conduct Medal in the Great War 1914–1918* (London: Blurb Publishing, 2010).

Wyrall, Everard, *The History of the Second Division, 1914–1918, Vol. 1: 1914–1916* (London: Thomas Nelson and Sons, 1921).

Zaloga, Steven, *Armoured Trains* (London: Osprey Publishing, 2008).

Ziegler, Philip, *Omdurman* (London: Collins, 1973).

Biographical Index

Acraman, William Edward – <u>Dates unknown</u>
Commissioned G. Gds; Quarter Master and Major G. Gds; MC, DCM.

Adeane, Henry Robert Augustus ('Harry') – <u>1882–1914</u>
Winchester College; entered army 1902; commissioned C. Gds; Lieutenant 1905;
Captain 1912; retired 1913; Captain 1 Batt. C. Gds August 1914; k.i.a. November 1914.

Alexander, Harold Rupert Leofric George – <u>1891–1969</u>
Harrow School; entered army 1910; commissioned I. Gds; Lieutenant 1 Batt. I. Gds
August 1914; Captain 2 Batt. I. Gds March–October 1915; second-in-command 1 Batt.
I. Gds December 1916; Major, Officers School July–September 1917; Lieutenant
Colonel 2 Batt. I. Gds October 1917–March 1918; Acting Brigadier General 4 Gds
Brigade March 1918; OC 2 Batt. I. Gds April–October 1918; subsequently Field Marshal
1944; Supreme Allied Commander, Mediterranean theatre; Minister of Defence 1952–54;
created 1st Earl Alexander of Tunis; KG, PC, GCB, OM, GCMG, CSI, DSO, MC.

Ardee, Reginald Le Normand Brabazon, Lord – <u>1869–1949</u>
Wellington College; entered army 1889; commissioned G. Gds; served S. Africa 1900–02;
Major 1906; Lieutenant Colonel 1912; transferred, following death of George Morris, as
OC 1 Batt. I. Gds September–October 1914, badly wounded at Ypres; employed under
Ministry of Munitions 1916–17; Colonel I. Gds Regimental District February 1917–
January 1918; Brigadier General (temp.) 4 Gds Brigade February–April 1918; succeeded
father as 13th Earl of Meath 1929; CB, CBE.

Asquith, Henry Herbert – <u>1852–1928</u>
Liberal Prime Minister of the United Kingdom 1908–16; 1st Earl of Oxford and
Asquith; KG, KC.

Bailey, Hon. Wilfred Russell – <u>1891–1948</u>
Eton College; entered army 1911; commissioned G. Gds; Lieutenant 2 Batt. G. Gds
August 1914; Captain & Adjutant 2 Batt. G. Gds 1915–16; Acting Major 1916; OC
1 Batt. G. Gds October 1918; Acting Lieutenant Colonel October 1918; retired 1924;
rejoined 1939; OC Training Batt. W. Gds; Colonel GHQ 1942; succeeded father as
3rd Baron Glariusk 1928; DSO.

Barrington-Kennett, Basil Herbert – <u>1885–1915</u>
Eton College; entered army 1906; commissioned G. Gds; Adjutant and Quartermaster
General of RFC 1912–14; transferred to 2 Batt. G. Gds 1915; k.i.a. May 1915.

Battye, Percy Lawrence Montague – <u>1886–1945</u>
  Charterhouse School; mining engineer; entered army in 1914; commissioned G. Gds;
  wounded February 1915; transferred W. Gds 1915; retired 1930 as Lieutenant Colonel,
  W. Gds; returned in 1940, as Major Royal Fusiliers; killed on active service May 1945; MC.
Bell, Arthur Clive Morrison ('Closh') – <u>1871–1956</u>
  Eton College; entered army 1890; commissioned S. Gds; Lieutenant 1894; Boer War
  1899–1900; ADC to Earl of Minto, Governor-General of Canada 1900–04; Major
  1908; retired army 1908; 1910–31 MP for Honiton; rejoined army 1914; taken prisoner
  February 1915; returned to England 1918; created baronet 1923.
Brabazon, Hon. Ernest William Maitland Molyneaux – <u>1884–1915</u>
  Entered army in 1904; commissioned C. Gds; Lieutenant 1906; Captain 3 Batt. C. Gds
  1912; Staff Captain 4 (Gds) Brigade; k.i.a. June 1915; DSO.
Brand, Thomas, 3rd Viscount Hampden – <u>1869–1958</u>
  Eton College; Cambridge University; entered army 1889; commissioned 10 Hussars;
  Captain 1898; ADC to Governor of New South Wales 1898–99; Boer War 1899–1901;
  Major 1903; Lieutenant Colonel OC 1 Batt. Hertfordshire Regiment 1913–15;
  Brigadier General 126 (East Lancashire) Brigade, Gallipoli 1915; commanded 185
  (2/1 West Riding) Brigade, France 1917–18; ADC to H.M. King George V 1920–31;
  Colonel 10 Royal Hussars 1935–39; GCVO, KCB, CMG.
Brooke, Bertram ('Boy') Sergison – <u>1880–1967</u>
  Eton College; entered army 1899; commissioned G. Gds; Boer War and served with
  Egyptian Army; First World War: initially served as Assistant Embarkation Officer and
  Brigade Major; commanded 2 Gds Brigade 1917 but was gassed; after First World War,
  OC 1 Batt. G. Gds; commanded G. Gds and Regimental District 1923; commanded
  15 Infantry Brigade, China 1927; commanded 1 Gds Brigade 1928; Brigadier on
  General Staff at Eastern Command, India 1931; Major General Brigade of Gds and
  GOC London District 1934; retired 1939; Lieutenant General recalled as GOC London
  District, retired 1942; KCB, KCVO, CMG, DSO.
Buchanan, John Nevile – <u>1887–1969</u>
  Charterhouse School; first-class cricketer, Cambridge University, MCC,
  Buckinghamshire; entered army 1914; Second Lieutenant G. Gds Special Reserve 1914;
  2 Batt. G. Gds December 1914–November 1918; retired army as temp. Major 1919;
  lawyer; DSO, MC.
Bulfin, Edward Stanislaus – <u>1862–1939</u>
  Stonyhurst College; entered army 1884; commissioned Yorkshire Regiment; Brigadier
  General 2 Infantry Brigade 1913–14; Major General 28 Division 1914–15; 60 Division
  1915–17; Lieutenant General XXI Corps Palestine 1917–19; promoted Major General
  and Lieutenant General for distinguished service in the field; General 1925; retired 1925;
  KCB, CVO.
Bury, Harold Sterndale Entwistle – <u>1888–1915</u>
  Eton College, 1st XI cricket 1907; Second Lieutenant G. Gds Special Reserve 1914; att.
  S. Gds; k.i.a. January 1915.
Buttle, R.W. – <u>Birthdate unknown–1915</u>
  Sergeant 2 Batt. G. Gds; k.i.a. February 1915.

Campbell, Hon. John Beresford ('Johnny') – <u>1866–1915</u>
    Eton College; entered army 1887; commissioned C. Gds; Lieutenant 1890; Captain,
    Reserve of Officers C. Gds 1914; k.i.a. January 1915; DSO.

Capper, Thompson ('Tommy') – <u>1863–1915</u>
    Haileybury and Imperial Service College; entered army 1882; commissioned East
    Lancashire Regiment; Commandant Staff College, Quetta, India 1906–11; Brigadier
    General 13 Infantry Brigade 1911–14; Major General 7 Division 1914–15; k.i.a.
    September 1915; KCMG, CB, DSO.

Cary, Hon. Philip Plantagenet – <u>1895–1968</u>
    Eton College; Second Lieutenant G. Gds Special Reserve 1914; Officer of Arms,
    Bluemantle Pursuivant 1913–23, York Herald 1923–32.

Cavan, Frederick Rudolph Lambart ('Fatty'), 10th Earl of – <u>1865–1946</u>
    Eton College; Oxford University; entered army 1885; commissioned G. Gds; Captain
    1897; Boer War 1900–01; Major 1902; Lieutenant Colonel OC 2 Batt. G. Gds 1908;
    Colonel 1911; retired from army 1913; recalled 1914; Brigadier General (temp.) 4 (Gds)
    Brigade September 1914–September 1915; Major General 50 (Northumbrian) Division
    June 1915; commanded Gds Division September 1915; commanded XIV Corps 1916,
    France 1916–17, Italy 1918; Lieutenant General 1917; Lieutenant of the Tower of
    London 1920; ADC to the King, 1920; GOC, Aldershot 1920; General 1921; CIGS
    1922–26; Field Marshal 1922; Colonel of the Irish Guards 1925; Colonel of the
    Bedfordshire and Hertfordshire Regiment 1928; KP, GCB, GCMG, GCVO, GBE.

Cavendish, Ralph Henry Voltelin – <u>1887–1968</u>
    Eton College; entered army 1906; commissioned G. Gds; ADC to Governor of Madras
    1912–14; Captain 2 Batt. G. Gds August 1914; Acting Major and Commanding Officer
    3 Batt. G. Gds; MVO.

Cecil, George Edward – <u>1895–1914</u>
    Winchester College; entered army 1913; commissioned G. Gds; Lieutenant 2 Batt.
    G. Gds August 1914; k.i.a. September 1914.

Cecil, Hon. William Amherst – <u>1886–1914</u>
    Eton College; entered army 1906; commissioned G. Gds; Lieutenant (Machine Gun
    Officer) 2 Batt. G. Gds August 1914; k.i.a. September 1914.

Cholmeley, Sir Montague Aubrey Rowley ('Monty'), 4th Baronet – <u>1876–1914</u>
    Eton College; Lieutenant 4 Batt. Lincolnshire Regiment; transferred G. Gds 1896; Captain
    (Reserve of Officers) G. Gds; 2 Batt. G. Gds November 1914; k.i.a. December 1914.

Churchill, Edward George Spencer – <u>1876–1964</u>
    Eton College; Cambridge University; entered army 1899; commissioned G. Gds;
    Lieutenant 1899; Boer War 1899–1901; rejoined army 1914; 2 Batt. G. Gds 1914–18;
    Captain 1915; wounded twice; retired from army 1921; MC.

Churchill, Winston Leonard Spencer – <u>1874–1965</u>
    Harrow School; entered army 1895; commissioned 4 Queens Own Hussars; served in
    India, Second Anglo-Afghan War, Nile Expedition, Boer War; retired from army 1900;
    rejoined army 1915; Major 2 Batt. G. Gds 1915; Lieutenant Colonel (temp.) OC 6 Batt.
    Royal Scots Fusiliers 1916; Under Secretary of State for Colonies 1905–08; President
    of Board of Trade 1908; Home Secretary 1911; First Lord of the Admiralty 1911–15;

Minister of Munitions 1917; Secretary of State for War and for Air 1919; active politician during interwar years; Conservative Prime Minister 1940–45 and 1951–55; KG, OM, CH, TD, DL, FRS, RA.

Clive, George Sidney – 1874–1959

Harrow School; entered army 1893; commissioned G. Gds; Sudan campaign 1898; Boer War 1899–1902; Major GSO 2 London District 1905; Head of British Mission French Army HQ 1915–18; Military Governor of Cologne 1919; commanded 1 Infantry Brigade, Aldershot 1919–20; Major General, Military Attaché, Paris 1924; Military Secretary 1930; Lieutenant General retired from army 1934; GCVO, KCB, CMG, DSO.

Clive, Percy Archer – 1873–1918

Eton College; entered army 1891; commissioned G. Gds; Captain 1899; Boer War 1899–1901; left army; MP 1900–06; rejoined G. Gds August 1914; Captain 2 Batt. G. Gds 1914; OC 7 Batt. E. Yorks. Regiment May 1916–April 1918; k.i.a. April 1918.

Colston, Hon. Edward Murray ('Ted') – 1880–1944

Eton College; entered army 1900; commissioned G. Gds; Captain 2 Batt. G. Gds August 1914–September 1914; Major March 1915; GSO 2 May–July 1916; Brigadier General (temp.) Infantry Brigade EEF; Colonel 1924; retired 1932. Succeeded his father as 2nd Baron Roundway 1925; CMG, DSO, MVO.

Congleton, Henry Pugh Fortescue Parnell, 5th Baron – 1890–1914

Eton College; Oxford University; entered army 1911; commissioned G. Gds; Lieutenant 2 Batt. G. Gds August 1914; k.i.a. November 1914.

Connaught and Strathearn, HRH Prince Arthur, The Duke of – 1850–1942

Third son of Queen Victoria; Royal Military Academy, Woolwich; forty years' service in army; Colonel of the G. Gds 1904–42; Governor General of Canada 1911–16; KG, KT, GCB, GCSI, GCMG, GCIE, GCVO, GBE, VD, TD.

Corkran, Charles Edward – 1872–1939

Eton College; entered army 1893; commissioned G. Gds; Sudan Expedition 1898; Captain 1899; Boer War 1900–02; Major 1907; Brigade Major 1 Brigade August–November 1914; GSO 2 1915; Lieutenant Colonel OC 1 Batt. G. Gds March–July 1915; Brigadier General (temp.) 5 Infantry Brigade 1915–17; commanded G. Gds 1919; Commandant Royal Military College 1923–27; Major General GOC London District 1928–32; KCVO, CB, CMG.

Corry, Armar Valentine Lowry – 1896–1916

Harrow School; commissioned G. Gds August 1914; 1 Batt. G. Gds; Lieutenant 1915; k.i.a. September 1916; MC.

Corry, Noel Armar Lowry ('Porky') – 1867–1935

Harrow School and Cheltenham College; entered army 1887; commissioned G. Gds; OC 2 Batt. G. Gds 1910; Colonel 1914; relieved of command of 2 Batt. G. Gds 9 September 1914 and sent home; OC 3 Batt. G. Gds September 1915–January 1916; Hon. Brigadier General 1920; DSO.

Craigie, John Churchill – 1890–date of death unknown

Eton College; Second Lieutenant G. Gds Special Reserve 1914; 2 Batt. G. Gds December 1914; Captain 3 Batt. G. Gds March 1917–November 1918; MC.

Creed, C.O. – <u>1880–1915</u>

Agent for Earl of Arran, Ballina; Master of the Ballin Harriers; managed sheep ranch in Patagonia; Second Lieutenant G. Gds Special Reserve 1914; 2 Batt. G. Gds; invalided home in March 1915; wounded May 1915; d.o.w. June 1915.

Croft, H. – <u>Birthdate unknown–1915</u>

Sergeant 2 Batt. G. Gds; k.i.a. January 1915.

Cunliffe, John Reynolds Pickersgill ('Jack') – <u>1895–1914</u>

Eton College; entered army 1913; commissioned G. Gds; Second Lieutenant 2 Batt. G. Gds August 1914; k.i.a. September 1914.

Cunliffe-Owen, Charles – <u>1863–1932</u>

Entered army 1883; commissioned Royal Artillery; Captain 1891; Major 1900; Lieutenant Colonel 1914; temp. commander 2 Infantry Brigade November 1914; Brigadier General 1915; CB.

Cunninghame, Alfred Keith Smith – <u>1891–1916</u>

Eton College; commissioned G. Gds from Special Reserve 1913; Second Lieutenant 2 Batt. G. Gds August 1914; Captain May 1916; k.i.a. September 1916.

Darby, Maurice Alfred Alexander – <u>1894–1915</u>

Eton College; entered army 1914; commissioned G. Gds; Lieutenant 2 Batt. G. Gds; k.i.a. March 1915.

Davies, Henry Rudolph – <u>1865–1950</u>

Eton College; served with army in Burma and India 1887–98; served in China 1900; Lieutenant Colonel OC 2 Batt. Ox.L.I. 1911 and 1914; Major General 11 Division 1918; retired 1923; CB.

de Crespigny, Claude Raul ('Crawley') Champion – <u>1878–1941</u>

Entered army 1900; commissioned G. Gds; Captain 1908; Staff Captain 4 (Gds) Brigade October 1914; Captain and Major 2 Batt. G. Gds 1915–16; Lieutenant Colonel and OC 1 Batt. G. Gds 1916–17; Brigadier General (temp.) 1 (Gds) Brigade 1917–18; succeeded his father as 5th Baronet 1935; CB, CMG, DSO.

Denny, John Anthony ('Jack') – <u>1889–1942</u>

Eton College; Second Lieutenant G. Gds Special Reserve 1914; attached S. Gds; severely wounded January 1915; Captain; ADC Viceroy of India 1917–19; went into family business E M Denny & Co. Ltd (bacon curers).

Derriman, Gerard Lysely – <u>1870–1915</u>

Eton College; entered army 1889; commissioned G. Gds; Captain; Boer War, retired army 1907; Chief Constable of Shropshire 1908; rejoined army 1915; Captain 2 Batt. G. Gds April 1915; d.o.w. August 1915.

Des Voeux, Frederick William – <u>1889–1914</u>

HMS *Britannia*; entered army 1910; commissioned G. Gds; Lieutenant 2 Batt. G. Gds August 1914; k.i.a. September 1914.

Digby, John Henry – <u>Birthdate unknown–1914</u>

Sergeant G. Gds; k.i.a. November 1914.

Dobson, Frederick William – <u>1886–1935</u>

Private (retired Lance Corporal) 2 Batt. C. Gds; VC.

Dowling, Charles Milne Cholmeley – <u>1891–1920</u>
  Rugby School; entered army 1911; commissioned G. Gds; Lieutenant 2 Batt. G. Gds
  1914; wounded 1914 and 1915, invalided home; transferred to Special Reserve 1920;
  killed by IRA in November 1920.

Esher, Reginald Brett, 2nd Viscount – <u>1852–1930</u>
  Eton College; Cambridge University; Liberal MP for Penryn and Falmouth 1880–85;
  Parliamentary Private Secretary to Lord Hartington, Secretary of State for War, 1882–85;
  Permanent Secretary to the Office of Works 1895; GCVO, KCB.

Eyre, J.B. – <u>Dates unknown</u>
  Stonyhurst College; Second Lieutenant G. Gds Special Reserve 1914; 2 Batt. G. Gds
  December 1914; wounded December 1914; Lieutenant Reserve Batt. G. Gds 1915–18.

Fanshawe, Robert – <u>1863–1946</u>
  Marlborough College; entered army 1883; commissioned Ox.L.I.; Boer War 1899–1903;
  OC 2 Batt. Ox.L.I. 1907–11; Colonel GSO 1, 1 Division 1911; commanded 6 Infantry
  Brigade September 1914; Major General 48 (South Midland) Division 1915–18;
  commanded 69 (2 East Anglian) Division 1919; retired army 1919; KCB, DSO.

Farquhar, Francis Douglas ('Frank') – <u>1875–1915</u>
  Eton College; entered army 1896; commissioned C. Gds; spoke French, Somali and
  Chinese; Lieutenant 1898; Boer War 1899–1900; Captain 1901; posted to the Chinese
  Regiment of Infantry 1901–03; Somaliland 1903–04; General Staff War Office 1908–13;
  Major 1910; Lieutenant Colonel 1913; Military Secretary to The Duke of Connaught,
  Governor General of Canada 1913; OC Princess Patricia's Canadian Light Infantry; k.i.a.
  March 1915; DSO.

Fergusson, Sir Charles, 7th Baronet – <u>1865–1951</u>
  Eton College; entered army 1883; commissioned G. Gds; Sudan 1896–1900; Adjutant
  General Egyptian Army 1901; OC 3 Batt. G. Gds 1904; Brigadier General Irish
  command 1907; Inspector of Infantry 1909; Major General GOC 5 Division in Ireland
  1912–14; commanded 5 Division August 1914; commanded 9 (Scottish) Division
  October–December 1914; commanded II Corps 1915–16; XVII Corps 1916–19;
  Military Governor of Cologne 1918–20; retired army 1922; Governor General of New
  Zealand 1924–30; GCB, GCMG, DSO, MVO.

Fisher-Rowe, Conway Victor ('Conny') – <u>1881–1923</u>
  Eton College; entered army 1900; commissioned G. Gds; Boer War; retired army 1902;
  rejoined August 1914; Lieutenant 1914; Captain 1915; 1 Batt. G. Gds; Major; wounded at
  Neuve-Chappelle 1915, badly gassed three times.

Fisher-Rowe, Laurence Rowe ('The Old Friend') – <u>1866–1915</u>
  Eton College; commissioned Queen's (Royal West Surrey Regiment); Lieutenant 1884;
  transferred G. Gds Second Lieutenant 1887; Captain 1898; Major 1906; Lieutenant
  Colonel OC 3 Batt. G. Gds 1911–14; OC 1 Batt. G. Gds 1914; d.o.w. March 1915.

FitzClarence, Charles – <u>1865–1914</u>
  Eton College; entered army 1886; commissioned Royal Fusiliers; transferred I. Gds 1900;
  served Boer War 1899–1900; twice wounded, awarded VC; Lieutenant Colonel I. Gds
  1914; Brigadier General (temp.) 1 (Gds) Brigade 1914; k.i.a. Polygon Wood December
  1914; VC.

Fleming, Rev. Herbert James – <u>1873–1926</u>

Oxford University; ordained 1897; entered army 1902; served at Aldershot, Ballincollig, Woolwich, Crete and Gibraltar; Major 1913; RMA Woolwich 1914; attached BEF August 1914; after First World War served at Woolwich and at Shorncliffe; appointed chaplain to the Royal Hospital, Chelsea 1923; CMG.

Fludyer, Henry – <u>1847–1920</u>

Eton College; entered army 1866, commissioned S. Gds; Captain 1869; Major 1877; Lieutenant Colonel OC 2 Batt. S. Gds 1884; OC S. Gds 1898; temporary OC S. Gds 1914–16; CVO.

Forbes, Atholl Laurence Cunyngham – <u>1882–1953</u>

Entered army 1905; commissioned G. Gds 1905; Adjutant 3 Batt. G. Gds 1913–14; Captain 1914; Regimental Adjutant G. Gds 1914–16; Major 1919; succeeded father as 21st Lord Forbes 1916.

French, John Denton Pinkstone – <u>1852–1925</u>

Eastman's Royal Navy Academy, Portsmouth; joined Royal Navy 1866; entered army 1870; commissioned Lieutenant 8th King's Royal Irish Hussars, transferred to 19th Hussars 1874; commanded Cavalry Division during Boer War; CIGS 1912, resigned following Curragh incident 1914; C-in-C of the BEF 1914–15; C-in-C Home Forces 1915–18; Lord Lieutenant of Ireland 1918–21; created Earl of Ypres 1922; KP, GCB, OM, GCVO, KCMG, ADC.

Gerard, Charles Robert Tolver Michael – <u>1894–1971</u>

Eton College; commissioned G. Gds; ADC 2 Division Staff 1915; Captain and Adjutant 4 Batt. G. Gds 1918; Lieutenant Colonel, Deputy Provost Marshal Second World War; DSO, OBE.

Gillette – <u>Dates unknown</u>

Company Sergeant Major 2 Batt. G. Gds; severely wounded November 1914.

Glyn, Arthur St. Leger – <u>1870–1922</u>

Eton College; entered army 1891; commissioned 3 Batt. Royal Fusiliers (City of London Regiment); transferred G. Gds 1891; Lieutenant 1895; Boer War 1899; Adjutant 1 Batt. G. Gds 1901–02; retired army 1907; rejoined army 1914; Major 2 Batt. G. Gds 1915; OC 1 & 2 Batt. G. Gds at different periods during 1916; Staff 1917; Lieutenant Colonel OC 10 Batt. Middlesex Regiment; killed motor accident 1922.

Gordon Lennox, Lord Bernard Charles – <u>1878–1914</u>

Eton College; entered army 1898; commissioned G. Gds; S. Africa 1900; played cricket for Middlesex CCC 1903; China 1904–06; Major 2 Batt. G. Gds August–November 1914; k.i.a. November 1914.

Gort, John Vereker, 6th Viscount – <u>1886–1946</u>

Harrow School; entered army 1905; commissioned G. Gds; Lieutenant 1907; Captain G. Gds August 1914; Brigade Major 4 (Gds) Brigade April 1915; Lieutenant Colonel (temp.) OC 4 Batt. G. Gds 1917; Colonel 1926; commanded Gds Brigade 1930–32; Major General 1935; Commandant Staff College, Camberley 1936; Lieutenant General (temp.) Military Secretary to War Minister 1937; CIGS 1937; Commander BEF 1939; Governor of Gibraltar 1941–42; Governor of Malta 1942–44; Field Marshal 1943; High Commissioner Palestine and Transjordan 1944; created Viscount Gort 1946; VC, GCB, CBE, DSO, MVO, MC.

BIOGRAPHICAL INDEX

Goschen, George Gerard – <u>1887–1953</u>
Eton College; Honorary Attaché Berlin 1911–14; Second Lieutenant G. Gds Special Reserve 1914; 2 Batt. G. Gds December 1914; wounded and taken prisoner December 1914; prisoner of war December 1914–June 1916; retired army due to ill health 1919.

Gosselin, Alwyn Bertram Robert Raphael ('Goose') – <u>1883–1915</u>
Beaumont College; entered army 1901; commissioned 19th Hussars; Lieutenant G. Gds 1902; Captain 1910; 2 Batt. G. Gds August 1914–February 1915; k.i.a. February 1915; DSO.

Gough, Eric John Fletcher – <u>1892–1914</u>
Eton College; entered army 1909; commissioned I. Gds; Lieutenant 1911; Lieutenant (Transport Officer) 1 Batt. I. Gds August 1914; Captain 1914; k.i.a. December 1914.

Graham, Henry Archibald Roger ('Archie') – <u>1892–1970</u>
Radley College; Cambridge University; Second Lieutenant G. Gds Special Reserve 1914; wounded February 1915; Captain 1917; Major retired army 1920; stockbroker.

Haig, Douglas – <u>1861–1928</u>
Clifton College; Oxford University; commissioned 7 (Queen's Own) Hussars 1885; served in India 1886–92; Sudan Expedition 1898; Boer War 1899–1902; Major General 1904; commanded I Corps 1914; C-in-C 1915–18; retired army 1920; created Earl Haig 1919; KT, GCB, OM, GCVO, KCIE.

Hamilton, Gilbert Claud – <u>1879–1943</u>
Harrow School; entered army 1898; commissioned G. Gds; Captain 1905; Adjutant 3 Batt. G. Gds 1906; employed with N.Z. military forces 1911–13; Major 2 Batt. G. Gds August 1914; Lieutenant Colonel (temp.) 4 Batt. G. Gds September 1915 and December 1916; gassed September 1915; Lieutenant Colonel commanding G. Gds 1919–23; CMG, DSO.

Hamilton-Fletcher, Gareth – <u>1894–1915</u>
Eton College, 1st XI cricket 1911, 1912; Oxford University; Second Lieutenant G. Gds Special Reserve 1914; att. S. Gds 1915; k.i.a. January 1915. Hervey-Bathurst, Sir Frederick ('Freddy') – <u>1870–1956</u>
Eton College; entered army 1889; commissioned G. Gds; Lieutenant 1896; Sudan campaign 1898; Boer War; Captain 1899; First World War, Major Staff; DSO.

Heyworth, Frederic James – <u>1863–1916</u>
Eton College; entered army 1883; commissioned S. Gds; Sudan 1885; Captain 1896; Boer War 1899–1902; Major 1902; OC S. Gds 1914; commanded 20 Brigade 1914–15; Brigadier General (temp.) 1915 commanded 3 Gds Brigade 1915–16; k.i.a. May 1916; CB, DSO.

Holness, Horace H.J. – <u>Birthdate unknown–1957</u>
Served G. Gds, Sergeant; commissioned 2nd Lieutenant Manchester Regiment 1915; Lieutenant 1915; warder Borstal B.I.; DCM.

Hopley, Geoffrey William Van der Byl – <u>1892–1915</u>
Harrow School, 1st XI Cricket 1909, 1910; Cambridge University, first class cricketer; Second Lieutenant G. Gds Special Reserve 1914; 2 Batt. G. Gds December 1914–February 1915; severely wounded February 1915; died May 1915.

Horne, Henry – <u>1861–1929</u>
Harrow School; entered army 1880; commissioned Artillery; Boer War 1899–1902; Brigadier General, Inspector of Artillery 1912; artillery commander I Corps 1914;

Major General 1914; GOC 2 Division 1915; executed evacuation of Gallipoli 1915; GOC XV Corps 1915–16; Lieutenant General 1st Army 1917–18; General, GOC-in-C Eastern Command 1919; retired army 1923; created Baron Horne 1919; GCB, KCMG.

Howell, Frederick Duke Gwynne – 1881–1967
Harrow School; Cambridge University; entered army 1906; commissioned Royal Army Medical Corps; Captain 1909; Medical Officer 2 Batt. G. Gds August 1914–15; Major 1918; continued distinguished career with Army Medical Services; Major General 1937; retired army 1941; CB, DSO, MC, MRCS, LRCP, DPH.

Hughes, John Salisbury – 1885–date of death unknown
Eton College; entered army 1907; commissioned G. Gds; Lieutenant 2 Batt. G. Gds October 1914; Captain November 1914; Major (temp.) 3 Batt. G. Gds 1918; Major 1920; Lieutenant Colonel OC 4 Batt. G. Gds 1930–34; Colonel 1934; MC.

Jeffreys, George Darell ('Ma') – 1878–1960
Eton College; entered army 1897; commissioned G. Gds; Sudan campaign 1898; Boer War 1900–02; Captain 1903; Major 1910; commanded Gds Depot 1911–14; Senior Major 2 Batt. G. Gds 1914–15; Lieutenant Colonel OC 2 Batt. G. Gds 1915; Brigadier General commanded 57 infantry Brigade 1916; commanded 1 Gds Brigade 1917; Major General commanded 19 Division 1917–18; commanded Brigade of Gds and GOC London District 1920; Lieutenant General 1930; GOC-in-C Southern Command in India 1932; General 1935; ADC to the King 1936–38; retired army 1938; Colonel of the Royal Hampshire Regiment 1945–48; Colonel of the G. Gds 1952–60; MP for Petersfield 1941–51; created Baron Jeffreys 1952; KCB, KCVO, CMG.

Kitchener, Horatio Herbert ('K') – 1850–1916
Montreux; Royal Military Academy, Woolwich; entered army in 1871; commissioned Royal Engineers; served in Palestine, Egypt and Cyprus; C-of-S then C-in-C Boer War 1900–02; C-in-C, India 1902–09; Field Marshal 1909; British Agent and Consul General, Egypt 1911; Secretary of State for War 1914; created Earl Kitchener 1914; KG, KP, GCB, OM, GCSI, GCMG, GCIE, ADC, PC.

Landon, Herman James Shelley – 1859–1948
Harrow School; entered army 1879; commissioned 6 Royal Regiment; Brigadier General 3 Infantry Brigade 1910–14; Major General 1 Division 1914; commanded 9, 33, 35 and 64 Divisions 1915–18; CB, CMG.

Lang, Arthur Horace – 1890–1915
Harrow School, 1st XI cricket 1906–09; first class cricketer, Sussex 1911–12; Cambridge University, 1st XI cricket 1913; Second Lieutenant G. Gds Special Reserve 1914; k.i.a. January 1915.

Lee Steere, John Henry Gordon – 1894–1914
Eton College; entered army 1914; commissioned G. Gds; Second Lieutenant 2 Batt. G. Gds August 1914; k.i.a. November 1914.

Littler, Joseph – 1876–date of death unknown
Rock miner; enlisted G. Gds 1899; Drill Sergeant; member of the Bearer Company at funeral of King Edward VII; Regimental Sergeant Major; retired army 1920; MC, DCM, RVM.

Loch, Edward Douglas, 2nd Baron – 1873–1942
Winchester College; entered army 1893; commissioned G. Gds; Brigade Major 3 Infantry Brigade 1910–11; second-in-command 2 Batt. G. Gds 1913–14; Staff August

1914; Brigadier General (temp.) 1915–18; retired army 1922 as Major General; CB, CMG, DSO, MVO.

Lygon, Hon. Edward – <u>1873–1900</u>

Eton College; commissioned G. Gds; Boer War, 3 Batt. G. Gds; k.i.a. at Karee Siding, March 1900.

Lygon, Hon. Henry – <u>1884–1932</u>

Eton College; commissioned Suffolk Yeomanry 1907; attached Royal Flying Corps 1915; Captain Suffolk Yeomanry; served France, Balkans, Italy 1914–18.

Lygon, Hon. Robert ('Bobby') – <u>1879–1952</u>

Eton College; commissioned G. Gds; Lieutenant 1899; Captain, retired army January 1914; Lieutenant Colonel attached Loyal North Lancashire Regiment, OC 2/4 Batt. 1916–17; MVO, MC.

Macdonald, George Godfrey Bosville – <u>1861–1930</u>

Page of Honour to H.H. Queen Victoria; Eton College; commissioned G. Gds; Lieutenant 1881; Captain G. Gds 1893; 5 Batt. G. Gds 1915.

MacEwen, Douglas Lilburn – <u>1867–1941</u>

Fettes College; Cambridge University; entered army 1889; commissioned Cameron Highlanders; Boer War 1900–02; Lieutenant Colonel 1912; GSO 1 War Office (temp.) August–September 1914; OC 1 Batt. Cameron Highlanders September–December 1914; temporary commander 1 (Gds) Brigade 11 November 1914; Brigadier General (temp.) 1916–18; retired army 1923; CB, CMG.

Mackenzie, Allan Keith ('Sloper') – <u>1887–1916</u>

Eton College; entered army 1910; commissioned G. Gds; Lieutenant 2 Batt. G. Gds August 1914; wounded September 1914; Captain 3 Batt. G. Gds April 1916; d.o.w. September 1916.

Maitland, Mark Edward Makgill-Crichton- – <u>1882–1972</u>

Eton College; entered army 1901; commissioned G. Gds; Boer War 1901–02; Captain 2 Batt. G. Gds October 1914; Major 1915; Lieutenant Colonel (temp.) OC 1 Batt. G. Gds July 1916; Lieutenant Colonel 1923; retired army 1928; recalled to active service as Colonel G. Gds 1939; CVO, DSO.

Manners, Hon. John Nevile – <u>1892–1914</u>

Eton College; entered army 1912; commissioned G. Gds; Lieutenant 2 Batt. G. Gds August 1914; k.i.a. September 1914.

Markham, Ronald Antony ('Tony') – <u>1870–1914</u>

Charterhouse School; entered army 1890; commissioned C. Gds; Lieutenant 1896; Captain 1899; Sudan Expedition 1899; Egyptian Army ADC to the Sirdar 1900–02; Major 1907; acting Lieutenant Colonel second-in-command 2 Batt. C. Gds 1914; d.o.w October 1914

Marshall, Frederick Guy ('Freddy') – <u>1893–1915</u>

Eton College; entered army 1912; commissioned G. Gds; Lieutenant 1914; k.i.a. March 1915.

McDonnell, P.H. – <u>Dates unknown</u>

Lance Corporal G. Gds; Sergeant W. Gds; DCM.

McDougall, Iain ('Lunga') – <u>1887–1914</u>

Eton College; entered army 1906; commissioned G. Gds; Lieutenant 1907; ADC to Governor and C-in-C New Zealand 1911–13; Lieutenant and Adjutant 2 Batt. G. Gds August 1914; k.i.a. September 1914.

Miller, William Joseph Macdonald ('Donald') – <u>1891–1914</u>
  Entered army 1912; commissioned G. Gds; Second Lieutenant G. Gds August 1914; k.i.a.
  October 1914.
Monro, Charles – <u>1860–1929</u>
  Sherbourne School; entered army 1879; commissioned Royal West Surrey Regiment;
  Captain 1889; served N.W. Frontier, India, S. Africa 1879–1900; Major General 1910;
  commanded 2 Division August–December 1914; Lieutenant General, commanded Third
  Army 1915; C-in-C Dardanelles 1915; General, commanded First Army 1916; C-in-C
  India 1916–20; Governor and C-in-C Gibraltar 1923–28; retired army 1928; created
  1st Baronet 1921; GCMG, GCB, GCSI.
Morris, Hon. George Henry – <u>1872–1914</u>
  Oratory School, Egbaston; entered army 1892; commissioned Rifle Brigade; served
  N.W. Frontier, India and S. Africa 1897–1902; Major I. Gds 1906; Lieutenant Colonel
  OC 1 Batt. I. Gds August 1914; k.i.a. September 1914.
Morrison, James Archibald – <u>1873–1934</u>
  Eton College; commissioned 4 (Eton volunteer) Batt. Ox.L.I. 1891; transferred to
  G. Gds 1895; Boer War; MP for Wilton 1900–06; MP for Nottingham East 1900–12;
  rejoined 1 Batt. G. Gds August 1914; wounded April 1915; rejoined June 1915; temp.
  OC 1 Batt. September 1915; severely wounded 1916 and invalided home; Lieutenant
  Colonel (temp.) OC Territorial Batt. Middlesex Regiment 1916; retired army 1919;
  his home, Basildon Park, was requisitioned as a convalescent hospital for injured
  soldiers; DSO.
Needham, Hon. Francis Edward ('Buddy') – <u>1886–1955</u>
  Eton College; entered army 1908; commissioned G. Gds; Lieutenant 2 Batt. G. Gds
  August 1914; wounded and taken prisoner September 1914; Captain 4 Batt. G. Gds
  October 1916–November 1918; retired army 1925; re-employed 1941–45; MVO.
Nesbitt, Frederick George Beaumont- ('Paddy') – <u>1893–1971</u>
  Eton College; entered army 1912; commissioned G. Gds; Second Lieutenant 2 Batt.
  G. Gds October 1914; Captain July 1915; ADC November 1915–August 1916; GSO
  3 May 1917–January 1918; Brigade Major January 1918–September 1918; War Office
  1922–32; Lieutenant Colonel OC 2 Batt. G. Gds 1932–35; Military Attaché Paris 1936;
  Major General Director of Military Intelligence 1939–40; various staff roles during
  Second World War; retired army 1945; CVO, CBE, MC.
Nevill, John Henry Gaythorne – <u>1884–1914</u>
  Ampleforth College; member of Stock Exchange 1911; Second Lieutenant G. Gds
  Special Reserve 1914; 2 Batt. G. Gds December 1914; k.i.a. December 1914.
Orr-Ewing, Sir Norman Archibald, 4th Baronet – <u>1880–1960</u>
  Eton College; entered army 1900; commissioned S. Gds; S. Africa, Egypt 1900–10;
  Adjutant S. Gds 1910–12; Acting OC I. Gds 17 November 1914; OC 2 Batt. S. Gds
  1916–18; Brigadier General 1918; retired army 1919; CB, DSO.
Penn, Arthur H. – <u>1886–1960</u>
  Eton College; Cambridge University; Inner Temple 1910; Captain and Adjutant 2 Batt.
  G. Gds; Regimental Adjutant G. Gds 1941–45; served Royal Household 1937–60,
  Treasurer to Queen, later Queen Mother; Chairman King & Shaxson; GCVO, MC.

Raglan, George Henry FitzRoy 3rd Baron – <u>1857–1921</u>
Eton College; entered army 1876; commissioned G. Gds; Lieutenant 1877; Second Anglo-Afghan War 1879–80; ADC to Sir James Fergusson, Governor of Bombay 1880–83; Captain 1886; retired army 1887; Under Secretary for War 1900–02; Lieutenant Governor of Isle of Man 1902–18; GBE.

Rawlinson, Sir Henry Seymour 2nd Baronet – <u>1864–1925</u>
Eton College; entered army 1884; commissioned King's Royal Rifle Corps in India; served in India and Burma 1884–89; transferred C. Gds 1899; Boer War 1899–1902; Brigadier General, GOC 2 Infantry Brigade, Aldershot 1907; Major General GOC 3 Division 1910; GOC 4 Division 1914; GOC IV Corps 1914; Lieutenant General, GOC Fourth Army 1916; suffered defeat in Battle of Somme 1916; General, GOC Second Army 1917–18; GOC Allied Forces at Battle of Amiens 1918; created Baron Rawlinson 1919; GCB, GCSI, GCVO, KCMG.

Rhodes-Moorhouse, William Barnard – <u>1887–1915</u>
Harrow School; Cambridge University; commissioned Royal Flying Corps 1914; d.o.w. April 1915; VC.

Ridley, Edward Davenport – <u>1883–1934</u>
Harrow School; Oxford University; entered army 1905; commissioned G. Gds; Captain 2 Batt. G. Gds September 1914–March 1915; Captain 4 Batt. G. Gds September 1915; Captain 3 Batt. G. Gds 1917; second-in-command Household Brigade Officer Cadet Batt. Home Forces 1918; Major 1919; Chief Instructor, Small Arms School 1925; Colonel 1932; MC.

Robarts, Jack – <u>No information available</u>

Roberts, Frederick, 1st Earl – <u>1832–1914</u>
Eton College; commissioned Bengal Artillery 1851; served in the Indian Rebellion, the Expedition to Abyssinia and the Second Anglo-Afghan War; C-in-C British Forces Boer War; Field Marshal 1895; C-in-C of the Forces 1901–04; created 1st Earl Roberts; VC, KG, KP, GCB, OM, GCSI, GCIE, KStJ, VD.

Rose, Ivor Sainte Croix – <u>1881–1962</u>
Eton College; entered army 1900; commissioned King's Royal Rifle Corps; resigned army 1907; Lieutenant Special Reserve G. Gds 1908; Lieutenant 2 Batt. G. Gds October 1914; Captain November 1914; employed by Ministry of Munitions 1917; retired army 1919; OBE.

Rumbold, Hugo Cecil Levinge – <u>1884–1932</u>
Eton College; Boer War; Second Lieutenant Special Reserve G. Gds 1914; 2 Batt. G. Gds December 1914–February 1915; Lieutenant Reserve Batt. G. Gds 1915–18; theatrical designer and impresario; died aged 48 from injuries sustained in First World War.

Sartorius, Euston Francis Frederick ('Snipe') – <u>1882–1915</u>
Eton College; entered army 1900; commissioned G. Gds; Boer War 1902; Lieutenant 1904; Captain 1908; resigned 1912; rejoined as Captain 1 Batt. G. Gds 1914; d.o.w. sustained in Battle of Neuve-Chapelle, March 1915.

Sawle, Richard C. Graves- ('Dick') – <u>1888–1914</u>
Harrow School; entered army 1908; commissioned C. Gds; Lieutenant 1910; 2 Batt. C. Gds August 1914; k.i.a. November 1914.

Scott, Lord Francis George Montagu Douglas – <u>1879–1952</u>
> Eton College; Oxford University; entered army 1899; commissioned G. Gds; Boer War; ADC to Viceroy of India 1905–11; Captain 1908; attached 1 Batt. I. Gds September 1914; wounded October 1914; Major November 1914; Lieutenant Colonel (temp.) Service Batt. Royal Fusiliers September–November 1915; retired army 1920; rejoined army 1941; Assistant Military Secretary to GOC East African Forces 1941; Kenya farmer and Member of Kenya Executive and Legislative Council 1924–48; KCMG, DSO.

Scott-Kerr, Robert – <u>1859–1942</u>
> Eton College; Cambridge University; entered army 1879; commissioned 24 Regiment of Foot, transferred G. Gds; Major 1896; Boer War 1900–02; Lieutenant Colonel OC 1 Batt. G. Gds 1904–08; Brigadier General (temp.) 4 (Gds) Brigade 1914; severely wounded 1914; DSO.

Seymour, Lord Henry Charles ('Copper') – <u>1878–1939</u>
> Entered army 1899; commissioned G. Gds; Boer War; Lieutenant 1900; Captain 1907; Major 1914; OC (temp.) 4 Batt. G. Gds 1915; Hon. Brigadier General 1930; DSO.

Smith, Bertram Abel – <u>1879–1947</u>
> Eton College; banker; commissioned Nottinghamshire Yeomanry; Captain South Nottinghamshire Hussars 1915; served Egypt 1915; Military Landing Officer Gallipoli August–December 1915; Major, Lieutenant Colonel (temp.) OC 23 Batt. Middlesex Regiment, France 1918; ADC to King George V 1926; Hon. Colonel 8 Sherwood Foresters 1937; Director of National Provincial Bank, Shell, and various other companies during 1920s–40s; MC, DSO.

Smith, Charles Jervoise Dudley – <u>1895–1915</u>
> Eton College; Cambridge University; entered army 1914; commissioned G. Gds; 1 Batt. G. Gds March 1915; k.i.a. June 1915.

Smith, Desmond Abel ('Dubby') – <u>1892–1974</u>
> Eton College; Cambridge University; Second Lieutenant G. Gds Special Reserve 1914; 2. Batt. G. Gds 1915–18; Captain and Adjutant, demobilised 1919; Major, Senior Military Liaison Officer, London Area 1939–44; Business career including Director of Equitable Life Assurance Society 1930–70 (Chairman 1940–47), National Provincial Bank 1948–69, Borax Consolidated 1937–69; MC.

Somerset, Norman Arthur Henry – <u>1894–1914</u>
> Eton College; entered army 1913; commissioned G. Gds; Second Lieutenant 1 Batt. G. Gds; k.i.a. October 1914.

Stephen, Douglas Clinton Leslie ('Tich') – <u>1876–1914</u>
> Eton College; entered army 1900; commissioned G. Gds; Lieutenant and Captain in service with Macedonian Gendarmerie 1906–09; Captain 2 Batt. G. Gds August 1914; d.o.w. September 1914.

Stewart, William Alfred Lindsay – <u>1892–1916</u>
> Eton College; entered army 1912; commissioned G. Gds; Lieutenant 2 Batt. G. Gds August 1914; wounded September 1914; Captain 4 Batt. G. Gds; k.i.a. September 1916; MC.

Stocks, Michael George – <u>1892–1914</u>
> Eton College; entered army 1910; commissioned G. Gds; Lieutenant 1913; Lieutenant 2 Batt. G. Gds August 1914; k.i.a. November 1914.

Stracey, Reginald G. ('Reggie') – <u>1881–1915</u>
Eton College; entered army 1900; commissioned S. Gds; Boer War; Lieutenant 1902;
Adjutant S. Gds 1904–05; Captain 1905; attached Egyptian Army 1907–11; Captain
1 Batt. S. Gds August 1914; Major (temp.) November 1914; k.i.a. January 1915.

Streatfeild, Sir Henry ('Stretty') – <u>1857–1938</u>
Eton College; entered army 1876; Captain 1885; Major 1893; Lieutenant Colonel 1900;
retired army 1904; recalled 1914 and commanded G. Gds 1914–19; Colonel; Private
Secretary to H.M. Queen Alexandra 1910–25; KCVO, CB, CMG.

Stucley, Humphrey St. Leger – <u>1877–1914</u>
Eton College; entered army 1897; commissioned G. Gds; Major 1912; Major 2 Batt.
G. Gds August 1914; d.o.w. October 1914.

Symes-Thompson, Cholmeley – <u>1881–1914</u>
Harrow School; entered army 1901; commissioned G. Gds; Captain 2 Batt. G. Gds
August 1914; k.i.a. November 1914.

Thomas, George Henry – <u>Birthdate unknown–1915</u>
Sergeant G. Gds; transferred W. Gds 1915; DCM.

Thomas, W. – <u>Birthdate unknown–1914</u>
Sergeant G. Gds; k.i.a. December 1914.

Thorne, Thomas Fleetwood Joseph Nicol – <u>1888–1915</u>
Eton College; Oxford University; entered army 1909; commissioned G. Gds; Lieutenant
1910; Captain 1915; k.i.a. September 1915.

Trefusis, Hon. John Frederick Hepburn-Stuart-Forbes- ('Jack') – <u>1878–1915</u>
Eton College; entered army 1901; commissioned I. Gds; ADC to GOC-in-C Eastern
Command 1904–07; ADC to GOC-in-C S. Africa 1908–09; Captain and Adjutant
I. Gds 1909–13; Adjutant RMC Sandhurst 1914; Adjutant 1 Batt. I. Gds September
1914; Lieutenant Colonel (temp.) OC 1 Batt. I. Gds November 1914; Brigadier
General (temp.) 20 Infantry Brigade August–October 1915; k.i.a. October 1915;
DSO.

Tritton, Alan George – <u>1882–1914</u>
Winchester College; entered army 1899; commissioned C. Gds; Boer War 1901; Adjutant
to 3 Batt. C. Gds in Egypt and ADC to GOC-in-C, Western Command; Captain 3 Batt.
C. Gds August 1914; k.i.a. December 1914.

Trotter, Gerald Frederick – <u>1871–1945</u>
HMS *Britannia*; entered army 1892; commissioned G. Gds; Boer War 1899–1902,
severely wounded 1900; Captain 1902; Major 1907; retired army 1912; Major 1 Batt.
G. Gds 1914; wounded March 1915, arm amputated; Brevet Lieutenant Colonel OC 1
Batt. G. Gds July 1915; commanded 27 Brigade May 1916; ADC to Governor General
of Canada 1917; British Military Mission USA 1917; Hon. Brigadier General 1918;
Gentleman Usher to HM George V 1917; Groom-in-Waiting 1920 and Extra Equerry
to HRH The Prince of Wales 1925; CB, CMG, DSO.

Tudway, Hervey Robert Charles ('Tuddles') – <u>1888–1914</u>
Eton College; entered army 1910; commissioned G. Gds; Lieutenant 2 Batt. G. Gds
August 1914; d.o.w. November 1914.

Tufnell, Carleton Wyndham – <u>1892–1914</u>
Eton College; entered army 1912; commissioned G. Gds; Second Lieutenant 2 Batt.
G. Gds August 1914; d.o.w. November 1914.

Turner, H. – <u>1882–1914</u>
Sergeant G. Gds; k.i.a. September 1914.

Vereker, Rupert Humphrey Medlicott – <u>1894–1914</u>
Entered army 1913; commissioned G. Gds; Second Lieutenant 2 Batt. G. Gds August
1914; k.i.a. August 1914.

Vernon, Granville Charles FitzHerbert Harcourt- – <u>1891–1974</u>
Eton College; entered army 1910; commissioned G. Gds; Lieutenant 1914; Captain 1915;
Major 1939; Lieutenant Colonel 1940; DSO, OBE, MC.

Verschoyle, Edward Greville – <u>1866–1900</u>
Wellington College; entered army 1885; commissioned G. Gds; Captain 1897; Sudan
Expedition 1898; Boer War; d.o.w. received at Thaba N'Chu 1900.

Waggett, Philip Napier – <u>1862–1932</u>
Cambridge University; member of the Society of St John the Evangelist; appointed
temporary Army Chaplain December 1914; Warden of The Mission House, Cowley
St John, Oxford; author.

Walker, Cecil Francis Aleck – <u>1885–1925</u>
Eton College; entered army 1908; commissioned G. Gds; Lieutenant 2 Batt. G. Gds
August 1914; wounded September 1914; Captain 1915; 3 Batt. G. Gds September
1915–September 1917; Major 4 Batt. G. Gds January 1918–July 1918; OC 2 Batt. G. Gds
October 1918–November 1918; MC.

Walter, Sydney – <u>1893–1914</u>
Eton College; entered army 1913; commissioned G. Gds; Second Lieutenant 1 Batt.
G. Gds 1914; k.i.a. October 1914.

Warrender, Hugh Valdave – <u>1868–1926</u>
Eton College; entered army 1888; commissioned 5 Brigade Scottish Division; resigned
commission 1888; commissioned G. Gds 1889; Lieutenant 1894; retired army 1899;
rejoined army as Major, 1/15 Batt. London Regiment embarked for France March 1915;
Lieutenant Colonel (temp.) OC 15 Batt. Terriers 1915–16; DSO.

Welby, Richard William Gregory – <u>1888–1914</u>
Eton College; Oxford University; entered army 1910; commissioned G. Gds; Lieutenant
2 Batt. G. Gds August 1914; k.i.a. September 1914.

Wellesley, Lord Richard – <u>1879–1914</u>
Eton College; entered army 1900; commissioned G. Gds; Captain 1908; Captain 1 Batt.
G. Gds August 1914; k.i.a. October 1914.

Westmacott, Claude Berners – <u>1865–1948</u>
Eton College; entered army 1888; commissioned Worcestershire Regiment; served
in India with 1 Batt. 1888–1900; Lieutenant 1889; Adjutant 1892–96; Captain 1898;
Boer War 1900–02; Major 1904; Lieutenant Colonel OC 2 Batt. 1911–September
1914; Brigadier General 5 Infantry Brigade 1914; invalided home 1915; commanded
No. 6 District UK 1918; retired army 1920; CBE.

White, Godfrey Dalrymple ('Tit') – <u>1866–1954</u>
  Wellington College; entered army 1885; commissioned G. Gds; Lieutenant 1885;
  Captain 1897; ADC GOC British North America 1892–93; ADC GOC Home District
  1899; Boer War 1899–1902; Major 1901; Lieutenant Colonel (temp.) OC 4 & 5 (reserve)
  Batt. G. Gds 1914–16; Staff, France 1916; MP for Southport 1910–23; changed name to
  Dalrymple-White 1926; created 1st Baronet 1926.

Wiggins, A. W. – <u>Birthdate unknown–1915</u>
  chauffeur; Sergeant 2 Batt. G. Gds December 1914; k.i.a. March 1915.

Williams, Mervyn – <u>Birthdate unknown–1972</u>
  Second Lieutenant Special Reserve G. Gds 1914; Lieutenant 2 Batt.. G Gds October
  1914; wounded December 1914; Captain 1915; Major (temp.) 1919.

Index